Help Your Baby Talk

Help Your Baby Talk

INTRODUCING THE

SHARED COMMUNICATION METHOD

TO JUMP-START LANGUAGE

AND HAVE A SMARTER, HAPPIER BABY

● ■ ▲

Robert E. Owens, Ph.D.,
with Leah Feldon

A Perigee Book

A Perigee Book
Published by The Berkley Publishing Group
A division of Penguin Group (USA) Inc.
375 Hudson Street
New York, New York 10014

Perigee trade paperback edition / June 2004

ISBN: 0-399-52958-6

Visit our website at www.penguin.com

This book has been cataloged by the Library of Congress

Printed in the United States of America

10 9 8 7 6 5 4 3 2 1

ACKNOWLEDGMENTS

Dr. Owens

It has taken the help and encouragement of many people to bring this project from idea to book. Four individuals deserve special notice.

First is Leah Feldon, my cowriter and literary alter ego. Leah helped to organize my vision and enliven my somewhat dry academic prose with colorful phrases, witty examples, and a reader-friendly style. Not only did she bring order to my rambling ideas and crispness to my writing, but Leah should be credited with coining the term "Shared Communication." It is no wonder that she is a bestselling author in her own right. Her flair for writing is only exceeded by her personal style and grace.

Stedman Mays, cofounder of Clausen, Mays and Tahan, and now president of Scribblers House Literary Agency, deserves praise and my sincerest gratitude for his unwavering belief in the viability of *Help Your Baby Talk*. From the book's inception, Sted has been a continuing source of encouragement, a guiding hand through the sometimes unfathomable world of publishing, a true professional, a friend, and a source of genuine caring. He has been an advocate for this book throughout its gestation, birthing, and weaning process. There were many times when his calm, reassuring voice was all that kept me from giving up. Thanks, too, to Mary Tahan for her help and encouragement.

Sheila Curry Oakes and the folks at Penguin Publishing have been of inestimable help in manuscript preparation and review, and book design and layout. The creative process can be a messy one, but Sheila's professionalism helped to keep my focus on the goal.

Finally, my partner at O and M Education, Byung Choon Moon, has patiently and unwaveringly supported me with our little company's first endeavor. I could not have asked for or expected more.

In conclusion, I must recognize several friends and colleagues who helped with suggestions, critiques, and support, though I suspect in private they often questioned why I would want to take on yet another project. These troupers include Dr. Addie Haas, Irene Belyakov and Dr. Robyn Goodman, Linda and Mike Deats, Dr. Monica Schneider, Dr. Zhiming Zhoa, and Dr. Chris Dahl, President of State University of New York at Geneseo.

Leah Feldon

My sincere thanks and gratitude as well to the whole Penguin Group gang, as well as to agent/friend extraordinaire, Stedman Mays, and my loving personal support team, Adam, family, et al. And, of course, love, hugs, and special thanks to wonderful Dr. Bob—sharing communication with you has been a total pleasure.

CONTENTS

Help Your Baby Talk

CHAPTER ONE

New Beginnings

IF you're a new mom or dad or about to become one—congratulations! The experience of parenthood is like no other. It's filled with the wonderment of discovery, the joy of unconditional love, and the excitement of venturing into the unknown. As you settle in and get to know your new baby, you'll find yourself fascinated by the little creature who is now an important part of your family. As a new parent, I was so intrigued with my twin sons that I'd sneak into their room at night and watch them sleep for hours, just marveling at their tiny life forms. While you might not be quite as awestruck as I was, I can guarantee that when your baby first explores your face with his tiny hands, or grasps your finger, or smiles at you, you will be totally hooked. From then on, every development, from his first step to his first word, to his first crayon drawing, will become cause for cheer and family celebration.

One of the biggest developmental thrills of early parenthood is watching your child learn to talk. It's a fun adventure that begins with his early babbles, gurgles, and coos; and culminates with wonderfully imaginative and creative sentences. Somehow, our babies become little linguists right before our eyes as they learn how to examine the data in the world around them, intuitively hypothesize the rules of grammar, and experiment with bravado. Many of these first trial runs, as anyone with children will tell you, can be highly entertaining—and endearing. Creative words like *goed, wented,* and *jump-roping,* and delightful sentences like "I *eated* a ice cream cone," are enough to make any new parent forget the endless sleepless nights and countless diaper changes.

Interestingly, your toddler's verbal experiments are *not* errors. They're a natural part of learning how to use language; baby steps—both literally and figuratively—along the path to mature communication, and they produce indelible memories that last a lifetime. Although my daughter is now in her thirties, I can still picture her at the breakfast table when she was three saying, "I can't hear you, Daddy . . . I'm listening to my toast." The path to mature communication, it turns out, can take some surprising—and amusing—turns.

After more than twenty-five years as a professor of speech-language pathology, I'm still intrigued by the process of acquiring language and mastering communication. But for you as a new parent, communication and language acquisition go beyond academia. They're huge factors in your child's life—now and in the future. How your baby learns to talk and the way that you communicate with him during his first few years of life can have a tremendous impact on his lifelong psychological well-being, mental abilities, communicative skills, and academic and social success.

Good Early Communication Is Essential to Emotional Well-Being

Studies have shown that emotionally supportive environments produce well-balanced, happy children. For the first few years of your baby's life, you're his environment; you are his world. The sound of your voice is one of the first sounds your baby recognizes and responds to. The way you communicate and interact with him—even in the earliest months before he can imitate sounds or speak words; even before he can fully focus on you—sends him messages about how he's valued in this world. It tells your baby how you (and thus the world) feel about him. It lets him know whether or not his needs and desires count. All those messages are internalized and help shape his lifelong worldview.

The right kind of communication between the two of you creates a healthy life-confirming worldview. It teaches your baby at an extremely early age that he can influence others and have them respond to him and meet his needs. It tells him that he *can* effect change in his little world. It shows him that he counts in this world; that his existence matters. It is through your interaction with your baby that he gains the *positive self-knowledge* that allows him to internalize—*"I am me!"* These are invaluable, indeed crucial, lessons for future well-being and success. And they're the ones I want to help you "teach" your baby.

I want to help you steer clear of the kind of poor, albeit often well-intentioned, baby-parent communication that sends children the *opposite* kind of messages and fosters a less positive, less trusting view of the world. One of the biggest mistakes parents make is talking *at* their baby, instead of *with* him. Most of us are *not* instinctive *listeners*. We're instinctive *talkers* who are a bit intimidated by silences; and no matter how well-meaning we are, we tend to extend that behavior to our children. When you consciously change that, and learn to listen as well as talk to your baby, communication is greatly enhanced, and your baby develops a healthier psychological outlook.

My Shared Communication Method embraces a natural kind of rhythmic interplay of silences, words, and actions between you and your baby. It makes for an easy, natural exchange that dignifies your baby's early attempts to communicate, and helps you interpret his sounds and babbling. The method is a natural outgrowth of working with infants and young children as a language pathologist over the past three decades, as well as a passionate longtime study of multicultural parenting, and my personal experiences as a father and grandfather. As a young parent and a hands-on graduate student I often found myself in situations that called for inventive use of all and any teaching resources available—and thirty years ago, trust me, they were few and far between. As I worked with more young children and started to formulate my own theories, I very quickly realized the tremendous importance of parents' behavior on their child's mental development and communication skills—whether that child is normal or speaking-impaired. From then on my goal was, and still is, to maximize communication between parents and children as early as possible.

Over the years, I've refined and streamlined my techniques and shaped them into the Shared Communication Method that I share with you here. For me, developing the method has been a labor of love—and loving. As you practice the techniques and fine-tune your responses, you send your baby positive, life-confirming signals that will encourage his self-confidence, help shape the kind of healthy ego you want for him, and create a warm, trusting relationship between the two of you.

Shared Communication Creates Smarter, More Verbal Babies

If Shared Communication provided only psychological benefits it would be well worth adapting the principles, but it does much more. It also improves your child's mental ability and future communication skills. When you help your baby talk, you also grow his mind. Jean Piaget, the world's foremost child development expert, repeatedly found that during the first two years of a child's life, his language abilities run parallel to his mental and social skills. That is, the better he talks, the more advanced his mental abilities and social skills are. For example, children begin to play and use one object for another, as in using a shoe as a toy boat, at about the same time that they use words to stand for things. Likewise, children speaking in single words usually can concentrate on only one thing at a time, while those speaking in two-word phrases can hold two thoughts at once.

Language and cognition, in fact, are so closely associated that language is one of only two areas measured on most intelligence tests. This close connection is reflected in babies' behavior very early in the game. At about eight months infants begin solving problems at the same time they're using their burgeoning communication skills—mainly in the forms of sounds and gestures. An eight-month-old baby, for example, might pull on a tablecloth in an effort to reach something on the table—that's a cognitive skill (messy as the results might be). At the same stage in his development, he might also make sounds and gestures to get his mother to help him reach something—a communication skill. At about eighteen months, toddlers are able to concentrate on two mental images at once, and are also able to combine two words. The language skills–mental skills parallels go on and on and continue into the school years.

Your child's language skills when he first enters school are the best indicator of his academic success in later years, which isn't surprising since language is the primary means of instruction and gaining information. Numerous developmental studies show that children who speak better develop better writing skills, and children who comprehend speech better are better readers. Dr. Elizabeth Wiig and her colleagues at Boston University, for instance, reported in 2000 that approximately 60 percent of children who had *spoken* language difficulties had *reading* and *writing* problems as well. Furthermore, a study reported in 2003 by Dr. Ken Apel at Wichita State University in Kansas found that spoken language skills—sound awareness, and knowledge of word meanings and prefixes and suffixes—are as crucial to correct spelling as understanding which sounds and letters go together. These kinds of studies also indicate that youngsters with better language skills are more popular and more accepted by their classmates, which again makes sense when you consider that children use language to express their feelings and negotiate disputes with other children.

Children with poor communication skills, on the other hand, tend to lag behind in school, and initial difficulties in learning language often stay with them into adolescence. Over the years, I've seen hundreds of preschool children with language problems mature into school-aged children with academic problems—and often behavior problems to boot. Court statistics show that youthful offenders almost always have a history of academic difficulties.

Needless to say, all parents want to avoid those kinds of potential problems. We want our children to do well in school and thrive both academically and socially. And that's a good part of what this book is about—when you help your child get off to a good start by giving him a good communication base in these early years, you're taking a giant step in the right direction.

As a parent, you're a tremendously important part of your child's mental growth and development. You can help him grow the kind of active and imaginative mind you'd like him to possess. Some very simple things you do with your baby now will have a huge payoff for both of you down the line. When, for instance, you encourage your infant to look at an object as you talk about it, you're teaching him to focus his attention, an extremely important mental skill. When you play *hide the toy*, and talk about the object when it reappears, you're encouraging your baby to anticipate and connect certain sounds to certain objects and stimulating his brain. Language and cognition go hand in hand. As you help your child develop one, you help him grow the other—and the earlier you start, the more developed he will be later.

All this might sound like a big responsibility—and it is, in a way. But that doesn't mean it has to be onerous or difficult. Learning how to communicate effectively with your baby and helping to stimulate his language and mental development is easy, fun, and extremely rewarding. Most of the interactions and month-by-month activities in this book will fit easily into your everyday life—you can do them during diaper changes, feedings, and dressing. And as your baby matures and changes, the suggested exercises and activities do, too. Although most of us understand that mental development occurs with stimulation and learning, it's also important to note that the *type* of stimulation your baby needs changes as he grows. A mobile hung over his crib, for instance, will be exciting to him at two months old, but it will bore him to distraction at two years. Likewise, speaking to your baby in one or two words will stimulate language growth when he's six months old, but retard language development when he's eighteen months. That's why all the activities in this book are arranged month by month to coincide with and perfectly suit each stage of your baby's development.

All the techniques, games, activities, and exercises have been created, collected, compiled, and field-tested—or rather crib-tested—over the thirty years that I've been involved in child language development. They worked like a charm for my clients and my own kids, and I know your baby will benefit greatly from them, too. The important thing is to have fun with it all. As you'll soon find out, I'm a big believer in natural, relaxed interactions and simple techniques that use everyday objects creatively. Artificially staged games and expensive toys are really not necessary. The idea is to stimulate language, encourage mental development, enhance baby-parent bonding, and boost the growth of other physical and sensory areas crucial to early communication, and that's about love and caring, not money and artifice.

One last note: Because I often work with children with language impairments, I'm always conscious of parental concerns. Rest assured that no suggestions in this book would be harmful to any child with a disability. In fact, some of the activities I recommend are also prescribed by several early intervention programs. Still, this book is no substitute for the individual speech or language intervention that can be provided by a certified speech-language pathologist. While I respond to some special issues in Appendix A, I strongly advise that you check with a professional if you have particular concerns.

One *final* last note: In the name of gender equality I've alternated gender pronouns from chapter to chapter. So whether your baby is a boy or a girl, he or she will have his or her turn.

CHAPTER TWO

Your Baby's Growing Mind

CONTRARY to what child development experts once believed, the mind of a newborn is not a tabula rasa, or blank slate, upon which development is written. An infant's mind is a dynamic and expanding system that has already begun to acquire information before she's born. While a baby is still in the womb, her sensory systems are receiving data and feeding her information. Your new baby, for instance, has already learned to recognize your voice months before she is born. By the time she finally arrives, she's ready and able to learn even more from the world around her.

But although your baby's basic systems are all functioning at birth, her brain is relatively unorganized. There is no system set up yet to maximize the use of her one hundred billion nerve cells. The sections of her brain are like separate communities unlinked by roads or telephone lines. Because her nerve cells (or neurons) and senses are unconnected, it's difficult for her to reach for things she sees, or to track noises out of her view. Healthy adult brains in comparison are like superhighways, telephones, the Internet, and the most up-to-date tracking devices combined. Cells are in continual communication with each other, allowing information and data to pass easily between parts of the brain. Someone pitches you a ball, you see it, figure the distance, and signal your arm to move, your hand to catch it, and your fingers to clasp it—all in a split second.

Your baby's brain will operate that fast, too, someday. But first she needs to activate and organize her nerve cells and sensory and motor systems. That's an exciting part of development, and you have a big role to play in it.

The overall organization of your newborn's brain begins when specific working areas become activated—areas like visual processing, which is assigned to the back of the brain, and hearing, which is located close to each ear, among others. While many of these designated areas of her brain are *developed* at birth, they haven't been "switched on" yet. It's like they're on standby, ready for action but awaiting the cue to start. A newborn's memory is also extremely limited in terms of how much and how long it can hold information. As her memory circuits are "turned on" and her experiences increase, she's able to remember more, and do more, for longer periods of time.

Within a few months of birth, and with sufficient levels of stimulation—which at first is simply proper feeding and everyday TLC (tender loving care)—each of the functional areas within your baby's brain will turn on and start operating. The sensory areas—vision, hearing, smell, taste, and touch—activate first. But this is only a basic level of functioning. Further organization is the key to growth and development of your baby's mind—and that's where you come in.

Through interactions with you and the world, your baby will construct pathways that link all the different areas of her brain. By repeating actions like reaching for toys, and experiencing sensory stimulation, such as watching a mobile turn or feeling soft toys, she'll slowly build the brain network that will enable her to put sensory information to use; to perceive it, comprehend it, and to store and retrieve it at will.

Every new experience helps shape your baby's brain organization by allowing her another opportunity to connect sensory, motor, and memory areas of her brain. You can actually improve your baby's capacity to learn and to think by providing her with the kinds of experiences that stimulate her brain and challenge her to use and grow her mind. It may be gently stroking her skin when she's a newborn or reading books together when she's a year old—it's all about the *right* stimulation at the *right* time in her development.

Over the next few years you'll be able to watch as your baby's development unfolds one step at a time, and trust me, as a father of three, it's a thrilling process to behold—the first random reflexive behaviors that mysteriously metamorphose into early eye-hand coordinated reaching; the random sounds that become purposeful and transform into words. It's truly something, and it's even more exciting when you have an idea of the actual growth process that's taking place inside your little one's head. Understanding the nuances makes your multifaceted role of parent-teacher-supporter-cheerleader-partner (and more) even more gratifying and, in many ways, more effective.

Before we move on to the Shared Communication principles and their practical application, I want to give you a little background about your baby's various skills and how they are going to develop. I promise not to overburden you with a slew of academic, must-remember, developmental factoids here. My goal in this chapter is to let you know about each area of development so that you have the pleasure of consciously watching it blossom and a core understanding of your baby's needs at various stages.

Flowers in a Marvelous Bouquet

The areas of infant development are like flower buds in a bouquet. Every bud in the vase unfolds separately, but each contributes to the overall beauty of the bouquet. Any nutrient dropped into the water enriches each individual bud as it enhances them all and helps the whole bouquet bloom. Similarly, when you enhance your baby's skills in one area of development, every other area benefits and your baby grows and thrives. That's why encouraging your baby's overall development helps her to learn to talk, and vice versa. The areas of development that are important to nourish during these very early years are movement, reception, perception, cognition, and communication.

MOVEMENT

Movement is generally referred to as motor activity or neuromuscular activity. It involves your child's brain, nervous system, and muscles. It's the way she coordinates her actions; the way she breathes, sucks and swallows, kicks her feet, or bats at her mobile. Motor activity influences her ability to act upon her world, as opposed to just responding to it, and it greatly affects every other area of development, especially in the first two years of her life. Her ability to move her head and eyes, for example, allows face-to-face communication with you. Being able to physically create sounds is essential to producing language. And having the capability to sit without support later in development frees her hands to explore and learn more about her surroundings, which, in turn, helps grow her mind.

Your baby already had an impressive array of motor skills at birth, and has, in fact, had them for some time. You moms might remember those very early flutters of movement at about two months into your pregnancy. At about the same time, your baby-to-be might have given a startle or jolt in response to your sudden movements. By three months, she was rotating within your womb, making hand contact with her own tiny face, and occasionally sucking in and swallowing some of the amniotic fluid around her. So it's not surprising that she's capable of so much movement now. Birth actually resulted in relatively minor changes in your baby's motor abilities, but it did result in big changes in the types of challenges she faces in the brand-new world she's just entered; a world where the natural buoyancy of amniotic fluid is replaced by air and a much stronger gravitational pull.

Most of your baby's movements in the first few months after birth are reflexive, which means they're involuntary and somewhat beyond her control. When you put your finger in her palm, for example, she grasps it with her little fingers. While it would be lovely to think she's holding on because of filial affection, she actually has little control over this response. These kinds of reflexes are mostly reactive responses to the world. Touch your baby's lips, for instance, and she'll move them. Motor development, on the other hand, is proactive: The movement is purposeful. Your baby moves her lips so that you will touch them. That's a big difference!

Almost all your baby's involuntary reflexes will disappear by the time she's three to four months old, and she'll begin to reach out, explore, and coordinate her movements. Her purposeful control over her movements will begin with her head. First, she'll be able to hold it up all by herself for brief periods, and then have the ability to move it side to side. Within months she'll be able to sit alone, then stand, then walk, and then . . . look out! She'll be running around as fast as her little legs can carry her.

Each of your baby's movements send information to her brain about her spatial positioning—where she is relative to things around her, which in turn helps her know when she's secure and if she can attempt various movements safely. If she reaches for an object and misses, her little brain reprograms for the next try and stores that information for future attempts. Similarly, if she tries to say "Doggie" and gets it wrong, she tries again. This inner feedback is vital to her development because it teaches her what it *feels* like to say the word, as well as to hear it—an important part of learning to speak.

By one year of age, your baby will have enough motor control to start talking. That is, she'll have enough physical ability to coordinate her breathing with her mouth, tongue, and lip movement to actually produce words on purpose. But she'll need much more than that to become an accomplished speaker. That's where the other areas of development come in. Your baby will need *reception* to gather the experiences that give her something to talk about. She'll need the *cognitive* ability to know that a sound can stand for a thing or an action. And she'll need the *perceptual* ability to decipher the words she hears.

RECEPTION

Reception allows your baby to receive information from her body's senses: touch, taste, smell, vision, and hearing, as well as balance and muscle feedback. It gives her the ability to see, feel, smell, hear, taste, coordinate movement, and realize her position in space. Although, as I mentioned, all these senses are up and running at birth, some of them are more highly developed than others.

Hearing is probably the most highly developed at birth because it had the most stimulation of all the senses in utero. By five months into your pregnancy, the basics of your baby's hearing were fully formed and functioning, albeit within a liquid environment, and for the next four months, she was exposed to your voice and all the voices around you, as well as to environmental sounds—dogs barking, horns honking, music playing. During the late months of your pregnancy, she may have even given a slight startle in response to unexpected sounds.

Most newborns actually experience a slight hearing *loss* because of fluid in the middle ear, one of the ear's three chambers. You should know that the fluid is not the result of a cold or infection. It's simply one of the last vestiges of the fluid environment that was your baby's home for nine months, and has a relatively insignificant impact on overall hearing. It usually drains within a week or so.

Your baby's sense of *touch* and *feel* are also well developed, although somewhat less than hearing. Studies have shown that fetuses are able to respond to some touch as early as eight weeks after conception, and by fourteen weeks their entire bodies are responsive. You moms may recall gently stroking your distended abdomen and the calming effect it seemed to have on your baby-to-be. That's because by six months into your pregnancy, your baby already had tactile and temperature receptors, although, of course, there was little opportunity to use the latter because of the protective nature of your womb.

The senses of *taste* and *smell* are somewhat less developed at birth since they receive less stimulation in utero, although we do know from studies that fetuses respond very differently to sweet and noxious substances introduced into the amniotic fluid.

Not surprisingly, *vision* is the least stimulated sense in utero. Eye movements begin about four months into pregnancy, but at most, fetuses are capable of responding only to strong contrasts of light and darkness, sort of like the light-dark contrasts you'd see through tightly closed eyes on a sunny day. At birth, your baby will be near-sighted. She'll be able to see best at about eight inches—the perfect distance for feeding and cuddling. As the muscles around the corneas of her eyes mature, she'll be able to focus on things farther and farther away. By about twelve weeks, she'll have full range of focus from near to far.

Finally, *balance* and *muscle feedback*, both very important for your baby's coordinated movement and spatial knowledge, are quite limited at first. She won't sense when she's near the edge of a sofa, bed, or changing table, for instance, until she acquires some *experience* with heights. There's a reason cribs have sides.

PERCEPTION

None of these reception skills would mean much without perception. While *reception* is your baby's ability to receive information, *perception* is her ability to interpret that information. Perception allows her to distinguish likenesses from differences and recognize stimuli or incoming information that she may not have experienced before. Simply put, perception is your baby's attempt to make sense of her world, to categorize it. Typical newborns can perceive differences and likenesses in taste and smell, colors, sound pitch and loudness, and speech sounds. Although these characteristics won't mean much to your baby yet, she's already begun to process the data and learn from the sensory information—and she's already formed some very strong preferences.

You've probably noticed that your baby prefers you to other people. That's not because she already knows what a great mom you're going to be, it's because so much of the sensory information she's received so far has come directly from you, and she has strong associations with the information and the patterns they form. Your baby can identify your scent and the sound of your voice, and thus likes them better than anybody else's. After repeated exposure to your sensory information, your baby has started to remember the information. Quite a feat, when you think about it. If you remain a nurturing, caring, loving parent, she will soon prefer your face to all others, too. With continual proximity to you and a bit more memory development, your baby will not only recognize your scent, voice, and face easily, but will also associate them with all the warm, safe feelings they impart. It won't be long before just seeing or hearing you will trigger warm memories in her. So there is a rich dividend to staying positive and hanging in with the 2 A.M. feedings.

COGNITION

Cognitive skills are intellectual or mental. While perception allows your baby to make sense of sensory information, cognition allows her to comprehend the information and give it meaning. Cognition is the way she solves problems, organizes and remembers information, and approaches new input. When your little one swats a soft, squeaky toy for the first time, she may be startled by the noise. But after a few more swats, instead of being surprised she'll *expect* the toy to make a noise when she touches it. Then she'll touch the toy for the explicit purpose of making the noise. That's cognitive learning. She has processed information and is using it to alter her world.

As you watch your baby over the next few years, you'll be able to see these kinds of cognitive abilities develop almost step by step. First she'll start to pay attention (or "attend"); then she'll learn how to *discriminate*, *organize*, and *remember*. You'll notice as you go through the exercises and games in chapters Five through Eleven that many of them are earmarked "cognition." Those activities are designed to help grow these various aspects of your baby's mental awareness at just the right stage of her mental development. A quick word about how these specific cognitive elements operate.

Attending ◆ Attending is the very first step in cognition. In order for an infant to begin to process incoming information, whether it's the sound of a rattle or the colors of a mobile, she has to pay attention to it. Interestingly, humans aren't born with the ability to attend. Newborns cannot actively direct their attention; they're neither able to look or listen purposefully, nor stop looking or listening once something has captured their attention. So for the first few weeks, while you may not be able to draw your infant's attention to your face, you could find her staring intently at some especially colorful or visually interesting object. While she might seem totally engrossed and intrigued with it, the truth is she is simply physically incapable of stopping herself from looking.

After those few weeks, though, your baby *will* be able to purposely pay attention to sounds, objects, and actions for short periods of time. By the time she's eight months old or so, she'll be able to share her interest with you by pointing to the things she wants you to see. It's these actions and objects that will become her first words. As she matures, her pointing will commonly be complemented with words. Gradually, pointing will decrease and words will increase until they replace pointing as the way to direct your attention. First the words will be related to things that are nearby and visual, but soon your child will start to talk about things that aren't necessarily present. She might say "Doggie bark," for example, when there's no dog around, just because she's got Fido on her mind and wants to talk about him. That's when you know you've got a true conversationalist on your hands.

Discrimination ◆ The next step in processing information, *discrimination,* requires your baby to hold information in her memory (rather like a computer's RAM) while she compares it to other incoming and stored information. This is where perception comes in. If your newborn hears the same sound over and over, she'll become used to it. She's made a comparison in her brain and noted that the sounds are the same, so she'll know when the sound changes.

But although your new baby has *some* ability to discriminate sights and sounds, both are restricted by her extremely short memory and limited knowledge. By about three months, though, she'll have begun to store familiar images so that she can recognize your face and other familiar images. Within weeks after that you'll be rewarded with a little smile when she sees you. Your face now matches the anticipated pattern in her brain. Soon even voices will help her retrieve this visual pattern. When she hears your voice, she'll be able to retrieve the visual pattern of your face, will anticipate seeing you, and will become excited when you finally appear. She's made a mental connection!

By seven months, your tot will be able to retrieve some images from her databank with a word. She'll hear "dog," for instance, search her memory for the correlating image, then look at and maybe point to Fido. By age one she'll be able to reverse the process; seeing the image will elicit the word. She'll see Fido, retrieve the word, and say "Doggie." Even more amazing, by eighteen months, she'll be able to access the word *doggie* even when the dog's not present. The key to that ability is increased memory and *organization.*

Organization ◆ Your baby is able to remember things about the dog because she has begun to organize all the information about it. Theoretically, all of us only have a limited—although huge—number of storage areas in our brains. You could think of these storage areas as file cabinet drawers. In order to store the ever-increasing amounts of information that flood our brains every day, we have to continually reorganize these drawers—constantly adding new folders and making new cross-checklists to access the information.

As you can imagine, the process of organization and reorganization gets rather complex. Your baby's notion of *dog*, for instance, has to be reconfigured with each new example of a dog she sees or hears. If Fido is a golden lab, for example, and your baby later meets your neighbor's dog, Muffy, a small black poodle, your baby's concept of dog will be expanded to include differentiations in size, color, fur texture, and so on. These new characteristics must then be linked to the word *dog,* as well as to scents and sounds that are also part of the concept.

Your baby—or maybe I should say her brain, since this takes place on a very subconscious level—organizes new information as it's acquired and as she gains new organizational skills. As she matures, she'll build an almost unlimited number of networks, and her ever-increasing collection of images and words and word groups will become connected. This cognitive organization helps shape her language, which, in turn, affects the ways in which she thinks about her world. Much later, she'll be able to form concepts purely from language, without actually experiencing examples of that concept. Most of us haven't experienced a deep-sea treasure hunt firsthand, but all of us have a concept of what it is—and given the chance, we could even act on that concept and sign up on the next ship going out.

Memory ◆ The next step in information processing, *memory*, is essentially retrieving information from storage. When your one-year-old sees you and calls "Mommy," she's withdrawing the word from her memory, accessing it through the image of your face that she's stored away. Now, that's organization! She also has memory from her senses, her muscles, and past mental events, such as how she's solved problems like getting your attention.

Your little one has three types of memory. *Working memory*—which lasts only a second or two—enables her to compare incoming information. When she hears two sounds in succession, for example, she uses her working memory to compare the two sounds. We also hold language in our working memory very briefly while we decode it and determine its meaning. When your baby hears you ask, "Want juice?" for example, she holds the phrase in her *working memory* for a second or two while she accesses the meaning for each word and then puts them together to get the overall meaning.

Short-term memory allows us to hold information for a longer time period—up to a minute—but is very limited in the *amount* of information it can hold. If your infant tried to repeat the phrase "Want juice?" from the last example, she'd be using her short-term memory.

Long-term memory consists of organized information that has been stored and cross-referenced. Stored information can be accessed as a result of external stimulation. If your child sees something in her environment, for instance, she'll have to go into her long-term memory to find the appropriate word for it. The information can also be accessed by internal searches—your child looks for a word so that she can tell you about something that happened.

A newborn has very little stored memory and almost no notion of how to retrieve the information that is stored. But slowly over the first year, your little one will build a memory store and a method of retrieval. The more she exercises her brain to retrieve information, the better it will work the next time—which again is why your Shared Communication role is so important.

Your baby's early memory will include past activities and routines, such as dressing and feeding, familiar faces like yours, and everyday objects like her bottle and toys. With continued exposure, by the time she's three months old she'll be able to anticipate your behavior in a simple game. She'll be able to guess, for instance, where a toy you've hidden is likely to appear next. The sequences stored in her memory enable her to predict your behavior. Later she'll be able to predict the words that accompany your behavior in various routines. When my children were babies, I used to finish up a diaper change with the phrase, "Well, good as new!" They learned very quickly that those words meant the changing was finished and a game was about to begin.

As your baby's memory gradually increases, she'll be able to find objects that are completely hidden, and by eight months, her memory will have advanced to such a degree that she'll search in the location where an object was *last seen*. She'll be able to hold the image of the object and to recognize it when found.

Her growing ability to memorize sequences rather than just single events enables your baby to *imitate* first herself and then others. When she hears herself say "Bah" at six months, for instance, she quickly retrieves the motor patterns from her memory and does it again—that's when you start hearing a lot of babbling. By about eight months, she'll be able to hold the sequence of a simple action you do in her memory while programming her muscles to imitate you—you clap your hands, she'll clap hers! After performing the action, she'll scan her memory again for correctness, matching it to the remembered sample of your clapping.

Memory also influences your baby's problem-solving skills. Initially, she'll discover cause and effect by chance. She'll kick her feet and the mobile over the crib will shake. Gradually, she'll make the connection: Kick = mobile moves. She'll kick again and again with the same result. Eureka! New information to store away in her memory! Next time she sees a mobile over the crib, she'll kick in expectation of the remembered result.

This is also the time, developmentally, that she'll begin connecting other behaviors to consequences, such as your response to her crying, and will begin to predict consequences *prior* to her actions. "Hmmm . . . If I pull on the tablecloth, I can get the glass of juice." This is just a short step away from gesturing and vocalizing to achieve the same end—"Mommy, juice."

It's easy to see just how closely cognitive growth is linked to the ability to use words . . . and talking is just around the corner.

CHAPTER THREE

How Your Baby Learns to Talk

Talking—The First Baby Steps

"Language is the inner voice of thought."
—Dr. Lev Vygotski

THE wonders of cognitive development take on a whole new dimension as your baby learns to talk. Language gives him a brand-new way to express himself and communicate his needs and thoughts. Your baby's first communications with you will be unintentional. He'll simply cry because he's wet or hungry; make little gurgles and gulps when he's relaxed; or make cooing sounds in the back of his throat when he's alert and satisfied. Essentially, these are just sounds he's making in response to his body. He's not trying to communicate or influence anybody else. In fact, he doesn't know yet that he can affect others, but in the beginning that doesn't really matter. What's important is that you respond. Your responsiveness completes a circle of shared communication between the two of you and nourishes a very important part of your baby's mental, physical, and emotional well-being.

Long before your baby understands the meaning of your words, he'll respond to the gentleness in your voice and your caring touch. Long before he says his first words, you'll respond to his crying, cooing, and sound making. Through shared experiences with your baby, you'll come to understand his protests, requests, signals of interest, and nonverbal questioning. You'll be able to differentiate between the loud, shrill cry and series of whimpers that characterize his pain cry, and the quieter crying interspersed with silent periods of sucking that make up his hunger cry. And you'll laugh together over the funny things he does.

This kind of early communication in the first year of your baby's life sets up a powerful bond between parent and child and forms the foundation on which your baby will build speech and language. Within months, his behavior will become more purposeful and he'll make noises to get your attention. Then, week-by-week, as his communication matures and becomes more complex, your baby and you will begin taking turns with sounds. Turn taking is an important early communication skill, and one that's essential for communication all through our lives. Your baby will start practicing this fundamental skill as early as three months old, as he makes sounds in response to yours—just as we do in real conversations. As we'll discuss later, even during these very early oral exchanges, it's important to provide a silent pause so that he has time to respond.

By about his sixth or seventh month, your little guy will respond to a few words and to everyday gestures like holding out your arms to signify that you're going to pick him up. He'll even begin to gesture himself and check to make sure that you're paying attention. In fact, don't be surprised if he develops a whole system of gestures for the messages he wants to convey to you. He'll reach for things he wants, hold his arms up when he wants to be picked up, point to things he fancies, and hand you things. He'll look at you very intently to make sure that you understand what he's "saying." He may squeal with delight during play, or make insistent grunting sounds as he reaches for Fido's tail, or regale you with a loud, insistent whine when Fido beats a hasty retreat. That might not be talking, but it's very definite communication. It's a beginning.

This early form of communication leads to talking before you know it—and that's when the fun really begins. On his road to verbal proficiency, your baby will produce hundreds of thousands of different utterances and soon be able to string words and thoughts together in ways that will make for some truly memorable moments. I remember one Christmas when my son Todd was about four. A recently widowed neighbor stopped by, and Todd was showing her his favorite Christmas tree decorations when he suddenly stopped in his tracks, gazed up at her with a look of real concern, and said, "I hope our lights will make you happy." It was so sweet my wife and I almost burst into tears. And talking about sweet—one of my favorite non sequiturs came from my granddaughter, who was then about two-and-a-half. During one of our regular phone conversations, she whispered, "I love you Gran'pa, but it's not my birthday." What could be better than being loved for yourself, not your presents? She had me wound around her little finger tight as twine—still does.

These kinds of magical moments are only a few short years away. First, though, your baby has to learn the rudiments of *speech* and *language*. Although these two terms are often used interchangeably, they are, in fact, quite different. Speech is the motor skill activity that we use to produce words. It's the physical act of speaking, and it's very complex. When your one-year-old says "Doggie!" for instance, his brain will have to coordinate all the little muscles in his throat, tongue, mouth, lips, jaw, and chest to form the sequence of sounds that make up that word. It's not easy. If you've ever been momentarily tongue-tied, you have a slight sense of how difficult speech can be—and you have decades of practice behind you. Your baby will be learning the process from scratch.

First Sounds

New babies cry a lot, but they also make lots of comfort or cooing noises. These sounds don't sound like adult speech sounds for a number of reasons. Although your baby can distinguish different speech sounds when he hears them, he can't yet program his little muscles to produce them. A newborn has great difficulty using his tongue, lower jaw, and lips independently. He also lacks the muscle control it takes to produce the precise movements that speech requires. His oral anatomy is different from yours, too—not just in size, but also in location and proportion. His larynx (voice box), for example, is very high, near the base of his tongue, which causes his tongue to fill his mouth much more than yours or mine does. It will take your child five to eight years to gain enough control and coordination to articulate all the sounds of the English language at will.

With growth, maturation, and learning, though, your baby will be able to produce many speech sounds (vocalizations)—first randomly, and then at will. He'll gradually begin to imitate the vocalizations he hears, and soon his repertoire of sounds will begin to reflect the language around him.

He'll also learn to string sounds together in predictable ways. The basic building blocks will be sounds formed by a *c*onsonant plus a *v*owel, or what we in language development call a CV syllable. When your baby's about six months old, he'll begin to produce strings of CVCVCV sounds, such as "ba-ba-ba." Many of his first words will follow this same CV pattern, such as *mama, dada,* or *baba (bottle).* It's easy to see how this leads to other words. *Baba* is very close to *baybay (baby).* Just a slightly different vowel sound and you've got a real word. Now you know why children say "doggie" instead of dog. They're simply following their pattern of CVCV sounds. *Dog,* which is a CVC sound (d-aw-g), is actually more difficult for an infant to say. Adults say "doggie" because children do, not the other way around—a little known fact.

HOW SPEECH WORKS

Of course, your six-month-old's first CV attempts—those irresistibly adorable *ba-ba-ba's*—have no meaning for him or anyone else. He's really just practicing the mechanisms of speech. The actual process of speech starts long before these practice runs. Your baby's first cries are the real beginning of the physiological learning process that will enable him to talk. Breathing *(respiration)* is the very first step of speech. As you probably know, the main function of breathing is to supply oxygen to the blood. But humans, as well as dogs and some other animals, have also adapted breathing for the purpose of producing sounds.

Exhaled air, in fact, is the energy that drives our speech system. That's why it's hard for us to talk when we're "short of breath," and why opera singers need good breath control to hold those impossibly long notes. If you watch your baby closely, you'll notice that even he takes a big gulp of air before letting go with a big wail. Babies naturally learn to coordinate breathing, swallowing, and sound-making. They make some mistakes along the way, of course, even choking a bit from time to time, but eventually they get it.

Because breathing is such a natural part of life, we don't think about it much, but it's actually a very interesting physiological process. As you watch your sleeping baby, you'll notice that he spends equal amounts of time inhaling and exhaling. Later, once he becomes more mobile, his breathing will change according to the level and type of activity he's engaging in—just like ours does. If at age two he's running around the house chasing Fido, his breathing will be louder and quicker, but his inhalation and exhalation phases will still be approximately equal in duration.

Talking, though, is another story. When we speak, our inhalation is quick, and the exhalation is long and drawn out, thanks to tiny muscles between our ribs that help slow expiration. Check it out the next time you're talking on the phone. You'll notice there's barely enough time for the quick inhalation, but the exhalation seems to go on and on. Your baby will be learning similar control as he learns to talk.

During exhalation, as the air leaves our lungs, it passes through a formation of spongy bony cartilage called the larynx, also known as the voice box. The Adam's apple is actually the protrusion of one of the cartilages of the larynx. Within the larynx are two folds of tissue that move either to block the air or to allow easy passage. During most breathing, these so-called vocal folds, or "vocal cords," are effortlessly moved to the sides. When we talk, our vocal folds are either out of the way or closed. When they're closed, air exiting from our lungs builds up until the pressure blows the vocal folds apart. They close tightly again and are blown apart again. This occurs several thousand times a second. The result is a little buzz, the beginning of a speech sound. The process of producing that buzzing sound is called *phonation*.

If you put your fingertips on your larynx, say "Ahhhhhhhhhhhh," and hold the sound, you should be able to feel some vibration. That vibration is the vocal folds being blown apart by air from your lungs and returning together again very rapidly. You can even feel the change in the vibrations as you change your pitch or loudness.

Right after you bring your baby home, you might hear his vocal folds making that subtle buzz as air passes back and forth through his larynx when he cries or even as he inhales. It doesn't take him long, though, to realize that it's not a very efficient way to use the larynx. Within a week or so the buzz will stop on inhalation as he opts to make crying sounds only when he exhales.

Since buzzing makes for rather limited communication, we humans modify the vocal buzz of the larynx into a speech sound by *resonating* it through our vocal chamber and funneling or blocking it with our tongues, teeth, or lips. The vocal fold buzz is carried along by our exhaled breath and changes as it passes through our throat (pharynx), mouth, and sometimes our nasal cavities. The shape of these passages modifies the resonated sound. When you say "Ahhhhhhh," for instance, the sound is being shaped by a relatively open mouth and exclusion of the nasal cavity. If you ever talked through a garden hose, tube, or pipe to one of your friends when you were a kid, or a bullhorn later on, you get the idea of how sound changes when it goes through different passages.

You can actually feel it when you use your nasal cavity for resonance. If you place your finger under your nose, and say "Mmmmm," you can feel a slight bit of warm air exiting through your nostrils. But when you say "Sssssssssss," there's no air from the nostrils. Your baby lacks the control and coordination that would allow him to switch between sounds as easily as you can, but as he learns to talk he'll learn to coordinate the shaping of these vibrating cavities. Meanwhile, even as a newborn he can entertain you with vowel sounds such as *Ahhhhh* and *Eeeee*, which are the easiest to produce. All he has to do is open his little mouth and *resonate*.

The next step in speaking is *articulation*, which we do by placing oral structures in the path of the resonated vocal breath stream. We can pass a stream of breath through a narrow constriction made by the tongue and teeth or tongue and the roof of the mouth, like we do when we say "Sssssss." Try it. You'll be able to feel the air pass over your tongue. We can also block the stream of air completely and let it explode, as we do when we utter the sound "Puh." Try placing your hand in front of your mouth when you say "Puh." Feel the explosion of air?

When you look at your baby it's amazing to think of all the intricate connections in his little brain and body that will allow him to coordinate these processes—all automatically, with no conscious thought. And think, his sound-making has to be coordinated with the processes of breathing, swallowing, and chewing, too. He'll learn all the basics rather quickly, but perfecting the process will take years. Most children are in kindergarten before they master some of the more difficult sounds, such as *r*, *l*, and *th*. Multisyllabic words take time, too, and are often shortened, treating us to such treasures as *efant* for *elephant* and *tefone* for *telephone*. Consonant blends, in which two or more consonant sounds are mixed together, as in *blend*, are tricky for toddlers, too, and are often simplified by leaving one sound out, as in *top* for *stop*.

Language

At the same time your baby is figuring out how to physically control the muscles that produce all these complex sounds of speech, he'll also be processing the information needed for *language*.

At the most basic level, language is a set of symbols (words) combined with rules on how they go together (grammar). Although your baby won't have any idea about the formal rules of grammar until he's well into his school years, he'll be learning language by hearing the speech of people around him—especially you.

During his first year, you are unequivocally your baby's most important source of language exposure. He'll learn specific sounds, syllables, and intonational patterns from you, and imitate your sounds long before he mimics the sounds of others in his environment. He may even invent his own words by combining speech sounds and syllables. It's interesting to note that even if a child had all the cognitive and physical skills necessary for speech, he wouldn't be able to communicate with words without being exposed to language. When you talk with your baby, you're providing him with the needed exposure. And the principles of Shared Communication in the next chapter will guarantee that you're maximizing that exposure in the most beneficial ways possible.

FIRST WORDS

Somewhere around the age of one, the momentous day will come when your baby will utter his first word—or maybe even words. His choice of that word or words will be influenced by many things: how important the word is to him, how many times he's heard it, and the syllable and sound structure of the word. My son Jason, who was totally in love with his toy train, said "Choo-choo" before he said "Dada"—which, now that I think of it, was terribly undiplomatic of him. Still, it was unquestionably preferable to other first words I've heard about. One student told me his niece's first little verbal gem was an unsavory four-letter word. That says a lot about that particular home environment, but it also serves as a caveat to us all—watch it! When you have a baby in your midst, someone is listening . . . and learning.

Your baby will continue speaking in individual words or small groups of words for the next year or two. By the time he's three years old, he'll be conversing in phrases and sentences. The interesting thing is that although your baby doesn't know a noun from a verb, or a preposition from a pronoun, most of his phrases and sentences will be properly constructed simply because they *sound right* to him. That takes impressive cognitive ability! This is not to say that your little linguist will immediately start sounding like a mini adult; he won't. It's only natural for babies and toddlers to say things like "Nana" for *banana and* "Mommy throw me" instead of the more mature "Mommy, throw the ball to me." Limited memory and skills, and a small vocabulary, will restrict your baby's language for some time—though happily, not his communication with you.

Once your toddler starts talking, he'll come up with some immensely creative words and sentences—many of them 100 percent original. One of my personal favorites came from my son Jason when he was about two-and-a-half years old. (Somehow our own children always seem to say the cutest things.) One night Jason staggered into our bedroom, rubbing his eyes and dragging his teddy bear, and sighed. "*I hate nightmaring*." *Nightmaring*, of course, isn't in the dictionary, but it seemed a wonderfully inspired word to this besotted dad. He'd even formed a perfect sentence! A friend's son, a little twenty-two-month-old baseball lover, came up with another good one. He invented the word *fast-a-baseball* to mean *quickly*. Quite ingenious, really—almost a simile! One thing I've learned—enjoy these precious moments when they happen; kids grow up so fast, these moments will be over before you know it.

THE NUANCES OF COMMUNICATION

Full communication often incorporates more than language and speech. Body language and posture, facial expression, gestures, reading and writing, and sometimes using sign language are all part of the picture. In face-to-face encounters, in fact, gestures, body language, and facial expressions often carry the bulk of the information. It's quite astonishing how quickly children learn to interpret the nuances. Remember when your mom planted her feet firmly, put her hands on her hips, and gave you "The Look." She meant business, and you knew it. The tighter her lips, the narrower the eyes, the stiffer her body posture, the farther away you wanted to be. A simple silence conveyed a wealth of information.

> CHILD: Hey, Mom, can Kim stay for dinner?
> MOM: (Silence)

Every child knows that a silent answer means "*NO!*" Your baby will be learning all these signals as he learns to talk. And he'll pick up others, too—our variations in speech intonation, speed, and loudness all carry messages. As adults, intonation is such an integral part of our speech that we rarely consciously think about it, but consider how it can color the meaning of one sentence.

You're going to the party.	Statement of fact.
YOU'RE going to the party?	We didn't expect YOU to go.
You're **GOING** to the party?	It was in doubt.
You're going to the **PARTY**?	As opposed to some other activity.
You're **GOING TO THE PARTY!**	You WILL go!

The emotional quality of our voices also seriously influences the message being conveyed. It tells us if the speaker is excited, nervous, angry, or being seductive. We've probably all played hooky from work at least once in our lives and called in "sick." We put on our best "on my deathbed" voice . . . then went out to play golf or maybe hit the mall.

You'd be amazed at the degree to which your baby is in tune with your intonations. Before he says his first word, he'll probably begin to imitate your intonational patterns. At around ten months, he may even sound like he's making statements and asking questions—but without words.

Now that you've got some background about what it takes to talk, we're ready to get practical and talk about how to get your baby started on the right path—how to help him to talk . . . and grow his mind.

CHAPTER FOUR

Shared Communciation Principles

The Best Ways to Talk to Your Baby

NOT too long ago, after a midday run, a friend and I were attaching a bike rack to my car when a little boy who looked to be about two years old approached us, his mother following close behind him. I smiled, dropped to my usual one-kneed toddler conversational stance, and said, "Hi."

No response. Instead, he touched the car.

"Car!" his mother shouted. "Car, Car. Show the man the car. Say 'car'!"

The little tyke continued walking silently around the car, touching it as he went. All the while, his mother kept up her incessant jabber. She never missed a chance to supply a word or to talk for him. "Door handle! Window! Antenna! Fender . . ." And on and on she went. No pause, no explanation, no breath. Words followed by more words.

When I attempted to interject a suggestion—after she screamed "antenna" a third time—she rolled right over me. "Antenna for the radio! Radio! We listen to the *radio*!" She was enough to try the patience of a saint.

Exasperated, I turned to the little boy. "Bob," I said pointing to myself.

"Tony!" the mother shrieked. "Tell the man your name is Tony!"

I was close to yelling, "Shut up for a minute, would you! Give the kid a break!" But a quick warning look from my friend kept me in check and stopped me from swinging into full speech language–pathologist professor mode. I tried to get the idea across by example instead, but not surprisingly, Tony's mom wasn't having any of that, either. The woman was well beyond learning from subtle examples.

While this overanxious mother wasn't doing her little son any good, she does serve a worthy purpose for us—she stands as the perfect example of exactly what *not* to do. She did everything wrong. Even if she had been concerned that little Tony wasn't talking much, which is my guess, talking *for* him was not the solution. Taking his turn in a potential conversation wouldn't teach him how to take his own turn and speak for himself. That's such an important point. Talking *at* or *for* your child will never improve her communication skills—and it won't help her to learn to talk. In fact, as we've seen with Tony, it quite often does the opposite. True Shared Communication is talking *with* your child, giving her a chance to express herself and validating her efforts, no matter how insignificant they may seem to be.

Although this chapter is not entitled "Teaching Your Child to Talk," it is in many ways what you'll be doing—you just won't be following traditional teaching methods. As a new parent, you're much too busy to take on teaching responsibilities, and the fact is, formal instruction isn't really needed. The best way to "teach" your baby to talk is to expose her to talking in natural everyday conversations. You're already your child's favorite and most frequent conversational partner, so all you have to do is talk in certain ways that are more beneficial than others—Shared Communication ways.

Wordsmiths among you might argue that communication is always shared, but it's really not true sharing when one person does all the talking and the other person does all the listening—and that's the way a lot of parents communicate with their children. Let me give you an example of some *nonsharing* communication that, while much less offensive and damaging than the kind of language-battering Tony's mom employed, is a lot more common.

Here's a mother changing her baby's diaper:

"Lie still, honey, while I change you. You sure are cranky. First, let's get rid of this dirty diaper, then clean you up. There, that's better. Now for a fresh diaper. You should feel better now. Okay, all done."

Now a mother using a few of the upcoming principles to turn this all-too-frequent task into a Shared Communication moment:

MOTHER: Ah, that's why you're cranky. (Pause)

CHILD: (Makes noise)

MOTHER: No, I wouldn't like that either. (Pause) Is this better? (Pause) Sure it is. (Pause) Now you're happy.

CHILD: (Gurgles)

MOTHER: (Gurgles) Happy baby. You talking to Mommy?

CHILD: (Gurgles)

MOTHER: Yes, you are. You're talking. (Pause) Talk to Mommy. (Pause) No? (Pause) Okay honey, all done.

This kind of *interactive* dialog—even when the baby contributes only a gurgle, coo, or smile—is constructed like a real conversation. The mom in this second example stops to allow her baby to respond. Even though the baby doesn't understand the words, she is being treated as a participant and learning about communicating. Cognitively, she's learning a routine and a script for the routine—essential intellectual skills. Both of these scenarios obviously result in a clean diaper—but only one results in communicative and cognitive growth.

The term *Shared Communication* is meant to convey an attitude of real partnership. My goal is for you and your baby to be true conversational *partners*. The principles that we're about to discuss are geared to help both of you participate to your fullest potential, and to make all the ordinary daily exchanges that you have with your baby enjoyable learning experiences for her, as well as fun bonding moments for you both.

Following the Shared Communication method may squeeze a little more time out of your already busy schedule, but most of the exercises and activities that I suggest in the upcoming chapters are designed to fit easily into your everyday activities—you can do a lot of them during feeding, dressing, eating, and bathing. And the principles themselves are simply superior communication techniques that really don't require any more time than inferior ones.

We've become such a multitasking society that our children are getting short shrift when it comes to true nurturing attention. The omnipresence of multimedia in our lives has lulled us into the false assumption that things like TV, videos, DVDs, and talking toys are a viable substitute for actually sitting down and relating to our children. Trust me, they're not. Passive entertainment, like television, is *not* quality communication. It doesn't teach children the kind of interactive communication that's necessary for engaging in conversations. In fact, television talks *at* children— the very thing we want to avoid. Certainly, there's some quality children's programming, but none of it, even the excellent show *Sesame Street*, is responsive to your child. If your little one watches television or videos, at least try to watch with her. Talk about what she's seeing, and use the conversation as a bridge between the TV and your baby.

In my work, I've seen an alarming increase in the number of children with delayed speech and language, and often there's no obvious cause beyond benign neglect. Not long ago I worked with a four-and-a-half-year-old child who was nearly three years behind in his language development! He was docile and passive. The look on his face was glazed, his speech sounded robotic, and he expressed little enthusiasm. With both parents working and an unemployed twentysomething brother hanging around the house, the poor kid was bombarded with nonstop TV from 6 A.M. to midnight! When we got the family to turn off the TV and taught them how to play with the boy, he made a miraculous recovery. (We can only hope that the long-term damage won't be too bad.) Obviously this is an extreme case, but incessant TV is certainly not unique to this home.

The good news is that where a steady diet of TV leaves children unprepared and reticent to participate in the give-and-take of classroom discourse, and one-sided parental communication produces passive, unchallenged, bored children, Shared Communication helps create bright, curious children who enjoy interactive conversation and are open to learning.

The Shared Communication Principles

Imagine yourself being airdropped into a strange but friendly country where the language is so different from yours that even the simplest word is indecipherable. You'd have to come up with a strategy for communicating with the people around you, while they in turn would try various ways to transmit information to you. Well, in a way that's what communicating with a baby is like. Many of the same strategies you'd use to exchange information and sentiments with non–English speakers are amazingly effective with babies. They are, in fact, the building blocks of Shared Communication.

BE ANIMATED

There's a wonderfully memorable scene in the movie *Dances with Wolves* where Kevin Costner, who portrays a lone solider at a deserted army post around 1870, tries to communicate with two members of the Sioux nation. He wants to talk about buffalo, but can't speak the language. To get his meaning across, he sticks his jacket under the back of his shirt to create a buffalo shape, gets down on all fours, makes horns with his hands, and snorts. At first the Sioux look at each other like he's totally nuts, but then one of them gets it. *"Tatanka!"* he says. "Buffalo," says Costner. *"Tatanka!"* says the Indian with a nod and a smile. They go back and forth a few times, each learning the other's word for the shaggy beast. It's a fabulous scene. The point? Kevin wasn't afraid to make a fool of himself in the name of communication—and you shouldn't, either.

The truth is your baby loves it when you're silly. No one, not even little babies, wants to have a conversation with a bore. Exaggerated facial expressions, voice variations, and movement hold your baby's interest. So act surprised, raise your eyebrows like Oscar the Grouch, widen your eyes, make big round O's with your mouth, smile a lot—show lots of teeth. You get the picture. Even very young babies will laugh and giggle at these kinds of carryings-on. Feigning surprise is especially effective when playing little games that introduce actions that aren't expected by your baby—like having a puppet suddenly appear out of nowhere or causing a squeaky toy to make a noise. Your baby will actually be comforted by the fact that you aren't frightened by these unexpected occurrences.

When you're talking, try varying the rhythm, pitch, loudness, and intonation of your voice. Pause more, use a slightly higher pitch, whisper occasionally, and exaggerate your intonation so it sounds a little more like singing. No need to overdo it, just a slightly varied way of speaking lets her know "This talk's for you, kid!"

The main purpose of these shenanigans, aside from pure baby-entertainment value, is that they help your baby pay attention, which, as we've discussed, is an important first stage cognitive skill. So liveliness and enthusiasm are the key words here. When you're playing on the floor together, you might even follow Costner's lead and try acting like a *tatanka*. That'll get your baby's attention for sure!

BE POSITIVE

I can't be more emphatic about this one. Positive feedback is incredibly important when dealing with infants. One of the most essential factors in a child's life is a strong, secure attachment to a nurturing adult. Young children, especially babies, look to us, their parents and caregivers, for comfort, nurturing, and a sense of well-being. Our kind words and deeds help them build trust, let them know they're loved and cared for, and are the building blocks of self-esteem. Children who receive positive feedback blossom like little flowers and have a much better shot at success in school—and in life.

Children who are constantly censured and denounced, on the other hand, become fearful, untrusting, and unsure. Their interactions with other people become tentative, and they may internalize the denouncements and come to think of themselves as bad people. I've heard more than one adult who was abused as a child say, "I guess I was a really bad kid because I made my mother so angry." My standard response is always, "No, you had bad parenting." Later in childhood, if the abuse continues, children usually either withdraw or become resentful and angry themselves.

I remember one incident from a couple of years ago that still makes me shudder when I think about it. My daughter, Jessica, and I were in a crowded toy store picking up something for my granddaughter when we spotted a toddler teetering on top of a bicycle. Apparently his mother had put him up there for safekeeping—if you can imagine. The minute we saw him, we naturally dropped everything and rushed to his aid. Unfortunately, we got there too late—the bike crashed and the toddler tumbled to the floor. Needless to say, the poor little guy started crying. Then along came the mother. You'd have thought she'd have been compassionate and concerned for her son, but no; she was steaming mad—ranting and raving. She slapped him and berated him with an unending stream of verbal abuse. She also got angry with Jessica and me for our concern. I have no idea what this mother's situation was. Maybe she sincerely cared for her child and was simply reacting to her own stupidity at leaving him on the bike; or maybe she was embarrassed by the subsequent chaos. Whatever her motivation, the message she was sending her child was negative, hurtful, and truly damaging to him in the long term. My daughter called it child abuse, and she wasn't far off.

The bottom line is this: The tone of your voice and the things you say to your baby have a tremendous impact on her and will all through her childhood. Babies learn to interpret intonation very early. Within just a few months of birth, your infant will react differently to the tonal quality of your voice. Angry or loud sounds might cause her to cringe or cry; happy sounds will bring smiles and giggles. So keep these positive feedback tips in mind—and keep those smiles and giggles coming.

- Always use a pleasant voice that conveys an upbeat, enthusiastic attitude. You love your baby—let her hear it in the tone of your voice and inflections. Respond with liberal praise, and always show interest in her and her communication efforts.

- The idea of communication is much more appealing to your baby when you encourage it through an accepting attitude and responsiveness in your voice, rather than by demanding it. Avoid overuse of commands like "Say _____" or "Tell me the word for _____." Children find these kinds of directives annoying and often just tune them out. On the other hand, although your baby won't *always* want to do as you ask, you'll be pretty hard to resist when you're being warm, accepting, and positive.

■ Follow your baby's early communication attempts with praise and enthusiasm. Use phrases such as "Yes, you're talking to me," "Tell me more," "Oh, I like the way you're talking." Remember, children whose noise-making is ignored stop making noises. Sure, your baby is producing some sounds purely for her own enjoyment, but a lot of it is for you. She wants you to react, and when that reaction is affirming, she'll be back for more.

■ When your baby begins to use real words, use *her* words as a bridge to *your* comments, like this:

CHILD: Kitty!
ADULT: Um-hm, that kitty. Pretty kitty.

■ Show your interest with eye contact as well as verbal responsiveness. I know it's not easy to drop everything when your baby talks, but try to give her your full attention if only for a short moment. Look at her and concentrate on the focus of her attention. And always respond with a positive word or comment.

■ Make it fun. You'll find that when you express genuine interest in your child and her interests, it *is* fun. Set aside the dishes for a minute and laugh together as you roll your baby over a soft, squeaky toy. The dishes will wait. Act surprised at your baby's discoveries, roll around together, make faces, giggle, snuggle and cuddle, and enjoy this miraculous little gift that is your baby.

■ Finally, be conscious of your own moods—it's part and parcel of staying positive. There are bound to be times when you're feeling overwhelmed or stressed or just not feeling well. We all have those days; just don't take your feelings out on your baby. If you see yourself becoming harsh or abrupt or a little prickly, *take a break*. Don't punish your baby for your momentary negative feelings. If you are prone to angry outbursts, negative comments, or binges of sarcasm, take action to learn to interact differently. You have to—it's not an option.

Many years ago when I was a graduate student, I volunteered to participate in a research project involving therapy for preschool children. As long as a child gave the correct response, I was instructed to respond with a genial "Good" or "Yes." But when the child made a mistake (which, of course, was inevitable) I was supposed to scream *"NO!"* It was horrible—for both of us. I became as frightened of the wrong answer as the poor child. I quit after only two sessions, and registered a strong complaint about the experiment. If you see yourself acting badly, quit, just like me. Give your child a positive start. Talk to your baby in an upbeat, calm, loving voice no matter how you're feeling. The important thing is to send her a message that she's loved and that communication is a positive thing.

COMMUNICATE AT EYE LEVEL

Being at the same level allows your baby to read the messages in your face. It gives her a chance to interpret the revealing quality of your eyes, the expressions on your face, and the positive feedback in your head nods and smiles. By watching your mouth she'll also gain knowledge about the ways sounds and words are formed and expressed. Most importantly, she'll be learning the value of face-to-face communication and of paying attention to others.

There's also the comfort factor. If you've ever watched a movie from the first few rows of the theater you know how unpleasant it is to be constantly looking up—a literal pain in the neck. Well, it's equally as uncomfortable for a child who is sitting or standing to have to keep looking up to talk with you. Even a very young infant lying on her back feels less at ease when she has to look constantly over her head or down toward her feet to find you. Needless to say, communication is less fun when you're not comfortable. So follow the basic rules of thumb: When she's on her back, approach from the side or near her feet and lean in so that your face is aligned with hers. During feeding or while holding her in your arms, angle your head so that she can see your full face when you talk. And if she's in an infant seat or on a low table, kneel in front of her so your eyes meet.

Being at the same eye level during your interactions also helps your baby's alignment. Alignment refers to the placement of her head, neck, shoulders, and spine; and being out of alignment is a common cause of crankiness in young children. Your baby finds it much easier to move and to be comfortable when these parts of the body are in a nice straight line.

It's also easier for her to make noises when her chin isn't sharply tilted up or pressed against her chest.

Face-to-face communication is more egalitarian and interactive. Whenever I meet a young toddler, I drop to one knee in an attempt to get lower than the child. It makes me less of an authority figure, conveys my caring and my sincerity, and shows that I accept the child on her own terms. In my work, I've found that this little move is often enough to convince a reluctant child to give old Dr. Bob a chance—and it will work like a charm with your child, too. And don't worry; she knows you're in charge even when you get down to her level.

A quick cautionary tale: I once asked a young mother to play with her nonspeaking child for a short time so I could watch how the tot responded to toys and other people. I had assembled a large array of toys on a nearby carpet. True to form, the child rushed for the carpet. Mom chose a chair off to the side, and proceeded to direct her son from above. "Pick up the car and put it in the garage," she said, "now move the man over to the house, put the woman . . ." The major thing I learned in those few minutes was that the child was fine, but Mom didn't respond well to others or to toys.

Children who learn language in environments where parents don't interact face to face but play by issuing orders instead will have smaller vocabularies, less developed language, and fewer social skills than children whose parents use shared communication methods. Your baby needs you to be *with* her. We're now learning that even infants with severely withdrawn behavior, such as those with autism, respond to gentle, soft-spoken, face-to-face communication and quiet interactive play.

Hold your newborn so that she can see your face easily, and when she gets a little older, get down on the floor with her whenever possible. If she's at the play table or high chair, sit next to her rather than stand over her. Even when she's feeding herself, sit next to her and have a nice chat. Remember, real conversations are *two-sided* and occur at *eye level*.

One final thought: I'm always amused by the way a lot of children draw adults with big, round nostrils. I've heard more than one parent protest, "But honey, that's a pig nose; people don't have pig noses!" Well, they sure look like they do to children who are constantly looking up into them. That's definitely not your most flattering angle—time to "get down!"

LISTEN, TAKE TURNS, AND KNOW WHEN TO STOP

You may have heard the expression "Listening is an art." Well, truer words were never spoken, especially when it comes to talking with young children. Knowing how to listen to your baby is every bit as important as being an enthusiastic and responsive conversational partner. Listening shows that you are interested in what your child is saying, even if it's just coos and gurgles. It's an incredibly important—and underappreciated—form of positive feedback.

Among the Navajo it's considered a sign of respect to wait a few seconds after someone has finished talking before you respond. That small period of silence gives you time to digest the words you've just heard and understand them fully so that you can respond from your heart, the source of all true communication. That's a good lesson to us all. We all know people who interrupt us before we're finished speaking. It's as if they just can't wait to tell us what *they* think, what's on *their* mind; and what we have to say couldn't matter less to them. Talking to these people is not fun. And it's not fun for your baby when you do it, either. Your little one wants to share her newfound sounds, and later her words, and she deserves an attentive, interested audience.

The best baby conversations are an interplay of quiet listening and simple talking, each of you taking a turn in a natural, easy manner. Even when your baby is too young to respond with sounds, pause to allow time for her turn—just leave a little silent space for her. Sometimes you'll get a coo or a gurgle, sometimes silence. But even if she doesn't make a move, she's learning that she's being invited to, and that helps her learn to talk. Learning to talk isn't just picking up words; it's learning how to participate within the normal rhythms of conversation—essentially taking turns. True conversations—even with a baby—are dialogues, not monologues.

No child can learn these very important conversational skills if she's hit with unceasing chatter. Remember little Tony and his mom on the bike trail? If only his mother had known how to listen, and understood the importance of giving her son a chance to talk, what a different scenario that would have been. Remember to offer your baby a turn to talk. Children need the chance to express themselves—even before they can actually speak—and they always need to be responded to.

Knowing when to stop talking is another related issue. It's important to strike a balance between not saying enough and talking nonstop. Use common sense—and take your cues from your baby. She doesn't like a conversational partner who drones on and on any more than you do. If you overdo it your baby will become tired, cranky, restless, and inattentive. She may fidget or fall asleep. Or she may simply move on to another activity, like a new toy, and seem to ignore your talking. Take heed if you don't want to become relegated to the ignominious position of background noise.

PROVIDE RICH INPUT

The richer your input into your baby's activities, the richer the rewards. Varied activities, comprehensible language, educational play, and rewarding interactions all make a huge difference in terms of your baby's language and mental development. Provide challenging, fun, and interesting experiences that keep her mind stimulated and active.

The idea is to stay on the edge of the curve so that your baby is never bored but also is never overwhelmed. The games and activities in the following chapters are geared to do just that—they provide the ideal intellectual and physical stimulation for each particular stage of development.

A couple of words about the kind of language to use as you play the games and interact with your baby. You want to challenge your child to stretch her vocabulary by staying one step ahead of her. When she speaks in single-word phrases, respond in two- or three-word phrases. When she begins to use three and four words at a time, that's your cue to move to five- and six-word sentences.

In the beginning, talking about what's happening in your immediate surroundings enhances your baby's comprehension of the words she hears and helps her to learn to talk. Have conversations about the things around you and the activities that you or your baby are engaged in. When she picks up a toy, tell her what it's called, describe it, and play with it together. That way she'll be getting language, sensory, cognitive, and social input together.

Here's an example of language that enhances a baby's experience and encourages her mind to grow in the early months:

MOM: Want juice? (Pause) Good juice?
CHILD: Juice.
MOM: Ruby want juice!
CHILD: Juice!
MOM: Ruby want juice. Mommy get juice. (Pause) O-o-o, good cold juice.
CHILD: Juice.
MOM: Yes, Mommy pour juice. (Pause) Juice in glass. Here's juice. (Hands it to Ruby)
CHILD: (Drinks)
MOM: Ruby drink. Mmmmmmmmmmmm. (Pause) Ruby drink juice.

Notice how Ruby's mother focuses on Ruby's current interest and the main event, juice. After Mom poses a simple question and Ruby responds, Mom expands on Ruby's answer. That's great feedback for Ruby. Then, as Mom gets the juice, she talks about what she's doing and describes the juice as she gives it to Ruby. As Ruby drinks, her mom describes in words what Ruby is experiencing. Throughout, the focus is on Ruby and procuring her juice. Her mom's language adds an extra dimension to Ruby's experience. If you're thinking that the grammar used by Ruby's mom is childlike, you're right. That actually helps Ruby's language grow. Using the important words that have meaning and neglecting the unimportant ones (articles like "the" and "a", for instance) keep things clean and simple and easy. There's plenty of time when Ruby is older for "Ruby wants *the* juice." Right now her mom's goal is to help Ruby's understanding and to give her a model of how to say just a little more than "Juice!" Ruby's mom gets an A+.

PICK THE BEST TIME TO COMMUNICATE AND GET YOUR BABY'S ATTENTION FIRST

Mind-growing interactions with your baby are best when she's awake but not agitated, and quiet but not sleepy—like after a feeding or changing, and when you're feeling relatively stress-free. Trust your instincts and watch your baby's behavior for clues that she's open to communication. Eye contact is a good signal. When she looks you in the eyes, it's usually a sign that she's ready to engage in play or quiet chitchat. And when she shows interest in a toy, that's the perfect time to slide gently into the activity and talk about it as you play together. Your interest and animation will make the toy-playing much more fun—and educational.

For maximum impact, always get your baby's attention before beginning an interaction. Methods will vary with your baby's age. Gently shaking something that's brightly colored or makes noise in front of very young infants works well. At three months or so, games like "peek-a-boo" are sure-fire attention-getters; at about six months, when your baby is able to sit unsupported, you can capture her attention by handing her toys and letting her hand them back to you; and a few months later, pointing and other gestures are effective. We'll talk more about this as we do the individual activities together later on, but trust me when I say it becomes very instinctual after a while as you and your baby get to know each other.

While attending is the first step in processing information and an important cognitive skill, *sharing* attention with another person is a precursor to sharing topics in conversation, and the basis of communication. When you help your baby learn to look and listen you're providing an excellent foundation for learning to talk. Of course, we don't want her staring at you—that's not the goal. The idea is just to get her interest so that she's able to receive information. If she's not paying attention she'll miss what's happening. It's that simple. As a consultant, I was horrified in one class to find the teacher timing the length of a child's stare. That is hardly the point. Get your child's attention and then quickly start your activity—and share communication. When your tot becomes tired, restless, and inattentive, it's usually a sign that she needs a nap or a change of activity. Be flexible and move on, but stay alert for another opportunity to talk with her.

ALWAYS RESPOND

By now you know how strongly I feel about responding to your baby. Whenever possible, respond to *all* her sound- and word-making. You're your baby's main source of validation, and your reactions to her communication attempts mean a lot to her. Your responses lend consistency to her world and let her know she's safe. They tell her someone is there who cares, and it gives her confidence that she can communicate and affect your actions.

What about crying? Well, that varies with age. Crying is one of the only ways newborns and young infants have to communicate with us, so it's very important to respond to those cries with ultimate TLC. Most babies let out a wail when they wake up in the first few months, especially if they're hungry or wet, but it usually stops by the third or fourth month. So hang in there! (Obviously, there are limits to your ability to respond. If your baby cries incessantly or extremely frequently, you should check with your pediatrician.)

As your baby matures, she'll have additional ways of communicating and her crying will become less important as a communication device, so that has to be factored into the crying response equation. Certainly, once a child begins to talk, it's still essential to be attentive to any crying brought on by fear or injury, but it's not necessary to respond all the time to anger or tantrum crying. Gently ask for an explanation and show concern, of course, but constant coddling until the tantrum stops is not required.

Crying aside, all talking and sound-making should be acknowledged. Most of us talk because someone responds. When we're having a conversation and we make a statement or ask a question, we expect a reply. It's rewarding. It validates our behavior. And it validates your child's behavior, too. Your reply says, "Continue. Go on, honey; I'm listening." Here's an example of a dad giving his daughter healthy, validating responses:

> CHILD: Ball! Ball!
> DAD: Becky want ball?
> CHILD: Ball.
> DAD: Want ball. (Pause) Here's ball. (Hands ball to child) Big ball!
> CHILD: (Throws ball to Daddy)
> DAD: Becky throw ball. (Pause) Daddy throw ball. (Pause) Throw ball, Becky.
> CHILD: Becky ball.
> DAD: Yes, Becky throw ball to Daddy.

In his first response, the father, who's seen Becky reaching for the ball, validates her attempt to communicate; he lets her know he understands what she wants. In his second response, as he gives her the ball, he revalidates in words *and* action. The next time around, Dad verbally connects the word for the object—*ball*—to the word for the action—*throw*. And finally, when Becky gives him a somewhat enigmatic "Becky ball," Dad quickly interprets her meaning, confirms he understands, and validates her communication attempt again. That's healthy, validating Shared Communication! Becky's dad gets an A+.

Naturally, the type of response and its effect will vary according to the situation, but in general, good responses:

- Affirm that you're paying attention.

- Reinforce your child's efforts. When you say "Yes" followed by a supporting comment, your child is rewarded for her attempt and is likely to communicate more. Plus, just the fact that you responded at all is reinforcing.

- Clarify her intentions. Because your baby has limited language skills, it's difficult for her to express a complete idea except in truncated form—like "Becky ball," for example. Your longer, more elaborate restatement of her idea clarifies her utterance and provides a more mature model of the way of saying it.

- Provide evaluative feedback. If you don't understand what your child means, ask her to "Tell mommy again." If she gets something wrong, correct her, but in a gentle, constructive way. If she points to a horse and says "Doggie," for instance, you might say, "No, honey, that horse." You could even add, "Like a dog (Pause) . . . but horse big." As a counterbalance, when your baby gets something right, she needs to hear that, too, as in "Yes! That horse."

- Model longer or more adult-like phrases. A child can learn quickly from a response that builds on something she's just said. If she sees a cow out the car window, for example, and says, "Dat bes cow," and you reply "Umhm, that's a cow," *she*'ll pay serious attention to your words because she's really interested in the cow and because she initiated the conversation. Result: You've just provided a prototype for her to use the next time she wants to express something similar. It works with older children, too:

4-YEAR-OLD: I heared it.
ADULT: Oh . . . you **heard** what?
4-YEAR-OLD: I heard the goose.

SPEAK IN SHORT, TWO- TO FOUR-WORD PHRASES . . .
BUT AVOID CUTESY BABY TALK!

As we discussed in the last chapter, in order to understand what someone's saying, first you have to pay attention and then hold the words you hear in your working memory while you compare each word to the stored concept it represents. Your baby has limited cognitive abilities and a very limited working memory. As a newborn, she has no stored concepts linked to words, so she won't be able to understand what you say. That will change in a few short months as she begins to link things with words, such as you with the word *Mommy* or *Daddy*. Gradually, she'll be able to comprehend more and more, first only as single words, and then in very short two- or three-word phrases.

Children at eight to twelve months of age, who are on the cusp of talking, understand one- or two-word phrases best. Longer utterances exceed their working memory. Although there's no way to know for certain, they most likely remember and comprehend only the last one or two words of a long string of words. Of course, their comprehension is greatly aided by the presence of objects being discussed, by context and routines, and by our gestures.

Once children begin talking in single words, they can usually understand short two- or three-word phrases. It's easy to shape these sentences by simply omitting articles (*a, the,* and *an*) *and* other short words. At first it may seem awkward to say "That kitty" instead of "That's a kitty," but you'll get used to it in no time. Think of it simply as economizing on words; using as few as possible to get the point across. "That kitty," you'll notice, contains all the essential information. After toddlers begin to combine words, they can easily understand short, four- or five-word sentences. Take a look at these examples of viable short phrases:

ADULT: Time to go. (Pause) Jimmy go car.
CHILD: Go car.
ADULT: Okay, go car. (Pause) Get coat. Cold outside.
CHILD: (Picks up coat) Cold.
ADULT: Yes, cold outside. (Pause) Jimmy has coat.

CHILD: Coat.

ADULT: Um-hm. Coat on.

CHILD: Help.

ADULT: Okay, Mommy help Jimmy. Coat on.

CHILD: Go car.

ADULT: Um-hm, go car now. Let's go.

Notice that the adult contributions are short and related in content and form to what the child said. Words are repeated and relevant to what's happening.

You're the one who serves as an example and shows your child how to expand her language—and that gives her direction. In the following exchange, watch how the parent stays just a little ahead of the child in the language she uses.

CHILD: Out! Out!

ADULT: Go out?

CHILD: Out!

ADULT: Outside.

CHILD: Out!

ADULT: Go out. Nattie go out.

CHILD: Go out.

While these kinds of short phrases are highly recommended, baby talk is *not*. Try to avoid saying things like "Ba-ba fawzy downzy" for "Bottle fall." Your baby's not a poodle—actually, vacuous baby talk would be pretty insulting to a poodle, too. This kind of cutesy, poorly modeled language is totally inappropriate and confusing and can be detrimental to your child's language development. If the bottle hits the ground—"Bottle fall" is the way to go.

SPEAK SLOWLY, PAUSE BETWEEN WORDS, AND KEEP YOUR VOCABULARY SMALL

You and your baby share a lot of experiences but *not* a lot of vocabulary. Infants' vocabularies grow very slowly in the beginning, then gradually increase to the point where they're picking up two or three words a day during their preschool years. It's important to stretch your baby's vocabulary but not confuse her by having too many words come at her too quickly. She's simply not yet able to remember them. Go slowly at first. Introduce her mainly to words that describe things she encounters most frequently, that are part of her little world. She'll remember the words easier when her other senses are involved, so try to make sure she sees, hears, touches, or tastes the objects that you're talking about. Experience is important.

At about seven months, your baby will most likely understand her own name, and a few other words that are part of her everyday life like Mommy, Daddy, and maybe Fido (if you have a Fido). Five months later, when she's starting to speak, she may understand ten to twelve words. Once she begins to talk, you can increase the number of new words you introduce into her vocabulary. There's really no optimum amount—just trust your instinct and judge by how your toddler seems to be absorbing and remembering the words, but remember, *repeated exposure and experience are key*. She'll need to hear the words and see the objects they represent many times before her little brain will be able to connect the dots. Also, it's very common at this age for her to understand many more words than she says, so don't become discouraged if she reaches for or looks at something when you call it by name but doesn't say the name herself. Give her time.

One of the big secrets to your baby's successful early vocabulary growth is to slow down your own speech. Your baby needs time to identify word boundaries. She needs to be able to figure out where one word ends and another begins, and that's not easy when you speak fast and all the words run together, as in

"Doyouwantohaveappleororangejuicewithyourcookie?"

That would be enough to confuse anybody. When you speak more slowly it allows her to hear each individual word and gives her time to process the message. You don't have to sound like a robot, just speak slightly slower than you do to other adults. Imagine that you're talking to someone who is just learning English—which in fact, you are. Pause very briefly between words, especially important words that carry the message. For example, in the phrase "Jeannie, see the bear," you would pause after *Jeannie,* to get her attention, again for a very short time after *see,* and longer after *bear* because he's important.

Articulation counts, too. The truth is, most of us adults are lazy speakers. We not only run our words together, but truncate them to death—gonna, kinda, gotta. We swallow the beginnings of the words—'fore ya go—as well as the ends—see if it's rainin'. Children aren't born knowing where words begin and end. When you enunciate clearly and complete each individual word, it's much easier for your child to understand the words, and she'll learn much faster. When a friend of mine reprimanded her two-and-a-half-year-old daughter by telling her that her behavior was inappropriate, the little girl responded, "No, Mom, it's out of a pwopwiate." Totally reasonable, I thought. It shows you how kids hear . . . and interpret.

REPEAT WORDS, BUT VARY YOUR LANGUAGE SLIGHTLY

Repetition is not boring for your baby; it actually helps language processing. When she hears a sentence or word repeated, she gets a second or third chance to decode it—to search her memory for the concept. If she decoded correctly the first time, the repetition gives her the opportunity to confirm it. One or two repetitions should do the trick, and, as always, comprehension improves when the words represent something present, visual, and interesting to your baby. With older toddlers, repeated sentences can be varied slightly to keep their interest and to provide additional language input. Here's a good example:

ADULT: Felipe, see doggie? (Points, looks at child for confirmation) See doggie?
CHILD: Doggie.
ADULT: See doggie, Felipe? (Pause) He's big doggie.
CHILD: Doggie.
ADULT: Yes, doggie. Big doggie?
CHILD: Doggie.
ADULT: Felipe, pet doggie! Pet big doggie.

This dialogue is particularly beneficial to Felipe's language development because there's plenty of variety with very few words and lots of repetition. The adult says "See doggie" three times, varying it slightly each time, followed by a description of the dog that is repeated later in the conversation. At the end, the adult describes the child's action as he does it, and then combines that with the previous description—"Pet big doggie." Each adult turn is short and there's always an opportunity for the child to respond. The adult has obviously kept the child's interest, as evidenced by the child's responses.

As with anything, repetition can be overdone. Let's look at the same example, but this time violating some the principles.

> ADULT: Felipe, see doggie? See doggie? See doggie?
> CHILD: Doggie.
> ADULT: Yes, see doggie. Felipe, see doggie. See doggie.
> CHILD: Doggie.
> ADULT: Yes, doggie. Felipe, see doggie. See doggie? See doggie?
> CHILD: (Looks away)
> ADULT: Felipe, see doggie!

The repetition is a killer. The child has tuned out and is looking for something more interesting.

FOCUS ON ONE TOPIC, AND FOLLOW YOUR BABY'S LEAD

It's confusing to your baby to talk about more than one thing at a time until she's about eighteen months old. So keep your conversations focused. If you're having a nice friendly chat about applesauce, don't suddenly change the subject to teddy bears—especially if the teddy bear is in the other room. Early communication is always most effective when you talk about an object or action or event that's happening right in front of you. On the other hand, if *your child* switches the conversation to the teddy bear, go with the flow.

When it comes to conversation topics and activities, you don't always have to be in charge—in fact, it's fun not to be. Let your baby indicate her interest in something, then move in. If she looks at something that's going on, or reaches for something, or picks up a toy, or eats food, talk about it. And if she graces you with a word, turn that word into a topic of conversation. If your little one reaches for her favorite toy and says "Bunny," for instance, a good conversation opener would be, "Want bunny?" By talking about what your baby is doing or what she's interested in, you'll be much more likely to get her full attention, and your speech and language will be more meaningful to her. You'll also often be able to combine concepts for a learning *two-fer* by chatting about both the object and your baby's actions. Say she picks up her teddy bear, for instance. You might say something like: "Shelly has bear (pause). Fuzzy bear (pause). Shelly hug bear (pause). Bear sleepy?" Lots of concepts laid out very simply = Lots of learning.

I was recently consulting at a nursery school and gave the teacher high points for her flexibility in following one of her little student's lead. The teacher was organizing a sort of toddler gym class. As all the little two-year-olds were getting ready to walk through this mini-maze of wee orange cones, one of the little girls, who obviously marches to her own drum, picked up one of the cones, put it on her head and danced around singing, "Happy Birthday party, Happy Birthday party!" Instead of criticizing the little girl, the teacher put a cone on her own head, did a few twirls, and sang "Happy Birthday," too. A few of the other children followed suit. They all had a great time. Four minutes later, the cones were back in place and all the kids were back on track. It was a perfect way to handle the situation. Moral: Children's agendas can be valid, too—we adults don't always have to run the show.

Teaching language also doesn't mean planning special teaching situations or circumstances. Teaching moments occur naturally all during the day and can be easily folded into your schedule. Diapering and feeding, for instance, are terrific teaching opportunities because they occur several times during the day (at least), and your baby knows the routine, which enables her to participate more easily. Let the events themselves guide you into conversation. During meals, for instance, there'll be feeding, wiping, burping, drinking, and the like. These can become your basis for communication. Two methods for including the actions within an event into your talking are called *parallel talk* and *self-talk*. Talking about what your child is doing is called parallel talk. Talking about what you're doing is called self-talk. Here's an example of each:

Parallel talk:
ADULT: Caitlin eat cereal.
CHILD: (Crunch, crunch)
ADULT: Yum! Yummy cereal.
CHILD: (Finishes. Looks in bowl for more.)
ADULT: Bowl empty. Cereal all gone. (Pause) Caitlin look for more.
CHILD: (Looks at adult)
ADULT: More cereal. Caitlin want more.

Self-talk:
MOM: Mommy mix paint.
CHILD: (In baby seat watching)
MOM: Shake can.
CHILD: Can.
MOM: Yep, can. Mommy open can. (Pause) Mommy stir.

In each case you can see that the conversations follow along with the action, and that Mom's phrases are short and mirror the child's actions, her talking, or both.

Of course, there will be times when you're busy and tasks need to get done. I don't expect you to follow *every* lead your child presents. You're still the boss and it's perfectly all right to let your little one know that it's time to move on. Just sweeten the medicine with the tone of your voice, and add a dollop of compromise in which you promise to do what the child wants after the task is complete. "Honey, do this now. Then we play walk doggie. How's that?"

GESTURE AND SIGN TO AID COMPREHENSION

Gesturing is a wonderful, natural accompaniment to language. We adults use gestures all the time. We might say, "I'm going to the store," as we point in the appropriate direction, for instance. Or say, "So I called him on the phone and told him . . ." And there we are, holding an imaginary receiver to our ear. If you asked some people to speak without their hands—it would be totally unthinkable. Gestures enhance spoken language. They make it more interesting, more fun, more emphatic—and definitely more understandable.

It's not surprising that natural gesturing helps your baby, too. It holds her interest, enhances your message, and helps her understand your words. Gestures also become an early form of communication between the two of you before your baby's able to speak. Babies actually begin to gesture instinctively at about eight months—simple moves like pointing and reaching to signal they want something, so other simple gestures are not hard for them.

There's an infinite variety of gestures you can use with your baby. For example, "Hear the doggie?" could be accompanied by a hand to the ear followed by a point in the barking dog's direction. When you say "car" you could move your hands in front of you as if you were steering. "Cold" could be signified by crossing your arms in front of you and moving your upper body back and forth as if you were shivering. And "Quiet" could be a forefinger to the mouth in a *shhhhh* motion—a pretty universal gesture.

Actions can be gestured, too: *Eat* could be moving your hand to your mouth as if spooning in a bunch of food; *run* could be pumping your arms up and down like a marathon runner in fast-forward mode, and *wash* could be pretend body scrubbing. And of course, pointing is a great substitute for the names of things. Once you start gesturing you'll find that some will come to you naturally. The simpler the gesture, and the easier it is to do, the more likely your baby will be able to copy it and use it to communicate with you. The other trick: Be consistent. Pick a gesture for an action or thing and stick to it.

Signs, such as those used in the deaf community, can also be used like natural gestures to enhance your child's comprehension. Children pick up sign language when they're exposed to it, just as they do natural gestures. A child may make her first sign at eight months, but not say her first word until twelve months. The explanation for that is simple—signing is easier for your baby's muscles and brain than speaking words. There's simply less brain programming needed for hand movements than for the coordination and precise movements needed for breathing and speaking.

But before you run out and register for a sign language course consider this: Most natural gestures are *iconic*—that is, they look like what they represent, so they're intuitive and easy to remember. Most sign language signs are not. That means that many signs are not as easy to learn as is often assumed. To use them effectively, you'd have to learn a whole new mode of communication, and most new parents are just way too busy to do that.

Your best bet, from my point of view, is to combine natural gestures with some of the most common and useful iconic Signed English signs that are illustrated on page 56. As you can see, they're quite instinctive and baby-friendly.

You can even invent your own natural-feeling signs and use them as gestures. For example, if you hold your cat and pet her a lot, you might want to make the stroking motion the sign for cat. If your child is interested in a physical feature, such as her sister's pigtails, you might bring your fists down the side of your face as if tracing her braided hair when you mention her name. Body parts can be signified by touching them. Actions can represent themselves, such as pretending to wash yourself when you say "bath time." Don't be too surprised when your baby begins to sign. More than likely, she'll do it before she speaks her first word—and it will be a thrill to see.

I'm a real believer in parenting that feels comfortable to parents and children. The amount of gestures or signs that you use should fit the type of person and the type of communicator that you are. Try some natural-feeling signs, try inventing some signs of your own, and try using gestures and words. See what feels right for you—and your baby.

Here's an example of a conversation using gestures and signs to get you started.

ADULT: Go (Points) get coat (Signs coat). Coat (Signs coat again).
CHILD: (Points) Coat.
ADULT: Yes, get coat (Signs coat).
CHILD: (Complies)
ADULT: Good. Now, go (Point) car (Signs car).
CHILD: Wet!
ADULT: Yes, rain (Move fingers down to simulate rain falling).
CHILD: Wet.
ADULT: Mommy and Julie (Points to herself and Julie) run (Pretends to run) to car (Signs car)?

Note how a sign or gesture accompanies only the important words. These are signals to the child that this is important information, and the visual symbols help the child comprehend better.

Some parents worry that if their baby uses signs and gestures she'll begin to talk later than other children, since she'll start to depend on signs and gestures and neglect speech. Actually, the exact opposite is true: Signs and gestures enhance your baby's ability to communicate and motivate her to begin to speak. Once she begins to experience the "benefits" of communicating with you, she'll want even more. She'll notice that most of your communication is accomplished through speaking and she'll want to become a part of that.

It's never too early to begin using gestures and signs, but you certainly want to start before your child begins to make her own gestures at about eight months old. A few other guidelines:

- *Don't overwhelm your baby with signs or gestures.* Decide on signs and gestures for particular things, actions, and events in which your baby has shown an interest.

- *Speak at the same time you gesture.* It's important for your baby to get both the visual and verbal input.

- *Sign and gesture in context.* Always sign or gesture when the thing you're signing or gesturing about is within view. This makes it easier for your baby to associate the word she hears with the sign she sees and the thing to which they refer.

- *Offer repeated exposure.* Just as your baby needs to hear words many times before she knows what they mean, she also needs to see signs and gestures repeatedly.

- *Encourage imitation.* Just as you should encourage your child to copy your sounds and words, you should do the same with signs and gestures. You can help your child to make signs and gestures by gently manipulating her little hands.

- *Sign and gesture only important words.* Unless you are *superparent*—and you may be close to it!—you're much too busy to

Here are a few common Signed English signs that are easy to interpret. For maximum effect, remember to sign and speak at the same time. One-handed signs, such as *bed* and *throw*, can use either hand as long as you consistently use the same one.

Ball Make a spherical shape with your hands as if surrounding a ball. Fingers on top, thumb on bottom.

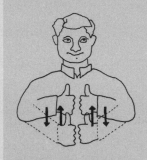

Bath Place your fists in front of your chest, palms inward, knuckles toward the center. Move your hands up and down as if scrubbing your chest.

Bed Rest your cheek on your palm as if placing your head on a pillow.

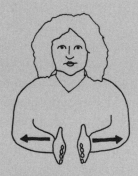

Big Begin with your palms flat against each other, thumbs on top, and slowly separate your hands by moving them laterally.

Book Begin with your palms flat against each other, thumbs on top, and separate your hands by rotating the upper portion outward while keeping the little fingers in contact, much as you would open a book.

Car Mime holding the steering wheel and rotating it side to side.

Drink Mime holding a big cup before your mouth and tipping it up as if having a drink.

Eat Your hand shape is fingers and thumb bunched together to resemble a flower bud. Tap your mouth twice with your finger- and thumb-tips.

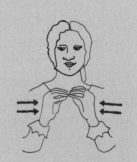

More Your hand shape is fingers and thumb of each hand bunched together to resemble a flower bud, palms toward the center. Tap your finger- and thumb-tips together twice.

Push Begin with your flat, open palms facing outward from your body at chest level and push away from your body slowly.

Throw Begin with a your fist raised slightly in front of your shoulder and move your hand away from your body while opening it so that you end with your hand spread as if you had just released the ball.

Want Begin with your hands in front of your chest, palms up, fingers curved slightly upward. Draw your hands into your chest twice.

learn a whole new way to communicate. I strongly recommend *not* trying to sign every word. As you talk with your baby, only sign or gesture as an accompaniment to important words. For example, when you say "Mommy and Lee going in car," you might just want to sign *go* and point to *car* when you say the words. "Kim eat ice cream" might be accompanied only by the sign for *eat*.

Finally, some grandfatherly advice: Be gentle with yourself. You may take to signs and gestures naturally—or you may not. Some people feel self-conscious or conspicuous gesturing, especially in public. It's okay not to use signs and gestures if you're uncomfortable. That doesn't mean that you're a bad parent. We're all different. Yes, the additional input will help your child, but many children learn to speak with very little gestural stimulation. So do what makes you happy. Happy parents are usually the best parents.

LIMIT YOUR QUESTIONS

Asking young children questions in an effort to engage them in conversation is a natural tendency for most of us—but it's not always the best idea. Questions put your child on the spot. Besides the fact that questions require an answer she may not be able to supply, they're also a bit more difficult for her to process than statements, because the grammar is different from what she's used to hearing in statements. The question "Is Daddy home yet?" for example, has a reversed word order from the more common statement "Daddy is home." So the little brain connecting those words has to go through a few more decoding steps to come up with a response.

Let me give you an example of a conversation with questions that would be difficult for a young toddler.

> CHILD: I got new bike.
> ADULT: Oh, what color is it?
> CHILD: Red.
> ADULT: Can you ride it?
> CHILD: Uh-huh?
> ADULT: Why did you get it?
> CHILD: 'Cause.

You can see how the questions constrain the child's behavior and lead to short, simple responses. Except for the child's original statement, she's confined to answering the adult and will bore quickly. She may be excited to tell her adult friend about her bike but can't. Here's a much better way. In this example, statements of interest take the place of questions.

CHILD: I got new bike.
ADULT: Hmm, wish I could see it.
CHILD: It's red and it gots a bell.
ADULT: A bell! Wow! Tell me more.
CHILD: I can ride.
ADULT: I want to see you ride.
CHILD: Okay, come on.

This time the child's much more enthusiastic and engaged. Instead of just answering, she's initiating comments on her own, providing new information, and, in the last utterance, giving a command. This kind of conversation stretches her language rather than confining it.

I'm not suggesting that you can never ask questions. Of course you can! But there's an art to it, and not all questions are equal. Some are much easier for children than others. In general, *what-* and *where*-type questions, as in "What's that?" and "Where's doggie?" are relatively easy for toddlers who are using single words. W*hen, how,* and *why* questions, on the other hand, are extremely difficult and beyond your toddler's cognitive ability to answer. So, take the simple *what* and *where* route in the beginning and use other responses that allow your child more latitude to respond.

In the long run, by not *relying* on questions, you allow your child to practice various ways of talking besides answering. She'll have the opportunity to explore all the other possibilities of conversation, and try her skills at commenting, making demands, naming things, exclaiming, even asking questions. And as she experiments her language grows, stretches, and expands.

TREAT YOURSELF WELL

This is mega-important! Being a new parent is exhausting. You need to do things for yourself that refresh your mind, body, and spirit. In other words, you need to make time to take care of yourself. In many ways it's as important as taking care of your baby. When you feel good you're more patient, more energetic, more insightful, more aware of your baby's needs, more emotionally available. In short, you're a better parent.

Trust me, as the father of twins—double the fun, double the diapers— I know parenting is tough. My wife and I didn't sleep for three months after the birth of the dynamic duo. We were practically hallucinating. And we had it relatively easy compared to the mother of sextuplets I read about, who actually had to check into the hospital every few days for rest and blood transfusions!

While one baby might not require your hospitalization, it is a serious full-time job. Don't wait until you're worn out to schedule some personal R and R. Nip the problem in the bud. Try to go out, alone or with your mate, at least once a week, even if it's just for a quiet stroll around the block. Make sure your child is safe and asleep, then hire a sitter for a very brief time or ask Grandma or a friend to come over. Take a cell phone with you if it will ease your concerns, but try not to use it to check in every five minutes. Relax.

If you can't get out, give yourself permission to take a break and relax at home in ways that refresh your spirit. Even if it's only for five minutes, make it *your* five minutes. Listen to a favorite CD, watch a favorite TV show, enjoy a DVD of a great movie, settle into a bubble bath. Maybe you could finish that needlepoint or your latest half-read novel. Heck, put your feet up, have a cup of tea, and read the Sunday funnies. The most important thing is that you do it for you.

Don't be shy about enlisting the help of others. You *will* get tired of infant or toddler communication—it's impossible not to. You need some helpers and some other adults to talk to your little one, too. Don't let your partner use work-related fatigue as an excuse not to talk. Your baby needs to chitchat with both of you. Grandparents, siblings, kids in playgroup, preschool teachers, child-care workers, cops on the beat . . . all are potential baby conversational partners. They might not be the expert baby conversationalist you are, but they won't do any permanent damage, either.

I can promise you that if you stick by these principles during these first few years of your baby's life, she will blossom—emotionally and intellectually—and she will enjoy communication from the get-go. If you're already doing some of the things I've recommended—great! Keep up the good work and incorporate the others. If these ideas are all very new to you, apply one or two of the principles at a time, get used to them, then try two more, and so on, until you're practicing them all. Before you know it, they will all be second nature and you will be the best conversational partner a baby could ever have.

CHAPTER FIVE

Putting Theory into Practice

Working the Shared Communication Activites

PARENTING'S not easy, but it *is* a wonderful, exciting, and rewarding challenge. Every day offers a new opportunity for growth and new learning for both you and your baby. Now that you've got the basics of language and cognitive development under your belt, and are familiar with the Shared Communication principles, we're ready to put theory into practice and take full advantage of those opportunities. In the following chapters, I'll take you step by step through your baby's development and introduce you to plenty of games, activities, ideas, and suggestions that will encourage your baby's language and mental development as they nourish his little spirit. Most of the activities will fit easily into your everyday routines, and all are perfectly age-appropriate—fine-tuned to suit your baby's abilities as he grows each month. As you'll see, sometimes just a subtle tweak in an exercise or simple adjustment in your interactions is all that's needed to give your baby a developmental boost from one month to the next, while at other times, he'll be ready for a whole new approach.

I've earmarked each activity to let you know just which area of your baby's development it encourages so that you'll better understand the developmental nuances and just which ways you're helping your baby talk and flourish. While your little one will have fun no matter what category the games and activities fall under, my feeling is that the more you know as a parent, the more proactive you can be, and the more exciting the whole process of parenting will become for you. A quick reminder why these different developmental areas are so important for your baby's learning:

- *Cognitive* stimulation and development helps your baby organize his brain as he "builds" critical links between functions and areas of his brain. Cognition and language grow on parallel tracts. Changes in one are reflected in the other.

- *Hearing and Attending* stimulation helps your baby communicate because learning to talk requires learning to listen. Most children learn speech and language by hearing. That's why you'll find various suggestions here that provide a variety of "noise" experiences for your baby. The noise experiences become even more meaningful when you name and discuss the noises. For example:

CHILD: *(Startles. Looks around)*
ADULT: *Loud noise! Airplane.*
CHILD: *(Looks around)*
ADULT: *Find airplane. (Pause) Airplane up. (Points)*
CHILD: *(Looks up)*
ADULT: *Yes, airplane. Airplane in sky. (Pause) Look up.*
CHILD: *(Searches)*
ADULT: *See airplane? (Pause, points again) Airplane!*
CHILD: *(Smiles)*
ADULT: *Airplane go up.*

- *Visual* stimulation helps your baby to talk because eye contact is a hugely important part of communication. We all gauge the importance and emotional strength of communication, as well as the intimacy of the communicants, by the amount of eye contact—either consciously or unconsciously. We don't want your little one to stare at you necessarily—although he'll probably do that without any outside encouragement. We want him to learn to look at you and transfer that ability to other people or to objects; to glance back, and to follow the conversation and the context. That takes some training. We all know at least one adult who doesn't get it.

- *Sensory* stimulation. When a child begins to talk about the world around him, he talks about experiences. Most of these are sensory—things he sees, hears, feels, smells, and tastes. Sensory integration, such as being able to look in the direction of a sound or smell, or touch objects he sees around him, is important for brain development. An infant's brain has rather rough designations of where things will be. Motor control is across the top of the brain, vision in the rear, and hearing on the sides. What's missing is the organization. As your child reaches for objects or people that he sees, he begins to connect two areas and to organize them. The connectors aren't "hardwired" like an electrical appliance. They're more like paths through the woods. When your baby uses the path enough times, he'll soon find it easily and access it more. And soon enough it will become second nature.

- *Motor Development.* Your child's body is a little machine. All the parts move with the help of muscles. Muscles can only do one thing—contract. It's up to the brain to control the contraction. It has to figure out what muscles to contract, how fast, and how much. That only comes with practice. The motor activities in these upcoming chapters provide your baby with lots of fun practice.

    While physicians might be more interested in your child's muscle strength, it's his muscle *control* that's the big issue in his development. Overall motor development is very closely linked to cognitive development in the first few months of a child's life. Your baby's motor experiences, such as swatting at suspended objects over his crib, or turning to look at a noise, strengthen his cognitive pathways and forge links between the sensory and motor sections of his brain.

    The connection between sensory and motor aspects of development is easiest to understand when you think of it as *stimulus* and *response*. Sensory perceptions create the stimulus that signals the brain, which responds with movements of the body. Say, for instance, you're in the garden and your senses tell you that there's a mosquito on your arm—stimulus. You program your muscles and swat at the location of the irritant—response. Likewise, your child sees a brightly colored object—the stimulus—and reaches for it—the response. We take these kinds of sensory-motor experiences for granted—but they're brand-new for your baby.

Teaching and Play

Together, the monthly activities are an integrated group, but feel free to alternate between activities or concentrate on one or another as you feel your baby needs them. You might want to play a few games one day and a few others the next—sort of like athletic cross-training where you vary exercises from day to day. In sports and fitness, cross-training makes exercising more interesting and gives you a chance to work various muscle groups in different ways. Same thing here. Varying activities will keep things interesting for your baby and encourage growth in the different areas. You could do a visual stimulation game one day, a motor skill activity the next, and a hearing exercise the next.

Don't try to do everything at once. Decide on a few activities, and then try them during play or at other times when your baby is awake and alert but not overly fussy. Many of the games are "anywhere exercises" that you can play in the supermarket, bank, waiting in line, or on a train or bus. But don't overdo it. A few repetitions of each activity are enough at any one time, unless your baby's excitement signals a real interest in continuing. If your baby is a little behind or ahead of the behaviors listed on the milestone watchlist for that particular month, adjust the stimulation activities accordingly. Relax. Let your baby grow at his own rate with your help.

Finally, you're a creative person. Having a baby didn't change that. Use your imagination to make these play activities or interactions interesting and progressively more complex and challenging to your baby if his responses call for it. Add your own twists and inventions.

Play is more than just fun for your baby; it's a very necessary part of his development. He'll use it to practice learned skills and to pick up new ones, and to explore the world and find out how things work. When he activates a noisemaker by touching it, for example, he learns about the object, cause and effect, and associations between objects, actions, and noises. Each new toy or activity is a chance for him to grow cognitively and to take in new information. A jack-in-the-box teaches about anticipation and a sequence of events—and just happens to be fun. With you to mediate the experience, play can expand into a huge growth opportunity. The learning-success ratio doubles when you hold objects in ways that make them easier for your baby to use and explore, supply needed materials, demonstrate, and talk with enthusiasm and interest about the objects and actions your little one experiences.

Over the years, I've found that some of us play better than others. I remember watching two parents in the clinic on a big mat full of toys going from toy to toy, suggesting to their child that he play but never interacting with him in any way. Your baby deserves better than that. Try to tap into your inner child and invite her to come out and play. A few play-time tips:

■ Stay in the moment. Play when you can. If you have other things to do, do them, but don't be picking at lint on the rug when you're supposed to be playing with a squeaky toy. If you only have a short time to play, set that boundary for yourself. Play hard, work hard—that's the motto—but always have fun.

■ Focus fully on your child and his experience. This goes along with the previous point. Give your full attention to your baby. Respond to his behaviors and sounds, encourage him to make sounds, take turns with him, mimic his actions.

■ Be a fun play partner. Yes, development is serious business, and being a parent is a serious responsibility, but play is the place to totally lighten up. Play and learning should be encased in fun. Your little guy will develop a sense of humor within just a few short months, and you want to encourage that. He'll laugh at unanticipated events, funny faces, exaggerated actions, and fun outcomes. Give him what he wants, and trust me, you'll have fun, too.

Developmental Watchlists

In the following chapters, you'll find monthly developmental milestone watchlists. It's really important that you understand that they're meant as a guide, *not as a diagnostic tool*. If your baby is not behaving as described, he may just be biding his time while he decides if he really wants to grow up. After all, being waited on hand and foot by doting adults is a pretty nice set-up. Remember that individual children differ greatly in the speed of their development. There is a *very wide range* of what is considered typical development, and there are a number of other considerations that need to be factored in as well. So please keep this in mind as you read on. All watchlists in this book *are guides to help you know what to expect*; they are not tests that your baby can pass or fail.

I tend to get pretty emphatic about this because I want to guard you against the kind of thing I ran up against when I first started teaching college language development courses. During a semester break, one of my students had blithely proclaimed her eighteen-month-old brother mentally retarded because he wasn't talking yet. When her frantic mother had questioned her diagnosis, my student insisted it was *absolutely true* based on . . . *what Dr. Owens said in class*. I nearly had a coronary when I heard about it and immediately called the mother to explain. Needless to say, a nonverbal eighteen-month-old is *not* necessarily retarded. I now leave very little doubt among my students that there is a very, very *wide* range of abilities that are considered typical. As a parent, I want you to be even more on top of that message. Children come in all shapes and sizes, and they develop at varying rates. Very tiny babies take a little longer. Babies who have a rough start—difficulty breathing, jaundice, colic—take a little longer. A premature infant isn't expected to perform in the same way as a full-term child. Children with disabilities may lag behind in some aspects of development. Boys are less mature at birth and may not reach developmental milestones at the same ages as girls . . . and so on. So relax. Enjoy your baby and watch the marvel of his maturation unfold before you. Treat these watchlists only as *guidelines*—they're developments to *watch* for, not die for. Your beautiful baby may be a little behind or a little ahead. Most babies who are behind catch up within a few months or years.

Now we're ready for our first "official" activities. Remember, above all, have FUN! Keep it light. It's fascinating to watch a baby's mind develop, and knowing more about how it's happening makes it even more interesting. If you ever need a quick, easy reminder of suggested activities for any given month, just flip to the instant activity referral chart at the end of each chapter. But now, let's get started!

CHAPTER SIX

Your Baby's First Three Months

Getting to Know Each Other

YOUR newborn may not be quite the cute, plump little cherub you imagined. But don't worry, most babies aren't. The airbrushed, perfect Gerber babies we're used to seeing in advertisements are, alas, a bit of a fantasy—at least those first few days. Your little gal might come home from the hospital wrinkled, a little misshapen, and might even remind you of your aging uncle (minus the cigar). But give your baby a few days and she'll fill out and blossom into the cutest thing you've ever seen. All babies are beautiful and truly wondrous to behold.

As you start out together on this new adventure, your baby will be on her own schedule. It's going to take her a while to adapt to the sleep schedule of the rest of the family, so if possible, go with the flow and adapt to her rhythms initially. Sleep when she does and let the housekeeping go—you're going to need all the rest you can get. By about sixteen weeks, she'll be sleeping through most of the night. Hang in there.

Development

MONTH ONE

Early Movement ◆ During the first few weeks, your newborn won't be able to control most of her motor behavior. She's still operating on *reflexes*, those automatic, involuntary motor patterns we talked about. Although some reflexes, such as gagging, coughing, yawning, and sneezing, remain for life, most baby reflexes—like the so called *plantor grasp* in which the toes flex when pressure is applied to the balls of the feet—disappear or are modified by four months of age as her brain matures, her nerves become more efficient, and she gains more muscle control.

Most oral reflexes, the precursors of biting, chewing, and speech, will also disappear after a few months. But they're fascinating to watch in these early months. There's a bite-release action called the *phasic bite*, for instance, that occurs when your newborn's gums are stimulated. Another is the *rooting reflex*, in which your baby's lips, tongue, and jaw move together toward a point of stimulation, such as a gentle touch at the corner of her mouth. And there's the *rhythmic suck-swallow* that occurs when her mouth is stimulated. Sucking is primarily accomplished by up-and-down jaw action. To swallow, she'll extend her neck, open her mouth slightly and protrude her tongue, then retract it. She'll have a hard time operating her jaw, mouth, and tongue separately. Believe it or not, she won't be able to swallow independently of all these other oral movements until she's about three years old.

Early Sounds ◆ Your newborn will produce some sounds, but they'll be predominantly reflexive, such as fussing and crying, and so-called *vegetative sounds* associated with eating like burping, gurgling, and swallowing. You'll also occasionally hear some brief vowel utterances, such as *ah*s and *oh*s. By the end of the first month, you'll be able to recognize the meaning of your baby's different cries by their sound pattern. In these early months, it's the only way she can let you know that she needs something, her only way of communicating. By responding consistently and quickly, you let her know that her signaling has been successful. It's the very beginning of your shared communication. On a physiological level, crying helps your little one become accustomed to airflow across her vocal folds, and gets her used to modified breathing patterns. The good news is that crying typically decreases as your baby becomes more aware of the world around her, learns to communicate in other ways, and develops movement skills, such as rolling and creeping where she's almost crawling, but still on her tummy.

Early Vision ◆ Your infant will be nearsighted at birth—she'll focus best at about eight inches, but will be sensitive to both brightness and color. She'll rely mostly on visual patterns for recognition, and prefer to look at angles and light-dark contrasts, which are exactly what your eyes look like to her. She'll see the angles at the corners of your eyes and the contrast between the darker central area of your pupil and the outer white of the eye. So don't be surprised if you find her staring intently into your eyes as you interact face to face. As her depth of vision increases over the next few months, she'll start to visually explore her world more.

Early Hearing ◆ Although your newborn's inner ears are ready to function, the portion of her brain that processes sounds isn't mature, and she still has some fluid in her middle ear (which will drain in a week or so). Within just a few days, she'll be able to distinguish different sounds, although she won't attach any meaning to them. But still, like most newborns, she'll prefer the human voice to all other sounds.

MONTHS 2 AND 3

Movement ◆ By two to three months, your baby will begin to develop control of her large muscles. It starts at the neck with the control of her head—she'll be able to raise it and hold it steady—then develops downward through the shoulders and back, which gives her the ability to control her torso and to sit (by about her fifth or sixth month). This control, and the further maturation of her brain, enables your infant to go from reflexive behaviors, like automatically grasping anything that touches her palm, to rolling and creeping and other purposeful behaviors.

By her second month, she'll have developed the oral muscle control to start and stop tongue and mouth movement on her own. She'll be able to move her tongue back and forth and open her mouth—although a little external tactile stimulation, such as your touching her lips, may still be needed to get it started. She'll also now be able to . . . smile! Get ready for an irresistible, unbeatable, delicious treat!

Although she'll be able to grasp things at two months, she'll be unable to control her reach. Her fingers will be relatively undifferentiated, too, almost as if they were in a mitten—not that this will stop her from bringing everything to her mouth for insta-baby-analysis. As her brain matures, she'll rapidly gain voluntary muscle control and begin to examine objects, people, and events that are close at hand. Vision and reach will become coordinated in the second month, and your little gal will be able to reach and grasp as her brain plans and directs the movement.

Social ◆ Social behaviors also change and improve as your baby's memory increases and she gains the ability to recognize and respond to familiar faces and situations. As early as the first month, she may become excited when she sees certain people or things, or quiet down when comforted by your soothing voice. By the second month, certain people—usually Mom—become associated with particular behaviors, such as feeding. Just seeing your face may cause your baby to remember the pleasure of being fed. Continue to be relaxed, comfortable, and comforting with her. Although she won't understand your words, she'll definitely respond to the tone of your voice and your body movements. And as you interact with her and respond affectionately to her behaviors, your infant will learn early that if she makes a noise someone responds in some way—the rudiments of communication.

Vision, Hearing, Communication ◆ By the time she's three months old, your little one will be able to discriminate people visually and to respond accordingly. As she becomes more responsive to people, she'll smile less at objects. At about the end of the first month, smiling will be less automatic and she'll tend to smile at interesting stimuli, especially people's faces, which she'll find fascinating. At two months, she'll look for you when she hears your voice but turn away from strange voices. (Nothing like a little recognition to reinforce great parenting!) Laughter and nondistress *gooing* or *cooing* also begin at about two months. You'll hear more long *gggguh*s and *kkkkuh*s. At times, her sounds will resemble gurgling or growling—like she's trying to "start her engine."

By three months, she'll be able to control the timing of her vocalizations and will make sounds in response to the speech of others. You may find her accompanying you when you make noises or alternating sounds with you—when you stop vocalizing, she'll start. Her vocalizations will now include more speechlike sounds, instead of isolated vowels, and will be accompanied by index finger extensions. Welcome to the world of *babbling*. Babbles are simple, single-syllable *consonant-vowel* (CV) sounds, such as *ba, ga,* and *ka,* or *vowel-consonant* (VC) sounds, like *uk,* that are usually produced alone. You baby's babbling will also include high and low pitches, glides between the two pitches, growling and throaty sounds, some nasal sounds, and a greater variety of vowels. Your girl is practicing! As her sound-making repertoire continues to expand, her crying will lessen—note, I didn't say disappear!

BABY PHYSIOLOGY

Now that you've got an overall idea of what to expect developmentally these first three months, we're almost ready for action, but just a couple of words on baby physiology first. It's very difficult for a child to attempt a new behavior or learn if she feels unsure about balance or support. Your new baby doesn't yet have the ability to hold her head up for long periods of time. She needs support. Also, although during the early weeks your baby's body will still be a little curled up, she'll soon start stretching out, and you'll want to start paying attention to her alignment. It will be difficult for her to coordinate body movements when her body is twisted in some odd way—it can also make her very cranky. A few alignment tips:

■ During these first three months, provide head support whenever your baby is in a position that would allow her head to flop back or side to side.

■ After the first month or so, try to make sure that her head, neck, and trunk are in a relatively straight line for maximum muscle control . . . and less crotchety behavior.

■ As she gains control of her head, shoulders, and back, gradually let her take control of some of her movements for short periods of time. While holding her upright, for instance, lessen your support of her head for a minute or so as you encourage her to look around, or, while she's on her tummy, see if you can get her to raise her head by herself.

SHARED COMMUNICATION REMINDERS AND TIPS

- **Accentuate your facial movement and expression.** Try to put on a good show—even if you're sleep-deprived. The fact is that no matter how gorgeous you are, your baby's going to get bored looking at you after a while. Keep her interest by exaggerating your facial expressions as you change your voice. Widen your eyes, move your mouth like Jim Carey, blink like crazy, roll your eyes, growl, whisper, pitch your voice high, low . . . you name it. This is baby entertainment at its finest—better than Broadway!

- **Treat your baby's movements or sounds as meaningful.** Remember our fourth Shared Communication principle. Be a good listener, don't talk nonstop, and respect your baby's contribution. Yes, she is very young. But this is the perfect time to establish a routine for just you two. "Talk" together at bedtime or after feeding. You won't be getting verbal replies, of course, but she will begin to anticipate your interactions just as you might anticipate coffee with a friend. She's also learning that speech accompanies most human activities.

- **Imitate your baby's noises and movements.** Infants often coo when interested or when eating.Coo with her. She may move her mouth and eyes as you do. She won't be able to imitate your sounds yet—that's way beyond her abilities at this stage—but in a few months, you'll be able to play vocal games with her. Even though she'll only be able to make her own kind of noise in response to yours, rather than echoing your specific sounds, she's learning a very important communication skill. Taking turns is what makes people good conversationalists. Think about the know-it-all you dated in college and dropped like a hot potato because he never gave you a chance to talk. Plus, cooing and babbling along with babies is fun and even a little stress-relieving.

- **Enjoy yourself.** We all know that talking to someone who doesn't directly respond can be less than exciting—and it's no different for your baby. It's up to you to make talking interesting and enjoyable. At this level of development, your child doesn't understand a word you're saying, so topics can be as free-ranging as you like. You can talk about your favorite movie star, the zen of motorcycle maintenance, or the state of the union—it doesn't matter, as long as you make it sound interesting. Enjoy this freedom while you can. Before long, I'll be asking you to talk about things in the immediate context and to modify your speech to enhance your baby's understanding. But for now—anything goes:

  YOU (in a soothing baby voice): So is Mommy crazy (Pause) or is the economy in the toilet? (Pause)
  BABY: Gurgle.
  YOU (playful voice): Oooooh, it is! (Pause) Big mess. (Pause)
  BABY: Gurgle, coo.

Sometimes, entertaining yourself like this is a good idea. If you're amused, your baby will be, too. The important thing is to be gentle and comforting, and pause to allow time for her to respond. At this stage, your baby is learning that people communicate and that she can have a turn, too.

Month One

Your precious little bundle is raring to get started. Don't believe anyone who tells you your newborn can't learn—or hasn't learned anything yet. Newborns are constantly learning. Remember, she's already learned how to breathe and suck and swallow, and soon she'll be coordinating all three. That's not bad! She's also already figured out to suck strongly for nutrition and lighten up when the object in her mouth is just a blanket corner or soft toy, and is already actively involved in exploring and testing things in her environment. This is a time of awe, emotion, and bonding for both of you, so take it slow and easy as you get to know your baby and discover her unique personality. Remember, crying is your baby's way of communicating with you and letting you know she needs something. Always respond when you can. This month is the beginning of lifelong Shared Communication.

● ■ ▲

MILESTONE WATCHLIST:
One-Month-Old

Does your baby. . .

❑ Startle (react to) or show interest in sound?

❑ Seem to recognize your voice? She might become excited if calm, or calm if excited when she hears it.

❑ Quiet down with she hears a soothing voice or when picked up? This may not happen if your baby is especially irritable or distressed.

❑ Make brief eye contact during feeding?

❑ Seem to prefer bright colors and black/white contrasts?

❑ Seem to enjoy feeling different textures against her skin?

SHARED COMMUNICATION ACTIVITIES: MONTH ONE

Communication ◆

Mosquito in your ear. Make gentle noises next to your baby's ear. While this is totally enjoyable for the physical closeness it creates between you and your baby, it also teaches your baby about sound production and stimulates hearing—the main pathway for language. Although noises of all types stimulate the brain, most babies would rather hear a human voice than any other sound. After feeding, before bed, or when just cuddling, rest your cheek against your baby's and hum a favorite song or lullaby, so that she can feel the vibration in your cheek. As she's comforted by the closeness, she'll be learning about the body as a sound source and that the human voice is soothing. Vary the pitch and rhythm to keep her interest. Low volume musical accompaniment is fine.

Isn't that incredible? Attract your child's attention with interesting objects. Start with yourself. Most children prefer the human face to other visual stimuli. They love the animation and contrasting shades of color, especially around the eyes. Talk to your baby when she's alert and able to see you easily. If she doesn't look at you or fails to respond to your call, attract her attention by using a brightly colored item, a noise-making object, or a combination of the two, like a shiny red rattle. Shake it very gently in front of her, and then continue to jiggle it and slowly draw it to your face. When your baby looks at you, respond with a smile or eye blink and say something soothing in a pleasant baby-friendly voice, such as "Yes, you found Mommy," or "Oh, what beautiful eyes you have," or "Hi there, bright eyes."

Cognitive Development ◆

The amazing disappearing objects. Attract your baby's interest to objects by having them appear, disappear, then suddenly reappear. Even though your baby lacks the cognitive skill to search for missing or hidden objects, she still enjoys watching objects vanish only to miraculously pop up out of nowhere. Anticipating the location of objects is an early cognitive skill that also lends itself to lots of fun. Show your baby an interesting, colorful object like a stuffed animal or toy, and talk about it as you move it around. Then drop it out of her line of vision for a few seconds, and act surprised when it unexpectedly resurfaces. Cognitively, your baby will be learning patterns and anticipating behavior. Her memory will improve as she awaits the next appearance. Communication involves memory, routines, and anticipation.

Hearing Stimulation ◆

Those surprising noises. We've all been startled at one time or another. It's that little jump we feel when we're surprised by a loud noise or sudden movement, or are caught eating ice cream out of the carton when we're on a diet. It's also one of the first ways that children respond to sound. Your baby's little jump says, "Oh, that was a surprise, but I heard it loud and clear." When you make noises, you're actually helping your baby organize the auditory or hearing portion of her brain.

But please, keep the noises gentle—nothing thunderous or alarming. We don't want to frighten the little gal or create some kind of nervous tic; we simply want her to begin to notice sounds. Just make normal, everyday noises and look for signs that she's heard the noise. At bath time, for instance, you could drop the plastic baby powder container on the floor (make sure it's closed!), then act surprised and talk about the resulting noise. A ringing phone or doorbell can elicit the same response, and the remote control for the TV or CD player turns you into a first-class surprise noisemeister. Since almost any kind of everyday object can be used, this is a very versatile exercise that can be practiced any time of day, anywhere you are.

Visual Stimulation ◆

Follow that car! Looking at objects and faces is great, but your baby can do more. Visual tracking, which is basically a fancy term for following a moving object, is important for developing the visual portion of the brain. Think about how often you follow things in motion in the environment, especially when you drive.

First get your baby's attention and help her to focus on a squeaky toy, stuffed animal, puppet, or some other interesting object. Jiggle it in front of her face and talk about it. Remember that initially her best visual range is only about eight inches. When she focuses and displays some interest, shake the object and move it slowly so that she can follow visually. At this age, most babies will move their entire head, not just their eyes, so make sure that your child's head is free to move and that it's gently supported if she's in an upright position.

While this exercise is similar in some ways to the cognitive disappearing/reappearing toy activity above, it exercises a very different part of the brain: The *disappearing* toy encourages location anticipation, the *moving* toy encourages visual tracking. During these few first months, the difference in activity techniques can be very subtle, but the developmental results are profound.

Sensory Stimulation ◆

Texture touching. Awaken your baby's sense of touch and feel with different textures. Gently brushing different textured materials or toys over her skin provides sensory stimulation and cognitive input. Use items made of soft smooth fabrics, such as velvet, terrycloth, cotton, fake fur, Polarfleece, and the like. Fuzzy animals are perfect and fun for your baby to look at, too. Avoid scratchy or abrasive objects, and steer clear of very small scraps of cloth that could be dangerous if your baby put them in her mouth. *(Never leave your baby unattended with small pieces of anything!)*

If you're a whiz on the sewing machine or handy with a needle and thread you could even make a "texture blanket" or washable "texture mitts" from fabric store remnants. As you touch your baby or as she touches the soft fabrics, talk about the feeling. With my own children, texture stroking became a part of the bedtime ritual—and more often than not, put them right to sleep. Experiencing soft sensory input on various parts of the body can be very pleasurable for a baby.

Infant massage. If your little one seems to really enjoy texture touching, think about giving her a soothing infant massage. Babies love a good massage just as much as we adults do, and it helps them relax, aids digestion, encourages structural fitness, creates bonding, and generally stimulates their bodies and brains—just to name a few of the benefits. Begin naturally when your child is unclothed and calm—after a bath is a good time. Lay her down on her tummy, warm up a few drops of baby oil in your hands, and gently stroke her back, then move on to the legs and feet, arms and hands. Finish with several downward sweeps from her neck to her spine. Remember that she's tiny and sensitive to pain, so be very gentle.

(To learn more about nuances and massage techniques, check "Appendix E" for recommended books.)

Motor Development ◆

Swat and grab. This is another way to build those critical neuron-connecting pathways. Swat-and-grab toys, hung over the crib or playpen, help your baby develop eye-hand coordination—an important early skill that integrates two senses, visual and motor. As adults, we're always reaching and grabbing for things without even bothering to look or think about what we're doing. But we've had lots of practice; now it's your baby's turn. The visual and motor stimulation she gets from swatting and grabbing hanging toys will be welcome indeed. Lying on your back all day isn't all it's cracked up to be; it's much more fun—and stimulating—to be able to entertain yourself while lying in the crib or playpen.

There are a huge variety of commercial crib gyms and other interesting suspension toys on the market—or you can make your own. If you do take the homemade route, make sure that there are no small parts or anything that could come loose and end up in your baby's mouth. Don't place the mobile directly above your baby's face, since objects can become detached. Although ideal for newborns, swat-and-grab-type stimulation is not good after three months, because your more mature tot will quickly turn a swat-and-grab into grasp and pull—which means anything not secured will end up in the crib with her by the time she's through with it.

Lift those legs! While your baby lies on her back, gently move her legs as if she were walking. Push them up and then stretch them out, over and over. This exercises her limbs and instills the movement patterns that will be important later on. It's is a great little exercise after diapering, bathing, or dressing. Try it to music but keep the leg movements natural—and make it a fun game. One of my favorite tunes for this exercise was an up-beat version of the Hokey Pokey—I found the rhythm is perfect. But of course, feel free to follow your own musical muse.

Squeeze me, baby! Rest your finger across the palm of your baby's hand. Reflexively, she'll wrap her fingers around your finger and squeeze. This is actually quite beneficial for strengthening those little hand muscles. Soon she'll be picking up everything in sight. You'll only be able to do a few repetitions at a time, since your baby doesn't yet have the ability to release her grip voluntarily. She'll just hold on until she gets tired of grasping; then her little muscles will relax on their own.

Month Two

Get ready for a more communicative, responsive baby! Activities this month are a little bit more adventuresome—and a little more fun for you. Your baby is experimenting more with making sounds, smiling more, and, because her memory has improved, she's able to recognize you and other family members as individuals.

● ■ ▲

MILESTONE WATCHLIST:
Two-Month-Old

Does your baby. . .

❑ Have different cries for different reasons?

❑ Make pleasure sounds?

❑ Make some sound in the back of the throat, such as *g-g-guh* and *k-k-kuh*?

❑ Make noises when not crying, like grunts and growls or squeaks and squeals?

❑ Pay attention to speaking?

❑ Turn her head toward sounds?

❑ Smile at the sound of Mom's voice and/or sight of her face?

❑ Look and maybe smile at someone when they speak

❑ Make eye contact with Mom or Dad?

❑ Reach out?

SHARED COMMUNICATION ACTIVITIES: MONTH TWO

Communication ◆

Pleased ta meetcha! Establish a little routine of greeting your baby whenever you see each other again after being apart, even for a short time. In the mornings, after naps, after a stroll with Mom or Dad—all potential times for greeting anew. Say "Hi," smile, wave, and then start to talk. Besides being a warm, friendly interaction, your greeting will also become an expected routine. Your child will learn that Mom is predictable. She'll begin to anticipate your "Hi honey," and may even make her own contribution. Greeting people and starting conversations is an early baby communication skill—and one that we definitely want to encourage.

Hey, you! Call your child's name and get her attention before interacting. Although at two months your baby isn't yet able to recognize her name, it's still a good idea to start using it. She'll understand that it refers to her in a few short months, so let's get her used to it. Plus, who wants to be thought of only as *you*? Your baby might be tiny, but she's still an individual and deserves a little respect.

It's also good training. Using someone's name to get her attention when you want to engage her in conversation might seem instinctive, but it's actually a learned skill. I remember being surprised one day by a preschooler behind me who was chattering away to my rear end. It simply hadn't occurred to him to get my attention before he began talking—there's a lesson there. For maximum impact, get your baby's attention before attempting any kind of meaningful interaction. If you know she's awake, for instance, call her name softly as you approach her crib or playpen. Then reward her for looking your way with soothing talk, cuddles, or by sharing a soft, colorful stuffed animal or toy with her. If she fails to look when you call, try again or gently turn her head toward you by guiding her chin. Remember to give her positive feedback even if you have to move her head; smile, talk, and have fun.

Ahhhh, those pleasure sounds. Your baby makes lots of pleasure sounds—mostly coos and goos. You can encourage these by making similar pleasure sounds as you hold your child against your chest or face. This works best when your child is quiet but awake. When my children were babies, I used to lie on my back with one of them on my chest, his or her head resting next to my cheek. It was a definite feel-good experience. If your baby starts making pleasure sounds, either following your lead or on her own, join in softly. Try this little exercise whenever it fits naturally into your day, during down time when you're resting, or even while you're watching TV—it's a perfect diversion during commercial breaks. If lying down, make sure you don't doze off (which is easy to do) unless the baby is totally safe, sound, and secure.

I hear you! Respond to your baby's vocalizations as well as her cries. This is incredibly important now and all through your baby's early years. Let me tell you a quick story. I was once asked to evaluate a child who was forty months old—almost three-and-a-half years—but acted like a six-month-old. He was very lethargic, made no sounds, and spent most of his time staring at the ceiling, yet all tests came back normal. Once I started to investigate, I learned that his parents worked split shifts and someone was always sleeping while the other was at work. As a newborn, this preschooler had been placed in a playpen in the room farthest from the bedroom. He was fed and changed when an adult was awake—and that was it. Nobody bothered to play with him; there was little or no communication; there were no games, no other interactions—nothing. The poor thing simply gave up. Why cry? No one will come. Why make pleasure sounds? No one will pay attention. The parents were unconcerned for their *quiet, compliant* child. It was incredibly sad, but at least there was vast improvement once we educated the parents and enrolled their son in a preschool program. The little guy began developing more typically within about a year.

While this is an extreme case, it is illustrative. Babies need to know that the world is changeable and that they can make some of that change happen. So respond to your baby whenever you can. Change her when she signals that she needs it, feed her when she lets you know she's hungry, play with her, and show pleasure and respond when she makes sounds. This is not to say that you should continue this level of intense responsiveness into her adolescent years. In fact, you'll be asking for serious trouble if you do. At first, simply respond and gradually modify her feeding and sleep schedule to conform more to that of the rest of the family. You don't have to respond every time for her to maintain the expectation that you will.

Let the toys do some talking. As we've discussed, your baby has a natural interest in your voice and in talking. But after a few weeks she'll want something new. This little exercise makes your voice more interesting to her and keeps her mind active and alert. It usually works best with stuffed animals and dolls, but a talking "sock puppet" (insert hand in sock, move your fingers around, and start yakking), a chatty little wool hat, or a loquacious baby bottle will do just fine.

There are two variations on the theme. In the first version, the toy talks directly to your baby. You just jiggle the teddy bear (or possum, or whatever) a little in front of your baby, put on your friendliest high-pitched teddy-bear voice and say something like:

> *"Hello, Timmy. (pause) Do you want to play? (pause) You do? Oh goody! (pause) How 'bout the dancing bear game? . . ."*

In the second variation, you, your baby, and the teddy bear have a conversation; you in your regular voice, the teddy (you again) in his higher-pitched teddy bear voice, and your baby . . . well, you might get a coo or two. It would go something like this:

> TEDDY BEAR: Hello! Where's Timmy?
> ADULT: He's right here! (Pause)
> TIMMY: (Looks)
> TEDDY BEAR: Hi Timmy . . . You look cute.
> TIMMY: (Gurgle, coo)
> ADULT: Oh! Timmy talk to bear.

You get the idea—the scripts are limited only by your imagination—and maybe your ventriloquism. Enjoy the theatre of it and let the game evolve naturally. Try unexpected things like letting the toy dance around the crib, jump up real high, or appear in unexpected places. After a few times your baby will anticipate the next appearance and accompanying sounds. Confirm her expectations, or surprise her with a new location. This is a truly fun activity for infants and always holds their attention, so do it once or even twice a day if you can, for a couple of minutes or so— or until your baby seems to be losing interest.

Cognitive Development ◆

Hang 'em high. Hang interesting objects from a string suspended over your baby's feet. Interestingly, this helps develop a different part of the brain than the swat-and-grab toy I recommended for a one-month-old. While that activity helps develop hand-eye coordination, this one teaches *cause and effect*—a small change of placement, a big developmental difference. At this stage your baby can only relate a cause to the effect it produces in a very limited way, but it's enough for her to learn to anticipate events that recur when she moves in certain ways.

When you hang jiggling toys or objects close enough to her feet so that she can make them move by kicking them, you're giving her the opportunity to learn that she can cause things to happen—a very exciting development in her little world! She'll love to watch the different shapes bounce around. Being able to jiggle strange new objects by her very own movements is thrilling—and an important lesson. It gives her some control over her environment. Babies who have no control tend to give up and become listless after a while, as we just discussed.

Be sure to supervise this activity and remove the objects when you're not around. You can hang almost any object as long as it's interesting in some way—in color, shape, texture, patterns, and so on—and it's baby-friendly. Plastic kitchen utensils like ladles and spoons, soft stuffed animals, rattles, colorful mittens or socks will work—and as a bonus, they'll give you two lots to "talk" about.

Hearing Stimulation ◆

Roll on. Your baby is now beginning to integrate sensory input—this little game helps by combining movement with noise. At this age, she can roll from side to side, but may be unable to turn herself over completely. You can help her by putting her on your bed or on a soft pad on the floor, and gently rolling her over a *very soft* squeaky toy. The toy should be under her body but not near her ear. Act surprised when it squeaks, and talk about the noise. Ask your baby where it is. Don't expect an answer, of course, but remember to pause for one.

Encourage your tot to roll by giving her a little assistance. Then try some variations. Hold the toy to the side, squeak it, and encourage her to look at it, and then let her roll over and touch it. Don't make this too difficult, and don't expect her to grab and squeeze the toy yet—that won't happen for another month or so. Remember to always stay positive, and make it fun for your baby. This is not an everyday activity; once or twice a week will do the trick, rolling your baby over just three or four times each time you do it.

Whiskers on kittens and bells on your clothing. Attach bells to the sleeve or leg of your baby's clothing. This is another chance to integrate sensory information, reinforce cause and effect learning, and give your baby some more control. With this little bell trick, your baby can show her stuff as she produces "music" *accidentally* whenever she moves. If you move with her music and talk about it, she'll be encouraged to learn how to make music purposefully—and trust me, she will. Don't do this every day. This sensory game is only fun for a little while—then the novelty wears off. The last thing we want is for both of you to be thinking, "Oh no, not those #$@%;cr&% bells again!"

Noise, noise, noise, noise. Outside noises can present a golden opportunity to integrate vision and hearing input, and help build pathways between the visual and auditory portions of the brain. No more complaining about all the noise pollution—make use of all those airplanes, big trucks, trains, yapping dogs, and loud stereos instead. Call your baby's attention to the noise, point at its source, look in the direction of the source yourself, and talk about it.

ADULT (Pointing): Look Jeremy! (pause)

JEREMY (Looking): Gurgle, goo.

ADULT (Still pointing and looking): Big truck! (pause) Garbage truck.

JEREMY (Staring in wonderment): (Silence)

ADULT: Oh, very loud (pause) . . . So noisy! Noisy truck.

As brief as this is, it's a sharing moment. One caution: Very loud noises are frightening to babies. So be careful not to terrify her. This is meant to be a pleasurable experience, not a character-toughening one.

Visual Stimulation ◆

A sight for sure eyes. Hang fun pictures, objects, or a mobile over the crib or playpen. Giving your baby something to gaze at (especially complex or patterned images) stimulates the visual part of her brain. It gives her something to think about, and alleviates boredom as she's lying in her crib or playpen. Hanging mobiles and pictures is a great alternative to swat-and-grab toys—especially as your baby matures and is capable of pulling swat-and-grabs down. Because mobiles and pictures are typically hung higher, they're relatively baby-proof for at least the first six months. Still, make sure any hanging pictures or objects are well secured. There are all kinds of commercial toys and mobiles with brightly colored objects available in stores . . . but colorful magazine pictures, brightly colored gift-wrap paper, or fabric are plentiful—and also cheaper.

It's a good idea to change the pictures, mobile, or toy every week or so. Just like you, your baby will grow tired of the same visual stimulus day in and day out. If you're feeling creative and have a spare moment—I know it's a stretch—you can create your own mobiles. It's really easy. Cut a few shapes out of cardboard (circles, squares, triangles, you name it), paste some magazine pictures or wrapping paper on them with stick glue, punch a hole in them, run a string or ribbon through the holes, and attach the strings to a hanger. Voilà! It may not be a Calder, but it is inexpensive, easy baby entertainment. Or you could always offer to swap mobiles with a friend or check out a toy exchange. Again, make sure any homemade masterpieces are secure and harmless. Avoid plastic bags, balloons, or any small materials that might cause choking or suffocation, and check frequently to ensure that all is secure.

Looking for fun in all the right places. Being able to transfer eye gaze between objects and/or people is important for communication. Just watch people participating in an everyday conversation. They look at each other, gesture, glance around, and transfer focus to things they're talking about. We want to develop the same kind of flexibility in your child.

Once or twice a week try getting your baby to alternate her attention between a toy and your voice. Move a toy in a very animated manner until it attracts her attention, then hold it still and talk to your child or call her name. Your child should transfer her gaze from the visual source to the sound source. In another variation, you could use two noisemakers, one in each hand. Shake one, then the other, and look back and forth between the two with surprise—after three or four times, chances are your baby will be doing the same thing.

Sock it to 'em. Cover your baby's bottle with a clean sock. Alternate between different textures and colors. This will not only improve her grip, but will give her lots of extra sensory and visual stimulation.

Sensory Stimulation ◆
Scents sense. Babies, even newborns, have a relatively well-developed sense of smell. Research has shown that very young babies can recognize and are drawn to their mother's scent, so don't neglect this important sense. Olfactory stimulation will help develop yet another portion of your baby's brain, and scent will become part of her early definition of things in her environment. Although we take them for granted, there are wonderful scents all around us, so this is an easy activity to incorporate into your everyday routines. Let your baby smell spices when you're cooking. Imagine how stimulating and exciting it will be for her to smell cinnamon, nutmeg, curry, and vanilla. Introduce her to flowers in the garden, soaps in the bathroom . . . *very mild* perfumes, wet dogs . . . there's no end to the sensory pleasures that await her. Don't forget to talk about them, too. No need to overdo this one—once a week, or even once every two weeks, is plenty.

Motor Development ◆
Shake it up, baby! Give your infant things to hold and shake. Although she won't be able to hold anything at first except as a reflexive response to stimulation of the palms, let's give her a chance. Again, she can learn about cause and effect while she works on eye-hand coordination and builds those pathways in her brain. Don't hesitate to help her out—she won't be able to do it by herself yet. Stuffed animals are great for stimulation of the

hand muscles. Pick plush toys with contrasting colors for added interest. Rattles or other interactive noisemakers work for muscle development, too. Be careful not to use sharp or pointed objects—no drumsticks until high school.

Reach out and touch some . . . thing. Encourage your baby to reach for things at different angles to simulate different muscles and brain patterns, as well as eye-hand coordination. Instead of just holding something desirable—say a rattle or stuffed animal—right in front of your baby, try holding it off to the side a bit, or a little above or below the center of her body. Still keep it within her reach, of course. We want to encourage development, not frustrate the little gal.

Month Three

Curiosity is the name of the game this month, and your baby's growing control over her body, and increased knowledge and memory, allow her to take advantage of it. She's starting to use her hands for exploration—clutching and touching things that are interesting to her (including her own face)—and she laughs and smiles in direct response to things you do. She's also learned to expect a response from you for things she does.

● ■ ▲

MILESTONE WATCHLIST:
Three-Month-Old

Does your child . . .

❑ Take turns making sounds with you?

❑ Vocalize two syllables together occasionally?

❑ Produce several different kinds of sounds?

❑ Make sounds when you do?

❑ Laugh while playing with you?

● ■ ▲

MILESTONE WATCHLIST:
Three-Month-Old

Does your child . . .

❑ Look directly at you and watch your mouth?

❑ Try to find a speaker who is out of view?

❑ Show more interest in people than in objects?

❑ Signal distress, hunger, and pleasure consistently?

SHARED COMMUNICATION ACTIVITIES: MONTH THREE

Communication ◆

I'm game! Games are very important for communication development because they naturally incorporate so many conversational elements—shared attention, listening, and watching facial expressions, just to name a few. As you play together, your baby is also picking up social skills. She's learning about personal interaction; how to share—how to take her turn and allow someone else to take theirs.

Early games might include making eye contact, breaking it for a few seconds, and then making it again; making funny faces then looking away; and gently bouncing her on your knee, stopping, then starting again when she looks at you. "I'm gonna get you" is another favorite. You hunch down, hands toward the child, and say, "I'm gonna get you." Then pretend-lunge for your baby and "tickle" her sides gently. When she giggles, you've both won the game. Your baby may not understand games or even take her turn yet, but one thing is for sure—she'll always enjoy watching you be silly. Remember to pick the right time to play. Right after a diaper change is generally an excellent time, since the little tyke is usually feeling pretty mellow after a nice cleaning-up. She's also on her back, the ideal position for "I'm gonna get you."

As you can see, these kinds of simple games are super easy to incorporate into everyday life. You can make funny faces or play peek-a-boo and other eye contact games while giving your baby her bath, for instance, or even while you're putting on makeup or cleaning the house. Once you get going you'll be amazed at how quickly games become a natural extension of your shared communication with your baby—and they certainly give her something to look forward to every day.

Cognitive Development ◆

Search and rescue. Your baby now has the cognitive ability to search for sounds in the environment and integrate vision and hearing. As a newborn, she experienced sounds as fleeting stimuli that surprised her. Last month she began to coordinate hearing and vision and to look around for sounds out of her range of sight. Now at three months, she's mature enough to actually search for that sound, not just glance around. She can't search for a hidden object *physically* yet—that won't come for several months—but she can search *visually*.

So for now, don't hide toys; just hold them out of her sight for a minute. When you bring the toy back into view, she'll be happy and show surprise. This exercise stimulates her vision and hearing as well as cognitive development. You can use squeaky toys, mechanical noise and movement toys, or some of those rattles you got as gifts. Another variation on the theme is to try making the sound just outside her field of vision, then gradually move farther away. You may need to play the game a few times, staying partially in sight until she gets the idea. Tracking activities, like the ones I suggested for last month in which you move an object so that she can follow it with her eyes are very effective too. You can also attach rattles to her wrist or ankle for a couple of minutes so that she can shake them and make noise at will—another wonderful cause-and-effect lesson. Generally, babies lose interest in this sort of stimulation very quickly, so don't overdo it.

Hearing Stimulation ◆

Long-distance calling. Although as a newborn your baby could focus best at about eight inches, she now has nearly full focus and can see things at a greater distance. This visual focus will continue to expand over the next few months. That means you can move farther away, too. She still needs close-in cuddling, touch, and communication, of course, but occasionally it's fine to encourage her to look farther out. Again, use interesting objects or facial expressions and sounds to attract her. As your spouse or partner holds her, call your baby's name or make a noise while you jiggle or shake a favorite toy from across the room. Remember, she can follow a moving object now, too.

Up to this point, most of her eye movement has been side to side; now she can focus on objects in close and far away—just like a zoom camera. Babies love to have objects come close and snuggle their neck. Build anticipation and turn it into a game like "I'm gonna get you." For example:

MOM: (Shake rattle from across the room) Hi, Noah. Look Mommy. (Pause) Noah, look Mommy (Shake rattle).

NOAH: Babble, babble, babble

MOM: (Moving gradually closer) Here comes Mommy (Pause) . . . Closer (Pause)

NOAH: (Smiles)

MOM: . . . and closer . . . (Pause) . . . and even closer (Eyes widen)

NOAH: (Anticipating) Gurgle, babble (Kicks feet)

MOM: And here I am! (Kisses and cuddles baby)

Visual Stimulation ◆

Hidden masterpieces. Decorate the environment in new places. This will increase your baby's visual interest. As we mentioned last month, vision stimulation is important for development of the visual portion of her brain. Hopefully you already have interesting things for her to look at around her crib or playpen—like that mobile masterpiece you created last month. But your baby's been staring at her old environment for three months and is due for a change.

Now it's time to start putting interesting pictures in new but familiar places, such as next to the changing table, high chair, or even in the car. The car, in fact, is a natural art gallery. Whenever you drive somewhere your tot has to be in the car seat in the back and is usually facing the back of a seat—generally a pretty dull area. So liven it up! The seat back is the perfect place for a picture—just tape a bright, interesting photo or two from a magazine and bingo!—instant baby art gallery. She'll love it! Also think about putting visually interesting posters on the ceiling over her crib or playpen. Again—safety counts. Make sure all pictures are securely attached and with tape, not tacks. And lastly, you can be the ultimate decoration; brightly colored clothes and colorful prints will keep your baby's eyes on you—for a little while, anyway.

Sensory Stimulation ◆

Hey buds, taste this. As with all the other portions of the brain, the one concerned with taste also needs stimulation. Your baby will begin to take some semi-liquid nutrition at about this point in her development. Even mothers who breast-feed may supplement their infant's diet slightly. Although you can't vary the consistency much until your baby has better oral motor control, you can provide different taste sensations—even with bland baby food. Please don't try to really wow her senses by dumping jalapeños in the vanilla pudding. There will be enough taste differences in natural food to satisfy her need for stimulation, just vary tastes frequently. You could even try some recipes from a baby cookbook. Your baby would definitely thank you for that if she could! (Check Appendix E for some of my favorites—bon appétit!)

Crunch-a-munch. Fill a clean cotton sock with crunchy, crumpled cellophane and securely tie the open end closed. Then let your baby squeeze it and even chew it if she wants to—and I'm betting she will. This simple little homemade toy stimulates hearing—the crunch of the cellophane; touch and feel; and two motor skills—hand grasps and squeezes, and mouth movement. When your tyke's had her fill, remove the cellophane and toss the sock in the washer. A very easy toy!

Motor Stimulation ◆

With this hand, I . . . Talk to your baby about different parts of her body. Your baby is really on the go now. She's rolling over and creeping by pulling herself along on her tummy. As she moves about, talk to her about her movement, describe what she's doing and name her body parts. You could say things like, "Oh, look at those arms moving." Or, "Let me see that tummy." Make associations between body parts and movement— "Simone grab bunny with her hands." Your tot won't understand your

Shared Communication Activities:
The First Three Months

MONTHLY ACTIVITIES			
Age (Mos.)	Communication	Cognitive Development	Hearing Stimulation
1	▲ Mosquito in your ear ▲ Isn't that incredible?	▲ The amazing disappearing objects	▲ Those surprising noises
2	▲ Pleased ta meetcha! ▲ Hey, you! ▲ Ahhhh, those pleasure sounds ▲ I hear you! ▲ Let the toys do some talking	▲ Hang 'em high	▲ Roll on ▲ Whiskers on kittens and bells on your clothing ▲ Noise, noise, noise, noise
3	▲ I'm game!	▲ Search and rescue	▲ Long-distance calling

Shared Communication Reminders
- Accentuate your facial movement and expression.
- Treat your child's movements and sounds as meaningful.
- Imitate your child's noises and movements.
- Enjoy yourself!

Visual Stimulation	Sensory Stimulation	Motor Development
▴ Follow that car!	▴ Texture touching	▴ Swat and grab
	▴ Infant massage	▴ Lift those legs!
		▴ Squeeze me, baby!
▴ A sight for sure eyes	▴ Scents sense	▴ Shake it up, baby!
▴ Looking for fun in all the right places		▴ Reach out and touch some . . . thing
▴ Sock it to 'em		
▴ Hidden masterpieces	▴ Hey buds, taste this Crunch-a-munch	▴ With this hand I . . .
		▴ What a great pair of eggs!

words, but she'll begin to make associations, especially as she hears the words day after day. In addition, you're both focusing on the same thing—a valuable lesson for future communication.

Bath time, diaper changing, or dressing are also perfect times for naming body parts since you'll naturally be handling them, and it will make it all much more fun and interesting for your baby.

During dressing, for instance:

"This little arm here . . . (Pause) and this arm goes here . . . (Pause) . . . and this sock on foot . . ."

Or at bath time:

"Mommy washing Bradley's legs . . . (Pause) And his little toes (Pause) . . . and tummy (Pause) . . . and his ears . . ."

What a great pair of eggs! This is a terrific exercise for eye-hand coordination for you moms who may have some arts and crafts materials nearby. Fill the broad end of a L'eggs panty hose container (or any plastic egg) about half full of a mixture of plaster of Paris and water and let it dry overnight. The next day, fill the rest with crumpled tissue, and glue the two egg halves together well. Then let your child bat at it with her hand. When she knocks it over, it'll pop right back up again, and unlike a ball it won't roll away. If you want to add a little sound stimulation to this otherwise quiet toy, simply slip a few small bells (like the ones you find on cat collars) into the egg before gluing the halves securely together.

CHAPTER SEVEN

Months 4, 5, and 6

Babbling and Turn-Taking Games

Progress Report

MOVEMENT

Big motor changes are in progress from four to six months. Your baby's gaining a lot more muscle control. Now that his body control is progressing to the lower part of his body, he can crouch on his hands and knees, roll over, and creep. Early travel begins! Toward the end of this stage, at the end of his sixth month, your baby will be able to sit for short periods without direct support from you. These months also bring increased small muscle development, which will enable your baby to hold his own bottle, and—for better or worse—bring seemingly everything and anything to his mouth. This is the stage where everything holds potential for exploration by taste, touch, and smell, so be very careful what you leave on the floor as he rolls about. The days of baby-proofing the environment have begun!

LANGUAGE DEVELOPMENT

Although your baby can't talk yet, he's now getting a lot more control over the muscles that control speech. During these next few months he'll become capable of both curling up the edges of his tongue (called *tongue bowling*) and projecting it forward. He's not being difficult when he pushes all the food out his mouth, it's just that his tongue is strongest when moving in a forward direction. Just accept that you're in for some messy meals, and scrape the food gently off the little guy's chin with the spoon and put it back in his mouth again . . . and again and again. You'll also see changes in his tongue action when he's sucking. He'll start using his tongue more and relying less on the whole-jaw movement that he needed before. His bite will become more voluntary, too—he won't need the stimulation from your touch to get it moving—-and he'll be able to place his lips around a baby spoon and use them to ingest the spoon's contents. Now, that's progress! With his new lip control, your baby will be giving you lots of "raspberries" or "Bronx cheers" (that outboard motor sound you make by stickling out your tongue and vibrating it and your lips), but don't take it personally, even if he does it just after he's pushed food out of his mouth with that powerful tongue. Just smile, wash your face, and celebrate his progress in motor control.

VISION

During these next three months, as your baby gains better control of his eye movement, he'll be able to move his gaze more smoothly from object to object. He'll also form visual preferences; he'll be more attentive to specific people and prefer joyful expressions to angry ones. So stay cheery! Throughout these three months, your little one will be smiling, vocalizing, and examining faces—both visually and by touching—more and more. He may also be somewhat wary around unfamiliar faces. Mirrors are great fun at this age. Chances are he'll smile when he sees his own face, although it's doubtful that he has a sense of himself yet.

MEMORY

With his increased memory, your baby will now be able to store and retrieve images of familiar people and objects. His smile of recognition when he sees you means that your face matches the model he has stored in his brain. Your voice triggers the same recognition. As he becomes more aware of his environment, he'll begin to anticipate events in his everyday world. Just as he's now capable of storing images, he can also store limited event sequences. That allows him to anticipate familiar routines—bathing, feeding, diaper changing, game playing, strolls—and to play anticipation games like Peek-a-boo and "I'm gonna get you." Now when your baby sees you taking a towel out of the cupboard it may signal bath time to him; get out the stroller, and he may anticipate an outing. He may even begin to drool a little when he sees a spoon.

COMMUNICATION

Depending on his mood, your little one will either utter sounds at the same time you do or wait for you to finish and then take his turn (trading sounds back and forth is great fun!). He may even join in while you're singing. Both simultaneous vocalizing and turn-taking are important communication skills that he'll use later in conversations.

During these three months, your baby's *babbles*, those delightful random speech sounds that are like music to your ears, will become stronger and more varied as he experiments more and more with the *feel of saying sounds*. Although your baby will inadvertently make sounds that are used in many languages, he'll try to say sounds that reflect the language he hears most frequently—another reason your early communication is so important. (Those lucky children who are exposed to two languages are a special case. See Appendix A for more guidance in raising a bilingual child.) If you listen carefully, you'll notice a change in his babbling between his forth and sixth month. The throaty cooing and gooing—*kuh-h-h* and *guh-h-h*—will gradually give way to sounds he produces with his lips—*m-m-m* and *buh-h-h* and *puh-h-h*. Increasingly, as the weeks and months go by, his babbling will start to sound more like adult speech, especially in syllable structure and inflection. Don't get too excited. It will be a few more months before he can accurately imitate your words. At this age your little one still doesn't have enough muscle control to make a specific sound at will. He might say "Ma" or "Pa," but, alas, it's just a happy coincidence, not a meaningful word.

Many of his other baby noises won't resemble speech. You'll hear sustained laughing as well as high- and low-pitched whispers, shouts, and delight-induced squeals. It's a fun time. My granddaughter seemed to find the whole family particularly humorous at this age, and her delicious baby laughter pealed throughout the house. It was a real pick-me-up for everybody—it's hard to be down when a baby is laughing.

SHARED COMMUNICATION REMINDERS AND TIPS

- **Talk in a soothing voice.** The way you talk to your baby continues to be important. Your comforting, gentle voice helps him feel secure and conveys the message that communication is a positive thing. He'll continue to bond to his nurturing parents.

- **Spend more time playing and talking.** Your baby will be more alert and interested now. He'll be awake for longer periods of time. Use that time to communicate with him. When you talk and make sounds, he'll be encouraged to do the same.

- **Convince your baby that he wants to talk.** "You get more teddy bears with honey," if you'll forgive the paraphrasing. By making conversations fun and pleasurable, you'll show your baby the joy of talking. Use exaggerated intonation and facial expressions to grab his attention and hold on to it.

- **Talk to your baby throughout the day.** In our daily lives, communication occurs throughout the day, and so should your conversations with your baby. You don't have to talk all day, but converse with your little one frequently. Say a little something whenever you see him; pick the best times for little chats; enhance interactions by talking about whatever it is you're doing; and have fun by "copycatting" your baby's noises and movements

- And last, but definitely not least, remember to *treat your baby's movements and sounds as meaningful.*

Month Four

This is an exciting month. Your baby's becoming much more active during all your interactions. He's smiling more—especially when he sees you smile (called a "social smile"); and his giggling, laughing and sound-making are on the rise.. His gooing and cooing (those g-g-guh and k-k-kuh sounds) and vowel sounds (ahhh, ohhhhs, eeee) continue, but his vowel sounds are now more varied, and his consonants sound more like speech and less like noisy exhalations. He's becoming a more mature speaker! Thanks to his growing memory, he's also able to participate more in games and look forward to certain routines. While he's comforted by those routines and predictable actions and words, he also finds the expected especially interesting and stimulating, making this an ideal month for quick little games like "I'm gonna get you" and Peek-a-boo. Now that he can anticipate your actions and take his own turn—he's ready! Still, he's not yet capable of sustained interest, so keep it short—and sweet.

● ■ ▲

MILESTONE WATCHLIST:
Four-Month-Old

Does your child . . .

❑ Respond with distress to an angry voice?

❑ Babble vowels and *g* and *k*, sometimes in consonant-vowel (CV) syllables?

❑ Vocalize in response to your words and sounds?

❑ Vocalize in response to singing?

❑ Make a greater variety of sounds than in previously months?

❑ Smile or laugh?

❑ Turn toward familiar sounds?

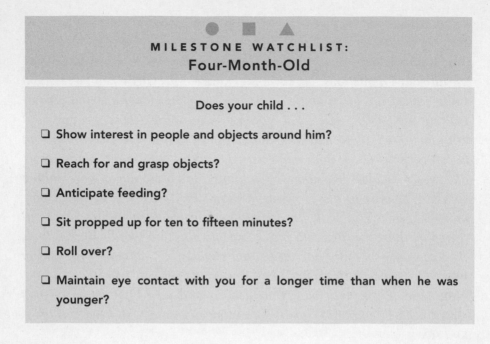

MILESTONE WATCHLIST:
Four-Month-Old

Does your child . . .

❏ Show interest in people and objects around him?

❏ Reach for and grasp objects?

❏ Anticipate feeding?

❏ Sit propped up for ten to fifteen minutes?

❏ Roll over?

❏ Maintain eye contact with you for a longer time than when he was younger?

*Remember, these watchlists are guides, not diagnostic tests. There's a broad range of normal development, and generally a month or so difference is not cause for alarm. If you have good reason for genuine concerns about your baby's rate of development, of course, consult a trained infant specialist.

SHARED COMMUNICATION ACTIVITIES: MONTH FOUR

Reminder: Feel free to alternate between activities or concentrate on one or another as you feel your baby needs them. Varying activities will keep things interesting for you and your baby and encourage growth in different areas.

Communication ◆
Back at ya, kid. Up to now, we've been focusing on imitating your baby's movement and noises. Now it's time to refine it a bit and echo his speech sounds specifically. See if you can mimic his babbles and all those *ahhhh, eeee,* and *ohhh* sounds. It will cheer him on and give him confidence to continue. Imitation, after all, is the sincerest form of flattery, and we're all

encouraged when someone thinks enough of what we did to follow suit themselves. When I'm working with young children, I find that reproducing their sounds and movements is the most effective way to get them to relate and interact with me. It becomes a fun game that babies really get into—yours will, too. After a few goos and coos, he'll begin to expect your reply and wait for it, and then laugh and smile. Have a good time with it. It's an important early turn-taking game that will soon lead to real conversation.

Join the sing-a-long. Your baby will be making a variety of noises. Happily, a lot of it will sound like little free-form songs. Join in; it's really quite therapeutic. Vary your participation. Sometimes "sing" in unison—a duet—and at other times chime in just after your baby stops—like alternating verses. It's fun to add your own soft melody or even words. My daughter used to sing in a whispered voice about how much she loved her baby, which was true music to the ears of this particular grandpa. Add some of your own movement, too—maybe some gentle rocking or head bobbing. Occasionally, if your little one's really cooking, you might just want to listen and sway to the sound of a baby serenade.

Silly time. Four months is a great age for self-expression, and you can help him along. Since he's already begun giggling and is capable of sustained laughter, give him a treat and be a comedian! Although he's already developing his own unique sense of humor, most young infants have a ball when you do silly things like making big, rude noises with your mouth on their tummies, dancing in some wacky way, acting wildly surprised at something they do, or making funny squeaky noises. You'll get more laughs than you'd get doing stand-up at a comedy club, for sure. I had my infant daughter practically in hysterics once by acting over-the-top shocked and amazed every time she hiccupped. Hiccups were never so much fun! It was just a chance event that I was able to turn into a fun shared interaction. Remember to keep your eyes out for those kinds of opportunities.

Don't be afraid to ham it up and have fun. Nobody's watching, and even if they were, so what? What will they see? A mom having fun with her baby. What they won't see—but what is terribly important—is that all this fun communicating, playing, sharing, and laughing is essential for your child's cognitive and social development, as well as his overall health.

My four-year-old granddaughter loves it when we act totally silly—it gives her permission to be goofy, too. We make faces; take roles from books, movies, and television; change our voices; and come up with whimsical games like comparing each other to various fruits and vegetables. Other favorites are suggesting outlandish clothing or food—"I really love ketchup on my ice cream." Sure, I'm a weird grandfather, but lots of fun to be around—and I can hide a lot of learning inside the fun. Our mismatching food and clothing game, for instance, helps her categorize her world—very important for a four-year-old. Your baby, of course, has some years to go before these kinds of antics, but you can begin to establish your fun personae now so that when your little one is a preschooler, he'll think you're a very cool, funny mommy when you jokingly suggest he plop Dad's sock on his head instead of his hat.

Cognitive Development ◆

Life is so routine. Little daily routines are tremendous learning tools. They teach your baby the predictability of human interactions. When he knows what to expect from you in certain situations, it gives him the confidence to venture forth and attempt communication, and helps him know the right time to participate. A learned routine, in effect, becomes his guide. As adults, we use routines to guide us all the time. If your spouse is a curmudgeon until he has his first cup of coffee in the morning, it only makes sense to steer clear until you see him sipping. Forewarned is forearmed. Likewise, your baby learns your routine behaviors and uses the knowledge to determine what to do. If, for example, you and your baby cuddle after lunch, or if you sing a soft song at naptime, your baby will begin to expect this to happen each time you repeat the situation. My eighty-something-year-old mom decided a few years ago to go back to work in an infant daycare center. Whenever she changed her little "clients," who ranged in age from six months to one year, she played "This Little Piggy" on their toes. She soon found that whenever she laid one of these babies down on his or her back, the baby's little leg shot up in the air in anticipation.

So use everyday events like diaper changing, feeding, baths, and dressing to teach your baby routines. Don't worry about trying to do exactly the same thing each time. You're a creature of habit and will repeat yourself without even trying. Help your child participate in the routine as you name familiar items (water, soap, towel), actions (wash, splash, dry), and feelings (wet, dry, warm). Play a little while you're at it, just to add a little spice—say splashing during the bath or a little tickling during changing. Here's a mom introducing something new to the already common routine of diaper changing:

ADULT: Time for a change. (Pause) Mandy wet.

CHILD: (Squeals)

ADULT: Yes, yukky diaper. Mandy have yukky diaper.

CHILD: Gggggah!

ADULT: Singing?

CHILD: Eeeeeeeeeeeeeee.

ADULT: Mandy singing. Eeeeeeeeeeee. She's happy. Eeeeeeeeee.

CHILD: (Giggles)

ADULT: More? (Pause) Eeeeeeeeeee. (Pause) Mommy wash. Stay still. (Pause) Mommy wash. (Pause) Now dry. Towel. (Pause) All dry. (Pause) Powder. Mandy all clean.

CHILD: Gggggah.

ADULT: Yes, clean. New diaper. (Pause) All done. (Puts hands up) A-boo!

CHILD: (Giggles)

ADULT: Mandy happy. A-boo!

CHILD: (Giggles)

Anticipation games. Babies always love anticipation games—any time of the day. "I'm gonna get you" is one timeless classic, but there are lots of other variations. Another all time favorite is "Here comes the _____." Fill in the blank with a fun little creature. It works like this: You announce the approach of the creature, say a butterfly, frog, kitty, birdy, or spider; then the "creature" (your hand or a pleasing object) crawls, hops, or flitters over your child in an entertaining, ticklish way.

Or try this one with your child on your knees:

Giddy up, horsy,
Go 'round and 'round.
But you better watch out
Or you might fall . . .
    Downnnnnn

On the last word, "Downnnnn," spread your knees, while holding your baby firmly, of course, as he mock falls through the opening space. Act really surprised as he goes through. His ability to predict the end of the game signifies his increased memory and knowledge of sequential events—important cognitive building blocks. Your little one is also predicting what your behavior will be. Like routines, these kinds of games help him know what to do, while providing opportunities for him to take turns and to share the game's agenda with you.

Here it comes! Aside from games, you can use your baby's new anticipation abilities to teach communication. Simply showing "signals" that an event is about to happen will teach him that one thing can represent another. For instance, if you show your baby his hat, and talk about it as you put it on for his daily stroll, he'll soon realize that "hat" means going outside, and before long he'll get excited when he sees the hat. As another example, if you show him a spoon, and talk about it as you're preparing his baby food, he'll soon associate spoon with an upcoming meal. Let's look at two examples, separated by a few weeks:

Child is in high chair after lunch. Mother is at kitchen sink with plastic tub.

ADULT: (Holds up soap and washcloth) Time for bath.
CHILD: (Looks at Mom)
ADULT: (Turns on water) Hear water? (Pause) Bath. (Splashes hand in water)
    Splash water. Warm.
CHILD: Ahhhhhhh.
ADULT: Yes, warm bath.

Same situation: Two or three weeks later.

> ADULT: (Holds up soap and washcloth) Time for bath.
> CHILD: (Becomes excited, kicks legs, smiles)
> ADULT: Yes, bath. Casey's bath.

Hearing Stimulation ◆

Outta sight noises. This little exercise helps your baby locate using his hearing and vision, further coordinating the two senses that began a few weeks after birth. Make noises with a squeaky toy, rattle, or some other gentle noisemaker out of your baby's line of vision, and encourage him to look in the right direction.

At this age, you can also hide the object—but he's still too young to find it on his own unless some of it is showing or you hide it under a cloth that conforms to its shape. Squeeze or activate the toy, put it under a napkin or piece of cloth, make the noise again, and ask your child, "Where's _____ (name the object)?" Pretend to be looking around. If your baby doesn't find it, activate the sound again or expose a little more of it—or better yet, do both.

Visual Stimulation ◆

Maintain your art gallery. Continue to place pictures and mobiles above your baby's crib. He still needs interesting things to look at. In fact, visual stimulation is even more important now as your baby is beginning to form expected images of familiar things and actions. The physical appearance of something is an important part of his understanding of it. To stimulate his interest, change the pictures and objects frequently. Trade mobiles or pictures with friends, use magazine pictures, print from the Internet, or, if you live in a large city, try a toy library. They're often located in child centers, churches, or city libraries, and you check out mobiles and toys just as you would books. (Be sure to wash them carefully before use.) Pictures should be big and colorful—Pop Art, for instance, is a smarter choice than a Matisse line drawing at this age. (We'll save the fine art education for later.) Also remember that mobiles and pictures should be higher up now to keep them out of your growing baby's reach and grasp.

The eyes have it. Encourage eye contact with your baby. Now that he's gaining more control of his ability to observe and concentrate, you shouldn't have to be quite as showy to attract and hold his attention. He'll focus on whatever attracts his interest. As you talk to him, varying your voice, look at him, look away, then look back at him again. Do it a few times. Before you know it, he'll begin to do the same thing. It's like a game, but he'll be learning about the importance of eye contact for communication. You could think of it as taking turns with your eyes, which is as important in conversations as alternating turns while speaking. We all know how disconcerting it is when a conversational partner either stares at us or fails to make eye contact. Both reflect poor communication skills. We want better than that for your child. It's best to do this exercise when you and your baby are quiet and relaxed and there's nothing going on around you to distract his attention.

Sensory Stimulation ◆

Let's face it together. Encourage your baby to explore your face with his hands. Although he's probably touched your face before, he now has more memory to store the information he perceives. Your little one is still learning to coordinate his senses, and multisensory stimulation and its integration in his brain are important for his continued mental development. This bonding exercise combines touch and vision. Say the word for each part of your face as he touches it. He'll be able to collect the sensory information and the word into the beginning of a definition of *face, eye, nose, mouth*, and *ear*. He may have a favorite part—your nose, lips, chin—but don't ask me why. I still have no idea why my granddaughter loved earlobes, or a friend's son fancied eyebrows. It's a mystery. Until further research, all I can say is, enjoy it. For variety you can also put a colorful sticker on a part of your face and name the area when your child touches the sticker. The sticker is guaranteed to attract his attention.

You can also further the sensory and cognitive learning experience with a little role reversal—explore your infant's face. Use a feather or a clean, soft, fuzzy piece of fabric. As you gently touch each part of his little face, give it a name—"This is your nose (pause) . . . and ear (pause) . . . and cheek . . . and lips . . ."

Anyway you do it, it's a "feel good" experience.

Cuddling duos. All of us need to feel loved, and cuddling says, "I love you" loud and clear. Tender hugs and snuggles help your baby learn to touch and be touched, an important part of communication, especially for a child. Most of us appreciate a gentle touch of sympathy or understanding, and dislike inappropriate or too-frequent touching. Your child is beginning to learn about that appropriateness and the value of touching in communication.

Talk about the cuddling as you do it. Your gentle voice enhances the warm feeling and stimulation of being held and touched, while adding information into the mix. Softly say the words for the body parts you touch—"Claire's little arm, (pause) soft arm, (pause) and sweet back, (pause) nice back . . . and oh, I found leg here" . . . and so on. If you don't feel like talking, you can make soft noises. Korean and Japanese mothers make little nonspeech pleasure sounds as they hug their infants. Whichever way you go, words and sounds during a pleasure activity help your child associate talking and sound-making with gratification. Bonus: You're not limited to duos. My kids loved gentle "sandwich cuddles"—Mom on one side, Pop on the other, and them in the middle. Soft cuddles and words can also be a lovely wake-up activity for a cranky four-month-old.

Rock around the clock. Rocking your child tenderly in your arms is the perfect time to cuddle and talk—a time of quiet and bonding. Talking or sound-making during the rocking attracts attention to your face, and gives your baby additional multisensory input—hearing, vision, and movement. The ideal time for rocking is before a nap, after waking, or after changing. Try introducing a little singing to your talk—maybe something about rocking. Put words to your own tune. Just make it up as you go along. You'd be surprised how the creativity will flow when you're not trying.

Motor Development ◆
Give 'em room to roll. Rock, and now roll! At this age, your little charmer should be a real pro at rolling over on his own. As a matter of fact, rolling will be his primary mode of "self-transportation." When your baby was younger, I suggested having him turn his head in order to locate a noise-maker, Now, we'll make the task a little more challenging by incorporating his locomotive abilities.

While he's on the floor or in his crib or playpen, call his attention to a soft, pliable object like a squeaky toy or small stuffed animal, then put it a little off to his side and encourage him to get it by asking, "Where ducky?" or saying, "Get ducky" (or whatever object you choose). As he looks at it, move it around a little or activate its noise making. Don't make this too difficult. Keep the object in reachable distance and not any higher than his shoulder or any lower than his waist. If you're doing this on the floor, also be sure that you're in a spot where he doesn't have to negotiate table legs. One final caution: If you opt to do this activity on a bed, be sure to stay with your baby at all times. He can roll now, and will, with little regard for the consequences.

Superbaby. This is a great muscle builder. Begin with your baby lying on his stomach on a bed. Place your hands under your baby's chest and hips. As you support his chest and hips with your hands, raise him into a "flying" position just a few inches off the mattress. Make sure you have a firm hold and that his chest and hips are supported, because he may squirm. Now all he needs is a red cape and blue tights. He'll instinctively raise his head and shoulders as he "flies" in your hands, which strengthens his neck, back, and abdomen. No need to prolong this activity—a minute or two every few days will do the trick, and no high flying—hovering just a couple of inches above the bed is plenty for this little superbaby.

Month Five

Your baby is even more responsive than ever now. He's smiling more—at you, in mirrors, and in response to pleasurable activities—and his speech sound repertoire contains even more consonants and consonant-vowel (CV) sounds—listen for gahhhh *and* bahhhh. *He's also squealing, yelling, whispering, and blowing raspberries at you—although he means no disrespect (at least I don't think so). He can't imitate your words yet, but he is able to parrot a few of your vowel sounds right after you say them. He still finds your face fascinating, but now other faces are starting to look pretty interesting too—he's ready to reach out to others and explore.*

● ■ ▲

MILESTONE WATCHLIST:
Five-Month-Old

Does your child . . .

❑ "Talk" to people by making sounds?

❑ Have more CV syllables in his vocalizations?

❑ Make sounds when alone or with toys?

❑ Smile and make sounds at his reflection in a mirror?

❑ Stop crying when he sees you?

❑ Smile when playing alone?

❑ Turn his head when his name is called?

❑ Make sounds when he plays with objects?

❑ Blow raspberries?

❑ Squeal or whisper?

❑ Make protest sounds when desired objects are removed?

❑ Initiate "talking" with eye contact and sounds?

SHARED COMMUNICATION ACTIVITIES: MONTH FIVE

Communication ◆

Guys (and Gals) and Dolls. Most all children enjoy dolls—yes, even your future quarterback—and it makes absolute sense. A doll is like a little person who's even smaller than the child. Wow, someone he can totally control! And a doll has all the body parts that your baby loves to look at on you—nose, eyes, hair. The best kinds of dolls for your baby at this stage are washable ones with no small or easily removable features, like button eyes that can look perfectly yummy to a five-month-old. As he plays with the doll, point out its various facial features and body parts, and chat about what the doll is doing—something like this:

> CHILD: (Touches doll's eye)
> ADULT: Eye. Jenna touch eye. (Pause) Touch baby's eye.
> CHILD: (Looks at adult)
> ADULT: What else you see?
> CHILD: (Bangs doll on highchair tray)
> ADULT: Doll jump. (Pause) Jenna make doll jump. Jump.

Dolls are so appealing to babies that this little exercise should have your little one's rapt attention—at least for a few minutes anyway. For variety, enhance the experience by moving the doll around in front of a mirror where your baby can see both himself and his little mini-me at the same time. A guaranteed winning combo.

"Knock, knock, who's there?" Here's a chance to use your theatrical training (or display your lack thereof). Make a knocking noise, show total surprise, then have a toy, puppet, or doll pop up and have a conversation with you and your child. Use your best cartoon character voice for the puppet or doll. The play-acting can be terrific fun—for both of you—and your baby will love the element of surprise and the feeling of anticipation as the knock becomes a signal of the main event to follow. This activity is a wonderful combination of your baby's burgeoning skills—anticipation, prediction of routines, greeting, turn-taking, paying attention, and sharing communication. Here's one knock-knock idea to get you into the mood.

> ADULT: (Knock, knock) Oh, who's there? (Surprised, looking around)
> CHILD: (Looks around. May startle at knocking.)
> ADULT: (Character voice) Snooopppppy! (Normal voice) Look, Snoopy!
>   (Pause) Hi, Snoopy!
> CHILD: (Babble) Eeeeee! Geh!
> SNOOPY: Hi, Manuela. (Pause) I love you. (Cuddles against child's neck)
> CHILD: (Giggles. Squeals.)
> ADULT: Snoopy loves you. Snoopy hug.
> SNOOPY: Hug Manuela.

CHILD: (Grabs Snoopy and bounces it up and down.)
ADULT: Manuela dance with Snoopy.
SNOOPY: More dance, more dance.

Variety vocalizations. Your baby is now making lots of varied sounds, squeals, shrieks, and whispers. Let's give some of the same back to him. He'll love hearing the sounds come from you, and will pay much more attention to you. This activity is similar to last month's *Back at ya, kid,* but because your baby's behavior and sounds are more complex now, the exercise involves more variety and new learning opportunities. Your tot will soon be mimicking your sounds as he learns to speak words; this sets the stage and helps establish the upcoming routine of imitation. Begin by copying his sounds. Before long it will be hard to tell who's imitating whom. One caution: Don't make any loud or sudden squeals or shrieks. We don't want to alarm him and make him fearful of noisemaking games.

After you. Take cues from your baby's moves. When he starts a "conversation," follow along. He's maturing fast and quickly learning how to engage you in shared communication—he'll make eye contact, move around, smile, or make noises to attract your attention. All these ploys signal a readiness to communicate. Respond with enthusiasm and interest. A neutral "Um-hum" won't do the trick! Engage him in a conversation as you note your surroundings and his actions. Is he looking at something? Is he touching something? Has something changed in the situation, like Fido entering the room? These are all clues that will give you an idea of how to respond. Pick what seems most likely to be the focus of his attention and begin the conversation by using that as the main topic.

At this age, your baby may initiate games, especially if he's in a very familiar situation or in the midst of a routine. For example, if you always play "I'm gonna get you" after changing, he'll begin to expect the game. He may laugh or even raise his arms as a signal to play. At this stage, it would increase his anticipation and make it more fun if you change the game slightly. Instead of saying, "I'm gonna get you" and then immediately tickling him, say it two or three times before making a move. Make sure to pause between each mock beginning. Chances are he'll giggle or squirm with excitement.

Cognitive Development ◆

Keep it fresh. This month it's especially important to provide a variety of stimulation activities. With his increased ability to sit with limited support (for short periods of time), your little cutie can now play and explore in an upright position (as long as you're cradling him) and he'll really want—perhaps demand—interesting objects to examine and play with. He'll still like some of his old toys, but supplement his collection with some new toys and objects that can be manipulated and have more parts to look at and touch. His grasp has also strengthened, so he's ready for a developmental step up. Kiddie gyms with rings to pull, and "busy boxes" with dials and buttons to spin and push, offer ideal stimulation for your little explorer. As always, be sure to add your commentary as he plays. Talk about what he's doing, seeing, touching, and feeling.

Hearing Stimulation ◆

Calling baby X! Always use your baby's name when you begin an interaction or want to get his attention. Although you've been doing this for a while, it's especially important now that he get used to the sound of his name. If he doesn't respond, entice him with a toy or other interesting object at the same time you call his name. Be sure to give him lots of praise when he looks at you. At this age, he doesn't have to be right next to you to respond. Talk more from across the room. The importance of using your baby's name will become evident within a few weeks. By seven months, he should be able to make the connection between a few words and the things they go with.

Visual Stimulation ◆

Mirror, mirror, on the wall. At around five months, babies love to focus on faces, and mirrors create an excellent opportunity. If you don't already have one, buy a shatterproof, washable, portable child's mirror with rounded corners. (There are some very cutely decorated ones in the toy stores.) You can't always anticipate your child's actions, and most likely, he'll want to bang on the mirror. So steer clear of regular handheld mirrors or wall mirrors that are fastened to the wall poorly. Fasten your child's mirror securely to his crib, playpen, or a wall in a play corner. When you see your baby looking at himself, name his face parts and talk about what he's doing. Touch his nose as he's looking in the mirror and say, "Nose. Rodney's nose." Follow this by touching your own nose and saying, "Nose." If, by chance, your baby touches his own nose after you do, be sure to make a joyful fuss and say, "Yes, nose. Rodney touch nose!"

Sensory Stimulation ◆

Touchy, feely. Add new tactile sensations to your baby's repertoire. Use small toys and items of new and different textures, temperatures, firmness, color, size, and shape. Try things like soft building blocks and balls of differing foam densities, warm and cool washclothes, ice chest cold gel-packs wrapped in a thin cloth, Jell-O, or your favorite faux fur. Tactile stimulation and exploration is still very important as he continues to mature. Widening the range of elements increases his store of sensations, and adds to his early definitions of things. Provide lots of input while you talk about how a particular object feels or looks. New words may include *scratchy, warm, cool, red, blue, big, little, round,* and the like.

Motor Development ◆

E-motional songs. Sing simple motion songs with your baby. Motion songs are little ditties that are accompanied by some kind of movement. Start with the most elementary one—help your child clap his hands to a rhythm. He'll be delighted with the sound and movement combination, and you'll be preparing him for the time—soon to come—when he can imitate your movements, a very important cognitive skill. Guide him in the beginning by clapping with your hands over his. He'll learn the movement, and in a few months, he'll be able to clap when he sees you do it.

As for music selection, try simple songs with repetitive lyrics, or modify the words for your own purpose. For example, you might clap your hands to "Mary Had a Little Lamb" or change the words to suit your situation, as in the following:

Mommy cooking chicken legs,
Chicken legs, chicken legs . . .

or

> *Kylie splashing in the tub,*
> *In the tub, in the tub . . .*

or

> *Casey sitting in her chair,*
> *In her chair, in her chair . . .*

Kiddie gym. Commercial baby gyms come in many shapes and types, and are terrific for helping babies coordinate cognitive and movement skills. The best ones offer lots of variety—things to grab, swat at, pull, or push. There are quite a few good ones on the market these days. (See my top recommendations in Appendix E.) If money is an issue, see if you can borrow one from a friend with an older child, or try a toy library or thrift store. If you have the time and patience, you can make your own gym. Please be sure you use objects that can't harm your baby in any way—nothing too heavy, easily breakable, or easy to disassemble. And always supervise its use. A couple of ideas:

- Suspend a beach ball over baby's playpen for swatting.

- Securely attach easy-to-grip knobs to a board or wall so that your baby can turn and spin them. Small cabinet handles of about one inch in diameter are just about right for little hands. Dials from an old CD player can also be used for spinning but must be firmly attached.

- Toys that talk or play music are terrific at this age. One of my favorites is a can that makes a mooing sound when it's turned over (available in most novelty stores). There are also refrigerator magnets that make noise when touched. Again, be careful that the talking toy has no small detachable parts or sharp edges. Safety is of the utmost importance; make sure that everything is fastened well and baby-proofed.

Splish splash. Water sports are good clean fun—especially mini ones in the bathtub. Once in the tub, your baby can be encouraged to splash the water either with his hands or a floating object. (Give that rubber-ducky a workout, too!) Start the game or, if he's already splashing around, join in. He won't appreciate water in his face, so don't go overboard here. Water play adds a new element to motor training and a new sensation. It also allows your baby to make forceful movements, such as bringing his hand down firmly, without any danger of hurting himself—excellent for those little muscles and self-assertion. *CAUTION: Never leave your child alone around water.* Your best bet—get in the tub with him! Bond and bathe.

Getting rattled. Even old toys can be recycled. By now, your child is probably very bored with his rattles, but they can still be used as teaching tools. While he's in his high chair or on the floor, give him a rattle and keep one for yourself. Then make noise by shaking them and encourage him to follow suit. This encourages motor skills and interactive play, a forerunner to shared conversations. Pause often to allow your child to make noise by himself. When he stops, jump in. Sometimes shake in unison. Add some music—recorded or self-produced. Sing. Make this a fun, shared interaction. It's a baby hootenanny!

Month Six

Your baby's hearing is of primary interest this month, as it becomes an important factor in his ability to produce speech sounds. In prior months he was making random sounds, but now he's starting to repeat himself—ba-ba instead of ba, for instance. He needs to hear that first ba, in order to purposely reproduce the sound. Now that he's gaining more muscle control in the front part of his mouth, lip sounds starting with b's, p's, and m's will predominate. You'll also hear a greater variety of squeals, grunts, and growls, but as his vocalizations become less random, they'll sound more and more like talking. Your little one is also beginning to recognize a few frequently used words (especially no and bye-bye), making your interactions and language examples increasingly important; and he's using his noisemaking skills to gain attention and to show enthusiasm or displeasure. Most impressively though, he's starting to build cognitive bridges between words and the things they refer to, and his ability to focus on an object and share his interest in it by using sounds—the basis of communication—is growing in leaps and bounds.

● ■ ▲

MILESTONE WATCHLIST:
Six-Month-Old

Does your child . . .

❑ Babble with more *b, p,* and *m* sounds?

❑ Repeat sounds, such as *ba-ba*?

❑ Vocalize when playing alone or with others?

❑ Grunt and growl?

❑ Make angry sounds of displeasure?

❑ Initiate babbling to people?

❑ Vocalize to show displeasure, get attention, or display enthusiasm?

❑ Recognize some word-action combinations such as *no* (with head shake) and *bye-bye* (with wave)?

❑ Respond to a pleasant voice with smile or laugh?

❑ Respond differently to strangers?

❑ Seem to know when he hears an angry or a pleasant voice?

❑ Sit and hold his head without support?

SHARED COMMUNICATION ACTIVITIES: MONTH SIX

Communication ◆

Talk and do. Remember not just to talk to your baby about what he's doing or what you do together, but also about what he sees you doing as you go about your everyday activities (called *self-talk*). While there's no doubt that talking about an activity in which your baby is a active participant *(parallel talk)* is most interesting for him, self-talk is still very conducive to shared communication and frees you up a bit—it lets you get things done. It's a very handy tool for a busy mom to have in her shared communication arsenal. Don't use self-talk *in place* of parallel talk; use it as a complement and, as always, keep the talk simple and repetitive and remember to pause after important words.

Lend a hand, kid. Let your baby participate and help you in your daily activities. While you might not consider washing dishes terribly exciting, your baby will find it endlessly fascinating. Everything is brand-new to him, and he's always very interested in the things you do. Letting him participate in your world is also very bonding and benefits healthy emotional development. So tuck him into a supported child seat or high chair while you do whatever it is you're doing—making dinner, retrieving your e-mail, putting on your makeup, you name it, and give him the lowdown on what he sees—in short two- to three-word phrases, of course. Whenever possible, let him hold and explore objects as you talk. If you have twin sinks in the kitchen, you could even sit him in one, give him a clean sponge and some warm water and let him "wash" some little plastic dishes while you do the real ones in the other sink. Here's a mom who's got another good idea:

> MOM: Mommy cut banana. (Pause) Make salad.
> CHILD: Ah-ya.
> MOM: Yes, make salad. (Pause) Mikey help? (Gives Mikey some banana and a rubber spatula.) Cut banana. (Shows him how)
> CHILD: Baba.
> MOM: Um-hm, cut banana. (Pause) Make salad. Mommy cut apple, too.

What if your future chef makes mush? It's great mush! Offer lots of praise and be a sport; put it in the fruit salad with flourish. You can always pick it out later when he's not looking.

Voice games. Remember how we talked about making a buffoon of yourself visually to get your baby's attention? Well, now that hearing stimulation has become more important, it's time to make a fool of yourself vocally, too! Go all out now with voice pitch variations, growls, tongue clicks, whispering, singing, funny humming, and any other interesting vocal possibilities you can think of. Indulge your dormant penchant for acting. Growl like a bear, moo like a cow, chatter like a monkey. Your baby will love the variety and just may chime in. If he does, imitate him. This is more than just being fun and silly. Communication includes a variety of sound production skills, and this is great introduction to a good many of them. Just so you don't think you're the only one to play the clown in the name of child development, when my children were this age, I was the king of multivoiced personas. My characters ran the gamut from an English grande dame with an overripe vibrato to a Brooklyn gangster with an underworld whisper. I'd also croak like a frog, oink like a pig, bray like a donkey, squeal like a . . . you get the idea.

Unintentional intentions. Your baby is not yet quite able to plan an action to achieve a desired end. He may see a toy or something else that he really wants but will fuss to get it rather than devise a strategy. He's just not quite to that planning stage yet; he's still *preintentional*, to put it in child development parlance. Still, some of his actions and sounds will send *unintended* messages—a reach for his teddy bear, for instance, tells you that he wants it. Reply to these behaviors just as if he were *intentionally* trying to communicate the message to you ("Oh, Kristin want teddy.") Here are a couple of other unintentional messages to watch out for:

Baby looks into a just-emptied cup	*Want more*
Cries when wet	*Change me*
Squeals when bounced	*Do it again*
Gets excited when sees the dog	*Let me touch*
Bangs spoon	*Meal's over, let me down*

It won't be long before he'll be giving you very "intentional" messages.

Sing a song . . . all day long. Sing about what you're doing as you do it. You may not be a Broadway musical diva, but don't hesitate to burst into song if the mood hits you—you will probably end up in a duet. Babies love making sounds at the same time you do—just as much as they love alternating sounds with you. But even if you wind up in a solo, your performance will definitely be entertaining to your baby. Don't expect him to know or learn the words yet. Use simple, repetitive melodies, such as "Row, row, row your boat," that will attract your baby's attention. Adapt the song to whatever you're doing at the time—for example, "Cut, cut, cut the apple . . ." This also works like a charm if your child is in a carrier. You may not be able to see his face, but you can still provide language input.

Bye-bye, baby. Your baby is now capable of some imitative actions in specific contexts. Although it's still a very limited skill, this is the perfect time to encourage it to grow. So as people leave the room or go outside, wave good-bye to them and encourage your baby to do the same. You can even move his hand for him at the beginning. Be gentle and pleasant in this maneuver—make it fun. Before long, he'll be a full-fledged waver. Waving, like gesturing and signing, comes well before babies can speak in words. Remember to only wave "bye" in appropriate situations. We want him to learn *when* to use this behavior, as well as *how* to do it.

Cognitive Development ◆
Outdoor explorer. Being out and about is a great time to begin to learn about the world. Talk about the places you go. Explore together. Keep your language simple as you name familiar objects, and always repeat what you say. Here's an example of a mom on a summer stroll with her baby.

> MOM: Listen Maree! (Pause) Hear birds? (Pause) Birds singing for Maree. (Pause) See bird. (Pause and point) Look! Big bird flying. Bird fly up. (Pause) Uh-oh! (Pause with look of surprise) What's that? (Pause) Doggie. Doggie bark. Doggies go "Ruff! Ruff!"

Hearing Stimulation ◆
Poised for noise. Because hearing stimulation is so important at this age for future speech, utilize sounds whenever you can in your play, and keep

them varied to hold your baby's interest. There're lots of toys that make noise, but don't feel limited to them. When you think outside the box, there is an infinite array of noisemakers at your disposal—pots and pans, toys that can clank together, plastic blocks, musical instruments, recorded music, whistles, bells, and the list goes on and on. So take advantage of them. Make noise with these and other handy items in everyday situations. And talk about the noises, too—"Oh, noisy pots! Listen (bang, bang)." Whenever possible, accompany sound with a real object or picture so that your baby gets both vision and sound stimulation. Listening to a baby CD about a cat while looking at pictures of kittens or cuddling plush kitten toys, for instance, would be a perfect paring. (See Appendix E for recommended baby CDs.)

Visual Stimulation ◆
Handy dandy. Most likely, your baby can sit for short periods of time unsupported, but he may still be wobbly. A high chair or infant seat is still best for short periods because it provides some support. If your child is still a little tottery, stuff small cushions between him and the chair for extra support. In either case, his hands will be free for exploring, so this is the time to give him visually interesting toys to examine and play with. Yes, he's explored before, and this may not seem like a big change, but now that he can explore from an upright position while holding an object on his own, it changes the entire dynamic. Imagine being only able to do things while lying flat on your back, then suddenly being able to sit while doing them—it's a different world! So bring on those toys and objects with interesting colors and patterns. Remember that although his hands are now free to explore, he'll still be looking to you to guide, explain, demonstrate, and make all his explorations feel safe and secure.

Sensory Stimulation ◆
Ooey gooey (Oy vey!) Introduce your baby to different substances. The world is filled with tactile pleasures—sticky, furry, hard, soft, and squishy—and they can be a thrill to explore. Dough, soft sponges, a partially filled beach ball, child putty, sponge balls, bean bags, sand, rice, ribbons, mushy bananas—the options are boundless. Make sure to always supervise when small objects are used and to never leave your child

unattended. If your tot is one of those mini-explorers who mouths everything in sight, wait a few months before delving into the gooier stuff.

I highly recommend my favorite kiddy dough recipe:

1 cup flour
5–6 tablespoons water
⅓ cup salt
A few drops of food coloring

Put it all in a bowl, mix together well. Then play! Just squeeze, touch, pat, handle, roll, pass back and forth, and have fun. Store it in the refrigerator when you're finished.

For variety, try Dr. Bob's not-so-famous "Almost Baby Putty." This stuff stretches a little easier and is more plasticlike than the dough, which is more claylike. The formula:

1 cup Elmer's (white) glue
½ cup Sta-Flo liquid starch
Food coloring (if desired, or suitable substitutes like washable, edible
*   kiddy paints)*

Using a spoon, mix ingredients in a bowl until mixture forms a ball. If mixture is not pliable enough, add more glue. If mixture is too sticky, add more starch. Store in resealable plastic bags in the refrigerator. Afterwards, be sure to wash baby's hands thoroughly. Parental presence and guidance are absolute musts.

Motor Stimulation ◆

Shake it up, baby! Fill a small plastic container or two with beans or bells to make great insta-noisemakers. Make sure lids are tight and very secure! Encourage your tot to give it a shake and make his own noise. He'll get grasping experience as well as shaking practice. The sound, especially since it's of his own making, will stimulate his hearing and add to his understanding of cause and effect. Again, supervision is important because small items like beans and bells can cause choking if ingested. If there's

MONTHLY ACTIVITIES

Age (Mos.)	Communication	Cognitive Development	Hearing Stimulation
4	▲ Back at ya, kid ▲ Join the sing-a-long ▲ Silly time	▲ Life is so routine ▲ Anticipation games ▲ Here it comes!	▲ Outta sight noises
5	▲ Guys (and Gals) and Dolls ▲ "Knock, knock, who's there?" ▲ Variety vocalizations ▲ After you	▲ Keep it fresh	▲ Calling baby X
6	▲ Lend a hand, kid ▲ Voice games ▲ Unintentional intentions ▲ Sing a song . . . all day long ▲ Bye-bye, baby	▲ Outdoor explorer	▲ Poised for noise

Shared Communication Reminders
- Acknowledge and confirm
- Talk in a soothing voice
- Spend more time playing and talking
- Convince your baby that he wants to talk
- Talk to your baby throughout the day
- Treat your baby's movements and sounds as meaningful

Visual Stimulation	Sensory Stimulation	Motor Development
▲ Maintain your art gallery ▲ The eyes have it!	▲ Let's face it together ▲ Cuddling duos ▲ Rock around the clock	▲ Give 'em room to roll ▲ Superbaby
▲ Mirror, mirror, on the wall	▲ Touchy, feely	▲ E-motional songs ▲ Kiddie gym ▲ Splish splash ▲ Getting rattled
▲ Handy dandy	▲ Ooey, gooey (Oy vey)!	▲ Shake it up, baby! ▲ Monkey see . . .

even any chance of the lid coming off, tape or glue it for extra insurance. Don't leave your infant alone with these kinds of toys.

Monkey see . . . Imitate your child. In my experience nothing ingratiates you faster to a young child than copying what he does. If your child coughs, cough. If he burps, pretend to burp. If he pushes a ball, push it back. If he does it, you can copy him! After you imitate him, watch for his next behavior and mimic that one, too. If he's doing the same behavior over and over and you're following suit, it will be difficult to determine who is imitating whom—and he's on his way to learning to imitate. This kind of monkey-see, monkey-do imitation sets the stage for your baby's later development, and sends the message that you are totally tuned in to him. He'll understand . . . and probably treat you to some priceless baby giggles and laughs, too. Don't expect your baby to directly copy your actions at this point. He's not quite to that stage yet, but he may surprise you by waving or executing other actions in the appropriate context. If you wave when you go out the door, for instance, he may do the same, if he's learned that it's part of that particular routine.

CHAPTER EIGHT

Months 7, 8, and 9

Intentional Communication

Progress Report

MOVEMENT

THESE are watershed months for your baby's motor skills development. During her seventh month she'll sit, creep, and make some worthy—if not all successful—attempts at standing. While sitting, she'll handle and examine things and experiment to see how to use them. She'll also be more interested in sharing toys and other objects with you, and get a real kick out of pushing things over the edge of her high chair tray—including, dare I say, food. As her fine motor skills become more refined, she'll be able to use her thumb and opposing fingers more to pick up things, which make finger foods, such as pieces of banana and other soft fruits, cheeses, and easily dissolvable graham crackers very viable food options during these months.

COGNITIVE

Your little dynamo will be awake now for longer periods of time, and be able to enjoy more activities for longer periods of time. By about nine months, she'll be an active game player and performer—maybe not at

soccer or Shakespeare yet, but a true-blue peek-a-boo and patty-cake afi-
cionado. When it comes to everyday routines, she'll be able to predict
what you're going to do and try to exert a little influence on the situation.
She might try to jump-start bath time, for instance, by tugging at her
clothes, or get agitated if you put her in her highchair and don't serve her
food "on time." She'll also make different kinds of sounds to see if she
can rouse a reaction from you. If you laugh or act surprised at one of
them, there's a good chance you'll hear her do it again. And she'll be able
to look around for a missing toy, even physically search for it for a short
time. Cognitively, that means that she can hold the image of an item in her
memory long enough to locate the item and recognize when it reappears.
That's amazing progress!

HEARING

Hearing ability has more impact on your baby's sound-making at this
stage than ever before. As she listens to you talking, she'll try to mimic
some of your words. Because she can't physically reproduce a lot of
sounds yet, she'll search her own small repertoire and come up with the
closest match. This probably won't happen out of the blue. You'll need to
get her started by parroting whatever sounds she makes first. That will
give her the idea—and once she's got it there'll be no stopping her. Even
though at this age your tot won't be able to duplicate your sounds and
words per se, just hearing them will encourage her to experiment with
new sounds on her own and, before you know it, you'll start hearing
noises from the crib and high chair that sound curiously like English.

By approximately seven months, your little cutie will respond more
consistently to your speech, and might even look around for a familiar object, like a ball or dog, when she hears you say the word. Although she
can't connect meaning to words yet, she's begun to recognize the *sound
pattern* of the words. She knows, for instance, that the four-legged thing
with the long furry handle on the back end and the bad breath on the
front end is characterized by the word *dog*. She'll pay a lot more attention
to *single words* than longer sentences, because a bunch of words strung
together are just a jumble of sounds to her little ears. That's why she may
seem distracted when you speak to her in regular adult sentences but

perks up, smiles, and makes eye contact when you use single words or very short sentences with lots of pauses in between the words.

<u>TALKING</u>

Her oral movements are also continuing to develop. By seven months, your baby will be able to pout and to draw her lips together. Don't expect big smooches yet, but in a few months prepare yourself for those sweet, wet, sloppy puckers that pass for infant kisses. By eight months, your little one will be able to keep her lips closed while chewing and swallowing semi-liquids—say, nice, smooth applesauce or yogurt. Note that I said, she'll *be able* to, not necessarily that she *will*. You'll probably still see food pushed out of her mouth onto her adorable chin—but a lot less than before, so let's look at the plastic cup as half full here. On a purely esoteric note, your baby's chewing will change from up-and-down to a more mature rotary pattern, much like our own. That's because she's gaining more control of her tongue and is acquiring the ability to move her lips, tongue, and jaw separately. Her chewing, to be perfectly frank, will resemble that of a cow.

Just about now, your baby will begin *repetitive* (or *reduplicated*) *babbling*—repeating CV syllables like *ba-ba* or *ma-ma,* and might occasionally say something that sounds like a word—maybe *Mama, Papa*, or *wawa* (water). Don't call the folks yet! It's just a lucky accident. She's not attaching any meaning to these "words" at this point, and won't be for at least a few more months. But keep your ears perked, because also during this time period an interesting thing happens; her CV syllables increase to longer units. Now, along with the *mama*'s and *baba*'s, you'll be hearing *ma-ma-ma* and *ba-ba-ba*. And as this happens and she willfully tries to reproduce your sounds, some of her other babbling sounds, like raspberries, will decrease. That's because while she initially babbled strictly for her own enjoyment, she's now learning that her new repetitive babbles can be used for communication. As babies imitate sounds and put them together in more wordlike ways, adults tend to pay more attention. So naturally, babies want to make more of those sounds, and gradually those wordlike sounds begin to resemble real words . . . and then real conversations.

Your seven-month-old has some limited knowledge of speech. She knows that when she hears talking, it means that humans are around. She realizes that speech produces predictable effects on others—her sounds bring or keep you near her. And she also knows that speech can represent a turn in interactions. That's not bad for having only seven months of experience—but around eight months, things really pick up. She'll often gesture as she "talks," and may even try to mimic some of your very easy words. If she can say the sounds, she'll repeat the syllables that are emphasized in the words she hears the most—*nana* for ba*nana*, for example. Give her lots of encouragement for these attempts, along with the adult word—"Yes, banana!" If the banana's nearby, pick it up, show it to her, eat some together, and talk about it. Now, that's teaching!

At about nine months, you might notice another subtle change in your baby's babbling. She may, on occasion, change the vowels in her repetitive babbling—*be̱ba* instead of *ba̱ba*—or, less frequently, change the consonants—*ba̱ma*. She may have done it by chance before, but now she can make these combinations on purpose! (Some children do very little of this kind of *nonidentical* syllable vocalizing, so don't worry if you don't hear it.) She'll also probably be adding some new sound sequences to her repertoire about now—VCV sounds like *ata*, and CVC sounds like *kek*. And she's experimenting with intonation now, too! Even though her "words" are indecipherable, she'll sound like she's making statements and comments and asking questions. Before long, her babbling will come to resemble the *patterns of English*.

<hr>

COMMUNICATION

The most significant change in baby communication comes with gesturing. (You'll remember that gestures are the physical movements that we use either along with or in place of speech.) At this stage your little one will point, show, and offer you objects, ask for things by reaching, and tell you "no" by moving her head side-to-side. There's a good chance these gestures will be combined with sounds, especially if she's trying to get your attention.

She'll probably show off, too. *Showing off* is another form of gesturing, and is, as you've no doubt inferred, basically trying to get others to notice you. Babies have an infinite variety of ways of doing it. They make faces, sound off, shake their heads, toss their little arms and legs all around—they can get quite creative. But all these shenanigans pale in comparison to tantrums—another unfortunate result of learning how to influence other people through gestures. Lock the doors and windows, and get ready for some real infant fury. Baby tantrums, like showing off, are as individual as the child herself, but whatever shape they take in your house they'll probably rank fairly low on your Joys of Parenting hit parade. I wish I could tell you that these outbursts will disappear quickly, but I'd be putting my credibility on the line. Tantrums and saying "No!" simply seem to be a step in the development of self and part of learning about how to control others.

Still, the positive side of gesturing far outweighs any minor inconveniences. Its advent is a very exciting milestone. It's the first time your baby moves beyond herself to consider you, her audience. Watch when she reaches for something beyond her grasp, for instance. She'll make some kind of insistent noise, and check to see if you're paying attention. Her purpose is to communicate with you. This is a big breakthrough! Up to now, she made noises only *in response to* being hungry, wet, tired, or angry. She'd cry even if no one was present. While she might have gotten excited when she spotted something to play with or eat, her excitement wasn't a *request* to play. Her actions weren't preplanned and she wasn't trying to influence you in any way. Now, she *decides* that she wants to share something of interest with you, *points to it*, and, if you're not paying attention, adds a squeal.

Expressing the intention to communicate is closely tied developmentally to recognizing cause and effect and planning ahead—both important cognitive developments. It's no surprise that jack-in-the-box type toys, very simple cause-and-effect devices, are very popular during these months. At this stage, your baby's burgeoning understanding of causality is still limited to things that have to do with physical movement—pulling tablecloths to get what she wants from the table, pushing buttons to operate toys, and the like. She's not yet able to figure out complicated, nonphysical problems or devise intricate, indirect strategies. So you have a few years before you'll have to deal with adolescent subterfuge around use of the family car.

SHARED COMMUNICATION TIPS AND REMINDERS

- **Show you understand.** When it comes to development, nothing happens instantaneously. Your baby's gestures and attempts at talking will be gradual. Just let her know that you understand what she's trying to tell you. When she points, look in the appropriate direction and talk about whatever it is she's pointing to. "Oh, I see. Doggie!" If she seems to be asking for something, give it to her if you can. Your acknowledgments and confirming actions strengthen her confidence in her communication abilities.

- **Keep it simple.** As your little one gets close to saying her first real word, your input becomes increasingly important. Aside from being a conversational partner, you're now also serving as a language role model for her. The words that you say to her will become the words that she will say—as long as they're not too difficult. Keep your baby-talk simple and your words short. This doesn't mean that you can't sometimes use longer phrases, it just means that your baby will understand the shorter ones best. At best, at this stage, your baby's short-term memory can only hold about two things. After that, it's difficult for her to remember the first item as new ones are added. It would be similar to you reading this sentence and by the time you get to the end, the only words you could remember are *the end.*

    Remember to repeat your words, varying the order a little or adding new words here and there—and, of course, don't forget to pause and leave some breathing space in between the short phrases. If you're reading a book together, for example, the "conversation" might sound something like this:

    What's that? (Pause) A bear. Big bear. See bear? (Pause) He's a big bear. (Baby Amy touches, then looks up) Yes, Amy touch bear. Big bear. (Amy puts arms up) Um-hmm. So big! Yes, big. Big like Amy. Big bear (Point). Amy big girl (Point).

- **Treat your baby as a real communicator.** You've been talking to your baby since birth, but now that's she's actually gearing up to talk herself, it's even more important to treat her as a true communicator. She'll never be silent again! Talk to her about the world in front of her—the things she sees, hears, smells, and touches. Reply to her efforts to communicate, no matter how elemental they may be. Follow her gestures, and give her a chance to contribute as you talk together. In short, be a real conversational partner.

- **Mimic your tot's reduplicated babbling.** This simply means that when your baby says *bababa,* you repeat it after her. There's a good chance she'll parrot you and you'll soon have a little game going. You can think of this as speech-sound play. If you get this type of response, encourage her to vocalize to her full potential, keep it going, smile, laugh, and make it fun. Don't worry if your baby doesn't respond or comes back with a completely different sound. That's perfectly okay, too. She's only just learned to imitate herself. So give her time and don't expect too much.

- **Use real words in conversations.** In about five months your baby will say words like *bottle,* only they'll sound like "baba." It's the logical progression from *bababab a.* Remember, babies build words with CV syllables. Bottle is CVCC (b-ah-t-l). That's a tough one, so in most cases they opt for *baba.* Many of these "babyisms" are easy to predict, like *wawa* for "water" and *bebe* for "baby." Remember not to use these baby versions when you have meaningful conversations with your child. "Here's your bottle, honey" is always better than *"Here's your baba, honey."* Later, as she tries to make her own speech clearer, she'll know to shoot for the word *bottle* that she's heard you say, since she wants to sound like you.

- **Respond to your baby's gestures.** Communication is a two-way street. Your little one can't communicate by herself. At this point in development she's looking for acknowledgement from her favorite partner—

you! Show her, with your actions and words, that you understand her communication attempts. When she points, look in that direction; when she reaches, give her what she wants (as long as you can safely do so). Pay attention and respond to her sounds, looks, gestures, and facial expressions, even body posture.

- **Use consistent words for things.** Imagine trying to learn a language in which they keep changing the words for various objects and actions. That's the challenge your baby faces unless you're consistent in the words you use for familiar objects. If it was a *bird* yesterday, don't call it *robin* today and an *avian* tomorrow. Remember, she'll have a limited memory for words at first.

    Your child's first words will most likely be group names . . . *dog* rather than *poodle*, *cup* rather than *coffee mug* or *teacup*, *chair* rather than *recliner* or *high chair*. It's important not be too specific yet. After your toddler begins to talk and slowly accumulates words, she'll need about six months to realize the boundaries of a word's meaning. For example, does *dog* refer only to the family mutt, or is the meaning wide enough to include horses, sheep, and cows? Once you've helped her decide on *dog*'s boundaries (I'll describe how to do that when we get to that point in development), she's ready to learn about different types. For now, a dog is a dog is a dog.

- **Gesture and sign.** As discussed in chapter Four, there are some definite benefits to using both signs and gestures with babies. Both work. If you gesture with her, she'll gesture. If you sign, she'll sign. Both will happen before she says her first word. But I'm a realist. Most parents don't have the time or energy to learn a new way to communicate with their hands, which is why I recommend using typical gestures, *enhanced* by a few natural-feeling signs. You'll be using some gestures anyway for *bye-bye, come here, yes, no*, and the like, and signing can be a natural extension of that. Do what's comfortable. Use some of the simple, easy-to-understand signs found on page 69, invent some of your own, and use gestures and words. Only do what feels right and fits your lifestyle.

Month Seven

This is still a major exploration month. Now that your baby can sit un-supported, and her hands are free to examine everything around her, physical exploration is her main source of incoming information. Give her lots of interesting stuff to squeeze, feel, manipulate, and explore (nothing small that can be swallowed or is too big for her tiny hands). Let her touch and feel different shapes and textures—a few possibilities:

Blocks	Wooden spoons
Yogurt	Dough (Play or edible)
Fake fur	Washcloths
Plastic containers	Applesauce
Your face and hair	Water (in small container)
Balls	Percussion toys
Bananas	Push-pull noise toys
Fuzzy stuffed animals	

● ■ ▲

MILESTONE WATCHLIST:
Seven-Month-Old

Does your child . . .

❑ Babble in three or more syllables; repeating her own sounds?

❑ Make speech sounds and shout for attention?

❑ "Talk" to toys by making sounds while playing?

❑ Look at some family members when their names are mentioned?

❑ Consistently respond to your voice and physical gestures?

❑ Recognize Mom or Dad on sight?

❑ Inspect, grab, and pull objects and toys?

❑ Sit unsupported?

● ■ ▲

MILESTONE WATCHLIST:
Seven-Month-Old

Does your child . . .

❑ Sit and use her hands to play or explore?

❑ Hold out her arms to be picked up?

She'll start sounding different this month, too. She says things like guh, *then imitates that sound to form* guh-guh. *Not one to be ignored, she may be very insistent and super-active when she tries to attract your attention. If you ignore her, she'll just up the ante, so don't spurn her attempts. She needs to know that you're receiving her message loud and clear. She's also paying more attention to your words, looking at family members and familiar objects when she hears their names mentioned, and beginning to look in the right direction when you point to something.*

SHARED COMMUNICATION ACTIVITIES: MONTH SEVEN

Communication ◆
Care to join me in a duet? Try "singing" a CV combination song. All you have to do is substitute a CV sound like *ba* for the song lyrics—one sound for each syllable. So "Mary Had a Little Lamb," when sung to the proper tune, becomes *ba-ba ba ba ba-ba ba.* Or you can sing CV syllables to a tune of your own choosing. Pick syllable sounds that you've heard your baby produce before so that she'll feel safe joining in. Before long, you'll be in a duet. Ah, the sweet music! Don't self-censor; sing from the heart. Your songs don't have to be loud, but they should have feeling. No one's rating your style and, from your baby's point of view, your singing is right up there with Linda Ronstadt's. Most importantly, she loves to be entertained and invited to participate.

AND YOUR POINT IS . . . ?

When you or your baby points to interesting objects, say the word for the objects and talk about them a little. If you see a big truck, for instance, point and say something like, "Look Alex. Big truck. Wave to truck (Wave). Truck go bye." Here's another example:

MOM: (Points) Mommy see squirrel. (Pause) Look, Mimi. See squirrel?
BABY: (Looks; squeals)
MOM: Yes, squirrel. Squirrel dig. (Pause) Now squirrel on tree.
BABY: (Reaches hands up)
MOM: Yes, squirrel go up. Squirrel up tree.

Because babies aren't born with the ability to follow pointing, it's up to you to show your little one how to do it. It's an important skill and a great way for you and your baby to share experiences. Watch to see what interests her, especially when you're outdoors. Follow her look with a point and a comment. Once you learn the kind of things your baby prefers, you can subtly change the procedure by pointing to an object, person, or animal before she spots it. Soon, there's no doubt, she *will* look where you point, and the next thing you know, she'll be pointing to things on her own.

Cognitive Development ◆
The purposeful life. A portion of your child's early definition of an object is what it's used for—its function. Ask a two-year-old, "What's an apple?" and she'll say, "Sumpin' you eat!" That's function. Even though a child might explore things on her own, she'll pick up most information about the purpose of things from the way they're used by the people around her. A child picking up a brush for the first time will have no idea what to do with it until she sees someone brush her hair with it. She wouldn't know what a spoon was for until she saw someone eating with it. So use objects for their intended purpose around your baby, tell her about the items as you use them, and include her in the activity whenever possible. It's a great teaching opportunity. You can make it a natural and organic part of any task you do throughout the day; any familiar house-

hold items will do the trick—kitchen utensils, soap and washcloth, toys, books, crayons, clothes, vacuum cleaner, food, and so on. Here's a quick example to get you started:

> MOM: Mommy wash dishes.
> CHILD: (Becomes excited)
> MOM: Yes, wash dishes. Suzanne help? (Pause) Okay, help. Wash with sponge? Suzanne touch sponge? (Pause) Sponge wet.
> CHILD: (Squeals)
> MOM: Yes, wet. Mommy wash with sponge. (Pause) See bubbles.

Helping Dr. Livingston. At this age your baby is a natural explorer, but she can always use some help on her adventures. Some things are too difficult for her to examine by herself, and some areas a bit risky. A ball, for example, may be too big for her to hold, water is too dangerous, and a dog could be too nervous. So lend a hand and help her out. Show her how to push the ball, splash her tub of water, and gently pat the dog. Hold objects so she can see and touch them easily, and even let her gnaw on them a bit if she's so inclined and it's safe. Touching and experiencing are all part of forming a mental image or concept of an object. Be sure to talk about the object as your little adventurer makes her way around.

Hearing Stimulation ◆

"Dance" to the music. Music is a pleasurable experience for most people— and that includes your little person. Almost all young children, no matter the culture, seem to enjoy music and accompanying rhythm activities. So give your baby a treat, as well as sharing and hearing stimulation experiences, by holding her in your arms and dancing around to the radio or your favorite CD. Rock her gently from side to side; just be mindful that although at this age she can support her head, you still don't want to snap her around. Talk or sing quietly in her ear as you dance. This will be a fun, shared, warm and fuzzy event for both of you. Do it a few times a week—and enjoy.

Percussion concussion. While your baby's sitting in her high chair, give her a wooden spoon and let her make her own music. Most children will do this naturally, but there's a difference between random banging and drumming together. Sit next to your little drummer and keep your own rhythm. Try adding some recorded music and play together. For variety, buy or borrow some percussion toys, drums, xylophones, tambourines, marimbas and the like, and have a go. Don't expect your tot to drum with you—she's not quite that coordinated yet. The important thing here is for your little one to experience different sounds, and for you both to share the experience and enjoy the fun.

Visual Stimulation ◆

Funny faces. We've talked about how babies are easily attracted by faces, so let's capitalize on that again and turn the predilection into a fun little game that includes taking turns, an essential element of communication; and imitation, an essential factor of cognitive growth. Get your little one to look at you, make a funny face, look away, then look back again with another silly face. Do it a few times and each time you look away, come back with a brand-new over-the-top nutty face. Puff out your cheeks, wiggle your eyebrows, waggle your cheeks, scrunch up your nose, make big O's with your mouth—the whole nine yards. Chances are your baby will get right into the swing of things by looking away and back, and will probably try to replicate your expressions. Needless to say, she won't be able to quite yet, but she'll definitely enjoy the fun. Get ready for lots of laughs and giggles. If she does manage to make an expression, copy it. This could easily turn into a fun turn-taking imitation game.

Sensory Stimulation ◆

Ooey, gooey (Oy vey!) Part II Play with all sorts of different textures, from soft and squishy to plush and furry. I suggested this last month, but it's just as viable now, and in fact will be for several months to come, so let's keep it up. Add some new textures this month (maybe spaghetti!) and, if you tried my favorite dough recipe last month, give my "Almost Baby Putty" a whirl this month (see recipes on page 123). In addition to strengthening her hands as she manipulates the putty, your little one will be using her arm muscles as she pinches, pulls, rolls, and stretches it. More importantly, all this movement stimulates her brain through new sensory experiences. And then there's our favorite bonus—the valuable social interaction time she gets with you as you play together and share communication.

Tête-à-tête. Your baby's natural inclination to touch you can provide wonderful interactions that are feel-good experiences for both of you. Lie or sit facing your baby and let her touch all the different parts of your face as you touch hers. Talk about each facial part—the nose, the lips, the cheeks, and ears—as it's touched. When I suggested this loving, bonding exercise, at four months, it was primarily to stimulate sensory and visual development, but now that your baby's learning level has increased and she's closer to connecting meaning to the words she hears, it moves into the realm of hearing and communication as well. You can add some sound variation to the exercise by occasionally repeating CV sounds in time to a melodic tune (as in the previous "Join me in a duet" exercise), or by making babbling sounds that you've heard your baby make before—*bababa*, or whatever. This can be a wonderful teaching moment, since you have your little one's full attention and she's hearing syllable combinations that she can actually produce—or will soon be able to.

Motor Development ◆

Roll on. Babies love to roll things at this age—balls, cups, bowls, toys, food, you name it. Anything goes—which is why they're constantly rolling things off their high chairs. You can turn your baby's fascination with this new skill into a fun shared interaction by rolling objects back and forth to each other on the floor. It's a great reciprocal activity that will help reinforce her understanding of taking turns. To give her extra communication stimulation, add a sound that you've heard her make before, like *ohhhhh* or *bababa*, each time you roll the ball or object. There's a good chance your baby will get the idea and start "talking" each time she rolls the ball, too. Making sounds is easier for young children if they're also doing something physically.

You are SO-O-O-O manipulative. Let's face it, your baby doesn't get to control much in her environment . . . unless, of course, you count her parents! But manipulation of things (not parents) is important for her motor and mental growth. At this age, she's able to grip and move objects and is perfecting her release of them. So give her the opportunity to handle and fiddle with safe, small objects. Let her play around with magnets on the fridge or a cookie sheet, or empty and fill a drawer with socks, or put small items, such as juice or pudding boxes, on shelves. Let her go to town with toys in a toy chest. (Needless to say, keep her away from any very small objects that can cause choking.)

Bounce and sing. With your baby on your knee, sing a song or nursery rhyme. Combine the motion of your bouncing knee with the song. If you're not in a singing mood, bounce her along to a CD or the radio. It's great fun for her and it combines two areas of development: motor and hearing. Although this activity may seem like one we've used before, there is a subtle difference in that we are combining song with overall movement, rather than just hand movement. For a twist, stand her on your lap while you support her by holding her wrists or hands and gently sway or bounce her. She'll find standing exciting and challenging, and it's excellent exercise! She's not too steady yet, though, so take it easy.

Reach for the stars. While your little one is sitting, encourage her to reach up at different angles by holding up a favorite toy or some other highly desirable object. This is terrific for eye-hand coordination and will strengthen and stretch that cute little back. It's a little touch of baby yoga!

Month Eight

You'll almost certainly see some of those gestures we've been talking about this month. Remember to respond to these communication attempts with words as well as your own gestures and signs. Your little one's sound-making becomes more insistent as she demands that you pay attention—she's really expressing her intention to communicate now! Because she's able to recognize her name and the words for one or more familiar objects, it's doubly important that you slow down your speech, pause after important words, and speak in very short sentences. In your conversations, she'll be paying attention to everything now—words, intonation, meaning, gestures, facial expression, and context.

● ■ ▲

MILESTONE WATCHLIST:
Eight-Month-Old

Does your child . . .

❏ "Sing" along with familiar songs?

❏ Produce nonidentical babbling? (Babbles in which the syllables are not the same, like *beba* or *bada*. Not all babies do this.)

❏ Imitate gestures?

❏ Sound like she's talking and having a conversation?

❏ Understand one or two familiar words, especially when accompanied by gestures?

❏ Recognize her name? (She may stop what she's doing to look at you.)

❏ Stop when you say "No"?

❏ Wave bye-bye?

❏ Look at a few common objects when they're named?

❏ Predict that it's time to play a game? (She may become excited, smile, or make eye contact.)

❏ Play patty-cake and peek-a-boo?

❏ Respond physically, orally, or with gestures when she sees a familiar person?

SHARED COMMUNICATION ACTIVITIES: MONTH EIGHT

Communication ◆

Play it again, Sam. This simple ploy gives your little one a bit of control over her world and a real use for her "talking." First engage her in some fun activity like telling a story or playing patty-cake, then stop and wait for her to vocalize before you continue. She'll probably catch on very quickly. If she's a little slow on the uptake, make a babble or some other baby sound first, or just wait until she makes one by chance. When she does, continue with your activity. If she doesn't seem to understand that her vocalizations can impel you to get on with the show, encourage her to hit the tabletop, or touch you, or do some other physical action. Once she can do that, add a sound to the action. It seems to be easier for a child to imitate a sound if it's attached to an action.

My favorite songs. While a baby's response to music will differ depending on her past exposure to it and her social experiences with it, all children just seem to naturally love it. So let's give your little one a treat. Pick a simple, repetitive song, such as "Old MacDonald," and move her to the music at the same place in each repetition. You could bounce her gently on your knee, pick her up, raise her little hands, or what have you. You're the choreographer. For example:

> *Ole MacDonald had a farm, e-i (Bounce, bounce), e-i (Bounce, bounce), oooo (Raise your baby's hands).*
> *And on his farm, he had a . . . (Clap her hands with each word) pig, eee-i (Bounce, bounce), eee-i (Bounce, bounce), oooo (Raise your baby's hands).*
> *With an oink, oink here (Make noise against child's neck) and an . . .*

You get the idea—lots of song, movement, repetition, silliness, and shared fun. Along the way, your baby will be making sounds, learning to predict movement and sound-making, and enjoying another loving, bonding interaction with you.

You're goin' to the dogs! Pretend play is always a guaranteed winner with babies—and parents, too. You get to do anything and be anything you want, and your baby will be thrilled with the surprise of seeing Mommy or Daddy behaving so differently than they usually do. So get down! Get on your hands and knees and pretend to be some sort of animal—your choice. If you opt for "caninedom," move like a dog, and bark, arf, ruff, growl, or otherwise sound like a dog. Describe your actions with simple commentary, such as "Doggie says 'ruff-ruff.'" If you've had a tough day and you're not up to getting down on all fours, use a stuffed animal stand-in. Move the fluffy dog around and talk about doggy things as before. After a few weeks, see if your baby can fill in the animal sound ("Doggie says . . .") or if she can point to the stuffed animal when you ask, "Who says 'ruff-ruff?'"

Cognitive Development ◆

The choice is yours. Your baby is gaining some independence now, and making choices will aid her cognitive development. All of us like to be offered options, and babies are no different. Present two baby-friendly things to your tot and let her pick one—the yellow squeaky duck or the scraggly talking rabbit. If she takes both, don't worry—she has a bright future with the IRS! But the next time, hold the choices far enough apart so taking only one is possible. Be sure to talk to her about whatever choice she makes and her reaction. It could go something like this:

> ADULT: Rosie in bathtub. Splash water.
> CHILD: (Splashing)
> ADULT: (Holding up rubber ducky and toy boat, looking at each and shaking it when named) Duck? (pause) Boat?
> CHILD: (Takes duck; pushes it under water)
> ADULT: Rosie take duck. (Pause) Duck in water. Splash. Duck splash. (Pause) Uh-oh, where duck?

Two at once. When you play with your baby, use two objects instead of one every once in a while—say a doll and doll clothes, or a dog and a brush. She's just beginning to be able to focus on two objects at the same time, which is an important step in cognitive growth and will be important for problem-solving, word definitions, and word combinations a little later on. Playing with two different associated items helps encourage development of this essential skill.

Try to pick objects that go together naturally. A few ideas to get you going:

Cup and bowl

Truck and block

Teddy bear and furniture

Car, bus, boat, or truck and passenger

Dog and bowl

Horse and rider

Hearing Stimulation ◆

Playback time. Record your baby's vocalizations—especially when she's in a particularly gregarious and chatty mood, then play the tape back for her. Kids get a big kick out of this, and in at least one study, babies were more likely to parrot their own chatter than the recorded sounds of others. She'll have a great time "talking" to herself, and it's educational and lots of fun to watch.

Coffee, anyone? Old coffee cans are great noisemakers. Children are fascinated by the fact that they can create different sounds by dropping blocks and other items into them. They can entertain themselves endlessly with this little activity and it's terrific auditory stimulation. Two cautions: Make sure the items are large enough so they can't be swallowed; and be sure that the metal left on the can after cutting the lid is not sharp. It's always a good idea to cover the top rim of the can with a nice heavy-gauge tape just to be safe.

Visual Stimulation ◆

Pinocchio knows. Kids love puppets, especially when they're visually interesting and appear and disappear suddenly. Some puppets can be refreshingly inexpensive. A few years ago I found a box of five soft, cloth puppets for my granddaughter for less than $10! You can also make your own with old colorful socks and pieces of brightly colored fabric. (As always, avoid buttons and other small adornments that can be pulled off and swallowed.)

A sock animal is one of the easiest puppets to make. Just hold your hand in the shape of a crocodile mouth, with the fingers on top as the upper jaw and the thumb as the lower jaw. Keep that shape as you pull a sock over your hand. Rather than push your fingers all the way in, tuck the toe of the sock back into the "croc's mouth." Take a needle and thread and run a quick line of stitches along the "cheek" on each side from the "lips" back for about two inches. This little bit of sewing will hold the shape of the "puppet." Your fingers and thumb are now in separate compartments. Open and shut the animal's mouth by moving your thumb and fingers apart and together. You now have a flexible start for a croc, dog, frog, cat, cow, horse or any other creature. Just add the appropriate colorful cloth eyes, ears, horns, tongue or what have you, and voilà!—a fun, interactive toy.

Puppet play is a perfect opportunity to use language in a novel way. You and your baby can "talk" with the puppet, who can be as outrageous or sassy as you want to make him. A colorful, active puppet is guaranteed to totally mesmerize your little munchkin. Here's a script to help you connect with your inner thespian.

> ADULT: Where doggie? (Bring out puppet) Oh, there he is.
> DOG: Ruff, ruff. (Puppet hides behind adult)
> ADULT: Where doggie go? (Looks around) Where doggie?
> DOG: (Peeks out from behind adult) Grrrrrr!
> CHILD: (Squeals, points, or looks)
> ADULT: Where dog?
> DOG: Ruff!
> ADULT: There dog. Nice dog. What dog say?
> CHILD: (Makes noise)
> ADULT: Yes! Dog say "Ruff!"

Sensory Stimulation ◆

Let 'em eat cake . . . or at least soft finger foods. Handling finger foods is terrific for motor control and a wonderful sensory experience. A variety of foods and textures provides taste and feeling stimulation and requires different types of chewing—perfect for sensory and motor growth. Just put your baby in her high chair and set the "feast" right on the tray. Avoid foods like whole hotdogs that break off in big chunks. (Hotdogs are fine, but cut them into very small pieces first.) Best-bet foods are bananas; berries; tiny apple, peach, watermelon, or pear slices; crackers; teething biscuits; soft cheeses; small pieces of toast; and even short pieces of cooked spaghetti with a little sauce. This is a full-parental-supervision activity—don't leave your child unattended.

Messy Bessy. This variation on the previous activity offers a plentiful dollop of one more sensory element—touch. Messy eating is a lot of fun for babies. Spread O-shaped oat cereal on the high chair tray with pudding, yogurt, whipped cream, applesauce, or other blended fruit . . . then step back! Your baby will experience the crunch of the cereal along with the smoothness of the yogurt or pudding and the chunkiness of the fruit. In addition, she'll have the motor and sensory experience of moving her hands through the muck. Keep the garden hose ready for clean-up! This is obviously not a daily activity—save for special times.

Motor Development ◆

Go fetch. Encourage your little one to throw or push soft objects like toy animals or balls, then retrieve them for her and give them back so she can have another go . . . and another, and another. Besides the obvious advantages of reinforcing the idea of social reciprocal actions (turn-taking activity) and training her throwing arm for Little League, your baby is learning to act upon the world rather than just respond to it. This is a valuable lesson that will encourage her gesturing development and communication skills. And as a bonus, it's a humbling, character-building experience for you to be the fetch*er* rather than the "fetch*ee*." Now, you'll see how exciting it is for Fido. Make it a fun game!

One for you . . . and one for me. At this age, babies love to hand objects back and forth, and handing objects is second only to rolling them for good turn-taking practice. Hand an object to your baby, and encourage her to give it back, until you're passing things smoothly back and forth between the two of you. Use toys or other things that differ in size and texture for added stimulation and motor development. This is an anytime activity—do it while getting her dressed (pass a sock or shirt), at breakfast (try a plastic cup), or in the playpen or infant seat (any kind of toy). Talk about whatever it is you're passing to each other while you're doing it. And every once in a while, make it a little more challenging or tease a bit—"Gimme that teddy."

A quick note: Don't concern yourself with whether your baby is using her right or left hand. At this age, she's not likely to have a preference. More exclusive use of either hand will begin to show up between the ages of three and four. Although handedness has some relationship to where language processing occurs in the brain, there's no indication that use of one hand or the other is better for language development. So let her use both and have fun passing objects back and forth.

Stack 'em up, knock 'em down. At this age, babies love stacking things up and watching them fall, so you'll definitely want to have some soft, colorful blocks in your bag of tricks. They offer endless hours of play and are great for motor development. Be sure to give your little one a hand—help her pick up the blocks, stack 'em, and show her how to knock them over. Naturally, you'll want to have a baby chat about the experience. As you're stacking, say "Uppppp," and as they're falling, say "Fall" or "Down." The language will be very meaningful for your baby because it occurs within an activity that the words describe. You'll find soft blocks at most toy stores, but you can also make your own by cutting squares out of an extra piece of foam and covering them with bright material. (Again, be sure that soft materials are safe and won't break off and be ingested.) Empty juice boxes can also be used for stacking.

Roll out the barrel. Encourage crawling, reaching, and sitting by using a rolling noisemaker that your baby can push ahead of her as she crawls or propels herself on her tummy. You can find mobile noisemakers in baby stores, or make your own from a cardboard cylindrical container, like the kind oatmeal and other food products come in. It's easy: Put beans, bells, or an old rattle inside the canister, glue on the lid, and decorate with contact paper. Just be sure that the lid is secure so your baby can't get hold of any of those items inside.

Month Nine

Speech and language input becomes especially important this month as your baby pulls out all the stops to vocalize and gesture with you. Don't be surprised, especially during regular familiar routines like dressing or eating, if your little one begins to sound like you—not your words, but your intonation. I have a friend who used to repeatedly say "Oh, my God!" with a raised pitch at the end. Right at nine months, she heard her baby using the exact inflection, just with different sounds in place of the words. It's a humbling experience!

● ■ ▲

MILESTONE WATCHLIST:
Nine-Month-Old

Does your child . . .

❑ Babble with more *b, p,* and *m* sounds?

❑ Speak in jargon (the string of sounds with adult intonation)?

❑ Use gestures, such as pointing, head shaking, or reaching?

❑ Mimic sounds and syllables?

❑ Whine when she wants something—either with or without a gesture?

❑ Respond consistently to "No?" (Ignoring you consistently doesn't count.)

❑ Look at pictures for up to one minute? (The important thing is that she notices pictures, not the length of time she looks at them. As usual, she'll pay attention longer if you talk about the pictures.)

❑ Hand things back and forth to you?

SHARED COMMUNICATION ACTIVITIES: MONTH NINE

Communication ◆

Don't say, "Say X." We still want to encourage your baby to mimic sounds—especially ones that you know are in her repertoire. The best time to get her to repeat a particular sound is immediately after she's produced it, but you can really do it any time you're speaking with her. The trick is *not* to ask her to "Say bababababa." You're using an extra word to get your message across, which can be confusing. Just say the sound you want her to repeat by *itself.* So, for example, if you want her to say "mama," all you have to do is utter the word *mama,* as opposed to "Say mama." If she wants to copy you, she will. You can try this with real words now, too, but they should be CV words like *key (keee)*, VC words, such as *eat (eeeet)*, or CVCV words as in *mama, dada, cookie,* or *baby.*

Babies often repeat a piece of a word rather than the whole thing. At this stage, if your little sweetie does actually say a word, she almost certainly won't know its meaning. Keep this exercise light and easy. Don't continually *insist* that your baby imitate you. Nobody likes constant demands. Once she starts making the same sound or word as you, do it a few more times, then change the sound slightly. If she follows suit, great. If not, go back to the original sound. She'll get it eventually—especially if you make a big deal out of it when she gets it right. We all like strokes.

My "special book." Start showing your little one photos of her favorite people, animals, or things. Maybe you already have a photo album you could use; if not, make up a small one with at least five personal photos. Point and talk about each picture as you "read" the book. "Look, Aunt Mary . . . (pause) Mommy and Aunt Mary . . . (pause) on a boat . . ." It will be a while before your baby has the cognitive ability to be able to comprehend two-dimensional images, but this is great practice for things to come.

Pretend "telephone." Since your baby is starting to use jargon (those indecipherable lines of babble that sound like language . . . kind of) give her a natural outlet. Let her pretend to use the telephone, or better yet, hand her the phone when you're talking to her grandma (or anyone else with saintly patience) and let them have a "conversation." This kind of phone play can be real fun and it is a great precursor to real conversation. My granddaughter was nodding appropriately and saying "um-hm" on the phone before she could speak. (Spoken like a proud grandpa, eh?)

"What see?" This is a more advanced variation on the pointing exercise that we did when your baby was seven months old ("And your point is . . . ?") In that one, you named whatever your tot pointed to. This month we up the ante by giving your baby a chance to name the item of interest—or at least offer a babble comment. When you see her looking at something, ask her, "What see?" or "What's that?" Give her full credit for any vocal or gesture response, then supply the name for her. The advantage here is that it gives your budding linguist the name for something that has already captured her interest—and even better, it

does it in a conversational context of question and answer. Since she won't be able to answer correctly yet, remember that it's your job to supply the name for her.

> ADULT: What see?
> CHILD: Bababa
> ADULT: Yes, (Pause) doggie!

Best not to overdo this little game—occasionally is better than constantly. Before long your little one will be using this word-learning tool herself, and you'll start hearing my very favorite child utterance, "Wassat?" She might say it as a ploy to engage you in a verbal game, or she may genuinely want to find out the names of things. Either way, it makes for fun communication. But don't worry if your sweetie never goes through the "Wassat?" stage. Some children simply ignore the strategy altogether.

Cognitive Development ◆
Hidden food. When you know your baby is watching you, pretend you don't notice, and "hide" some food under a nearby napkin or hanky—best to use finger food, such as a tiny piece of banana, cracker, cookie, or well-cooked vegetable. Then watch to see if she lifts the cloth to find it. This is great practice for her memory and recognition skills. If you see that she's having trouble finding the stash, leave some of it exposed as a clue. This is a perfect activity to do at snack time, since the reward for finding the tasty morsel is getting to devour it. Food for thought: If your little sleuth can do this one easily, make it a little more challenging by hiding the food under a solid object like a plastic cup or upside-down bowl.

Turn me on! Certain everyday occurrences, like turning on lights, are perfect demonstrations of cause and effect and planning—*if I do this, that will happen.* You can encourage the development of your baby's nascent planning skills by introducing her to the use of pull cords, switches, and levers. Turn on the lamp together and act surprised when the light comes on, or help her push the doorbell and act excited when you hear it ring.

Obviously, you want to stay away from wall sockets and plugs—we certainly don't want to encourage any action there. In fact, to be safe, make sure that all sockets have covers. My son Todd blew all the circuits in the house when he was eighteen months old by plunging a fork into a socket that had inadvertently been left uncovered after vacuuming. Luckily, he was unharmed . . . or, now that I think of it, maybe that explains his behavior during his teen years. Seriously, buy inexpensive plug covers and use them faithfully.

At the end of my rope! This one offers another excellent lesson in cause and effect. Attach one of your baby's favorite toys to a string and tie it to the high chair, then show her how to pull on the string to retrieve the toy, so she can get it whenever she wants. Or, on the same theme, attach a ribbon to a toy that's just out of reach on the floor, and show your little one how to pull the ribbon to get the toy. You could try popular commercial pull toys—the stores are packed with them—or even put things on a napkin or cloth and show your baby how to pull it close to acquire the items. Any way you do it, you're teaching causality, which is a hugely important cognitive skill.

Hearing Stimulation ◆

Poky-man—or woman. This is a twist on the causality theme—now we're adding sound into the mix. Get your tot an easy-to-operate baby CD or tape player, or radio. Children of this age love to poke with their index finger, and being able to poke a big button and produce your own music is pure ecstasy—and a powerful cause-and-effect lesson. There are a number of safe, colorful music players on the market, and most are reasonably priced. Baby's First Walkman, for instance, goes for about $25. Some baby tape recorders actually record, too, allowing you to record both you and your budding songbird for posterity. These recordings are priceless later on—and sometimes even more powerful than photos at bringing back the memories. A friend of mine, whose daughter is now in her thirties, just discovered a tape of her at three singing a John Denver song while picking it out on the piano. It was a true treasure, and just about brought tears to his eyes.

Visual Stimulation ◆

Peek-a-book. Your baby is now ready to begin sharing books with you. Don't expect long reading sessions—she's not ready for that yet. At this age, there's no way she's going to sit quietly as you read a story. For now, she just likes the visual stimulation. Use picture books with simple images of big, bright colorful things. There should only be one or two items pictured—too many on a page will confuse her. Help your fledgling reader turn the sturdy cardboard pages as you talk about the pictures. If she wants to move on and skip a few pages or go backwards, that's perfectly fine. Absolutely, let her take the lead—this is her introduction. The *hows* of the procedure can come later. (See Appendix E resources for some wonderful book recommendations.)

Sensory Stimulation ◆

Pots and pans band. This is a good one for social, motor, development, as well as sensory stimulation. Simply get out some pots and pans and a couple of wooden spoons and let the fun begin! Show your baby how to make "music" (I use the term loosely) by banging the different pots and pans with the spoon. Encourage her by saying things like, "Debbie make music!" If she doesn't seem to want to join in, leave the "instruments" in front of her and wait till you catch her starting to noodle around on her own (trust me, she will), then slip in and bang along. Obviously, you don't need anything fancy for this exercise. Pots and pans, their lids, cooking spoons, or rubber spatulas or ladles will do the trick. You can even introduce a woodwind section with an empty paper towel roll "horn" (which produces a divine sound when hummed into). This game is a natural for anytime you and your baby are in the kitchen, but it works anywhere, anytime. At this stage, your baby may not have the breath control for even elementary horns or whistles. If you'd rather buy infant instruments, just be sure to get very simple ones like shakers, drums, xylophones, or baby-style pianos with four or so large, easy-to-press keys.

Motor Stimulation ◆

Routine imitation. See if you can get your baby to imitate some of the simple actions you do during some of your everyday activities. Give her a little dustcloth, some safe food prep utensils, or even a little toy vacuum cleaner, and ask her to "Help Mommy (or Daddy)." She's aware of daily routines like washing, cleaning, making meals, etc., from watching you,

Shared Communication Activities:
Months 7, 8, and 9

MONTHLY ACTIVITIES

Age (Mos.)	Communication	Cognitive Development	Hearing Stimulation
7	▴ Care to join me in a duet? ▴ And your point is . . . ?	▴ The purposeful life ▴ Helping Dr. Livingston	▴ "Dance" to the music ▴ Percussion concussion
8	▴ Play it again, Sam ▴ My favorite songs ▴ You're goin' to the dogs!	▴ The choice is yours ▴ Two at once	▴ Playback time ▴ Coffee, anyone?
9	▴ Don't say, "Say X" ▴ My "special book" ▴ Pretend "telephone" ▴ "What see?"	▴ Hidden food ▴ Turn me on! ▴ At the end of my rope!	▴ Pokey-man—or woman

Shared Communication Reminders
- Acknowledge and confirm
- Model language she can comprehend
- Treat your baby like a real communicator
- Mimic your child's reduplicated babbling

Visual Stimulation	Sensory Stimulation	Motor Development
▲ Funny faces	▲ Ooey, gooey (Oy vey!): Part II ▲ Tête-à-tête	▲ Roll on ▲ You are SO-O-O-O manipulative ▲ Bounce and sing ▲ Reach for the stars
▲ Pinocchio knows	▲ Let 'em eat cake . . . or at least soft finger foods ▲ Messy Bessy	▲ Go fetch ▲ One for you . . . and one for me ▲ Stach 'em up, knock 'em down ▲ Roll out the barrel
▲ Peek-a-book	▲ Pots and pans band	▲ Routine imitation ▲ Chase me ▲ Moving up in the world

- Use real words in conversations
- Respond to your baby's gestures
- Use consistent words for things
- Gesture and sign

and this knowledge (called a *script* in academia) will guide her play. Remember, routines are important for their predictability. Now we can combine *activities* that she knows with *things* that she knows—the routine of making peanut butter sandwiches with the names of items like bread, knife, and jar. Keeping things in context is one of the major elements for good learning at this age. When your baby uses common objects *within* known routines, the language you use to describe those objects will make more sense to her. When your words coincide with her actions, you'll be giving her labels for the things she knows. It won't be long before she begins to mimic daily domestic routines. Keep an eye out and soon you'll probably see her doing things like mock washing her face, stirring food, and wiping the table within her "play." It's a glorious thing to behold.

Chase me. Children love to be chased, and energetic movement is great for muscle development. When you see your baby starting to crawl around, get down on the floor with her and play "I'm gonna catch you." Be silly, crawl after her, and keep "threatening" to catch her. She'll giggle and squeal as you get closer and closer. When you catch her, hug or tickle her gently, then let her go and start all over again.

Moving up in the world. Your baby will be pulling herself up to standing position soon. Hoisting yourself up via a table leg isn't easy when you're nine months old, so let's help her out. A stack of cushions set at just the right height or a low step is just the ticket. Place a few firm sofa or chair pillows on the floor or use a carpeted bottom step to help her get into a kneeling position from all fours. From kneeling, she should be able to negotiate standing with a little assistance. To add a little incentive, set one of her favorite toys or something else irresistibly tempting on top of a stack of two pillows or on the second step, so she'll really want to stand to retrieve it. Don't abandon her on her way up. Stay close by and give her all the physical—and emotional—support she needs. Standing is a new phenomenon . . . and the beginning of a brave new word.

CHAPTER NINE

Months 10, 11, and 12 . . . Happy Birthday!

On the Cusp of Talking

Progress Report

MOVEMENT

LOOK out! During these three months, your baby will become even more active. By ten months he'll be able to push to a stand from a crawl, and then sit back on the floor again—quite an athletic feat! Two months later, he may walk unsupported for a few steps, although bona fide walking will take a bit more time and practice to perfect. When he's in a hurry he'll resort to crawling, which is still his most reliable mode of transportation— besides you, of course. Once he becomes mobile, his whole world perspective will change, and he'll want to get into everything! Your mantra: Baby-proof! Be sure to cover all electrical outlets; lock away harmful substances; put small objects out of reach; block stairways, doors, and windows . . . you get the picture.

As your baby's fine motor skills continue to improve, he'll imitate your physical actions more. He now has the ability to remember your movements while he programs his own muscles to mimic them, so when you're interacting he'll touch things when you do, clap his hands like you, and try to duplicate other hand motions. He'll especially enjoy taking things in and out of containers and touching your face—see if he doesn't squeal with delight when you blow raspberries on his hand as he touches your mouth.

There'll also be some advances in the kind of motor control he needs for speech. By the time he's eleven months old, he'll have enough muscle control to be able to bite into soft, solid foods. He'll also be able to raise the tip of his tongue a little, which will allow him to expand his repertoire of sounds, but he still has a few years to go before he has enough tongue control to make some of the more difficult sounds of the English language, like *th*.

COGNITION

Even though your baby's reasoning abilities and perception are maturing quickly, he's not quite capable yet of thinking through tricky problems like locating a hidden object. He can, on the other hand, solve problems by imitation. If you show him how to operate a mechanical toy by pushing a button, for instance, he'll get the hang of it pretty quickly and be able to apply the new strategy to other similar toys. His increased attention span and memory allow him to pay more attention to these kinds of problems, as well as to you and things around him for longer periods of time. He'll be absorbing a lot more now as you point out and talk about interesting things on walks and outings, and he'll really start to "see" the amazing new world around him.

COMMUNICATION

There's a dramatic increase in comprehension, as well as attention span, between six months and one year, and during these last months before his first birthday, your baby will just be starting to "understand" some words based on a combination of sound, gesture, intonation, and context. Within specific contexts, he'll associate the sounds of your words and actions with a particular item—when you say "doggie," for instance, he may look at Fido and even point at him. He'll be able to recognize a familiar word when it's mixed in with others, especially if he hears it in the context of an established routine—*soap,* for instance, during bathing.

And while at ten and eleven months he may point in the right direction when you ask him where something is, by his twelfth month, he'll be able to follow simple instructions like "Give Mommy Teddy." He won't understand the individual words as much as he'll be following a learned routine. The *sound* of what you say will tell him what to do more than the actual words . . . *this sound means I should do this.*

During these last few months of his first year, your baby will really enjoy the *feel* of sounds as well as hearing them. He'll imitate coughs or tongue clicks. It's fun for him. My granddaughter developed a "terrible cough" just before her first birthday. Of course, she giggled and smiled like crazy after she received the appropriate concerned attention, and the "cough" disappeared in a New York minute.

Even though junior will soon be talking, you'll still be hearing babbles and lots of jargon. By ten months, this splendid chatter can be four syllables or more. These syllable structures and consonant sounds are greatly influenced by you. Your little guy is basically parroting back the speech he's heard around him—his own baby version of it anyway. Just as he's approaching his first-year birthday, he may come up with the right combinations of sounds if you ask him for a specific word. (It's okay at this age to ask.) If he says "Mama" or any other word in place of the word you requested, just change your script and go with the flow. Ask him to "Say Mama." You'll have a better success rate if you request words he knows rather than asking for new words that he's never said before. If you want to try a new word, be sure that it includes sounds that you know he can produce.

Even before your baby says his first words—that milestone all we parents treasure—he may actually invent a few "words" of his own. Even though these aren't actual words per se, you can tell your tot thinks of them as words because he uses them consistently and in the same context. Every time one of my friend's sons saw a dog, for instance, he'd point excitedly and say *bedada*. It was pretty clear that dogs were bedadas. Within a few months, though, dogs were *doggies*. While these kinds of mock-words aren't based on actual words, they do function as words for your budding linguist, so accept his version but give him the commonly accepted word as well. For example:

CHILD: Bedada!
ADULT: Bedada. Yes, that doggie! (Pause) Doggie bark. Here comes doggie.

It's really not a problem if your baby suddenly starts speaking in this kind of mystery language. In fact, these kinds of *bedada* words show his creativity as a language learner. Now that he's got the idea that sound sequences stand for things, he just needs to understand that users of a particular language all use the *same* sound sequence to represent a meaning.

None of us are born knowing that a word is a word. The most popular developmental theory is that children make assumptions about the sound sequences that they hear. They might figure that words refer to things that are similar in some way, that they can apply new "words" to things they haven't heard named, that only adults use words in a consistent manner. Whatever's going on in those intriguing little minds, there are a few things you can do to help your fledgling speaker out.

- Say the words for things in context (when they are present and visual).

- Name the entire entity rather than specific parts. *Kitty,* for instance; save *tail, whisker,* and *claw*s for later—unless your baby asks, of course.

- Give multiple examples—for example, show him that cups of all different shapes and colors are still called cups.

- Be consistent. If it's *doggie* today, don't slip in *Pomeranian* tomorrow.

FIRST WORDS!

At around twelve months, most babies will say their first meaningful word. (The common range is ten to fifteen months, so there's leeway here. But twelve months is average.) A tot's first word usually refers to something that's visually present—a favorite toy, a certain food, a family member or pet—and it may have a specific function or purpose. He may say "Juice," for example, to indicate that he wants more juice as opposed to just naming the juice. This specialization will change as he gains more experience and you offer more examples of other uses of the word. Soon *juice* will be used to question, answer, request, name, and more. If junior is used to having apple juice every morning and you serve up orange juice one day, he may ask "Juice?" which loosely translates as "Wassat?"

But whether asking questions, making demands, or simply commenting on his world at large, your little tyke will now begin using a combination of gestures and words. If you've been using signs, he may sign and speak simultaneously. The important thing is to be aware of his different reasons for talking and respond accordingly. There's a common misconception that children use words only to *name* things. Nothing could be further from the truth. Remember to respond enthusiastically and repeat his words as you expand on them. For example:

CHILD: Juice!
ADULT: Juice! Yes, juice in cup. Michael's juice.
CHILD: Juice.
ADULT: Juice in cup. Drink juice.

SHARED COMMUNICATION TIPS AND REMINDERS

- **Be a good role model.** You are your baby's language role model, so remember to use short words and phrases plus gestures. Omit articles like *a, the,* and *an* for now; they add very little content to what you're saying. "Throw ball" gets the point across as well as "Throw the ball." If you're really uncomfortable with speaking this way, don't. It's not crucial that you leave out the articles; it just makes it a bit easier for your baby. Do what feels right.

- **Don't interrupt.** As your little one begins to add single words to his verbal repertoire, he'll go slowly at first and spend more and more time practicing sounds and sound-word combinations. Don't interrupt when he's practicing. It may seem like play, but in fact he's working very hard.

SHARED COMMUNICATION TIPS AND REMINDERS

- **Expand your baby's world.** Most of us talk about what we know—children do, too. *World* knowledge becomes *word* knowledge. Give your baby good quality experiences on which to base his language. Quality experiences are mediated by a caring adult who explains, helps, and participates.

- **Don't expect your tot to get it right each time.** Always respond positively, even if he makes a mistake, which will naturally happen more as he rapidly adds words to his vocabulary. Just gently redirect him, like this mom is doing as her child encounters his first horse:

CHILD: Doggie.
ADULT: Like doggie. But too big.
CHILD: Big.
ADULT: Yes, that big. Doggies are small.
CHILD: Big.
ADULT: Yes, big. That horse.
CHILD: Hawse?
ADULT: Yes, horse. Horses are big.
CHILD: Hawse.
ADULT: Horse. Big horse.

- **Try not to be critical of your child's speech.** When our speech is criticized too often, we talk less, and our goal for your baby is that he talk more. This doesn't mean you can't laugh *with* him at the truly funny things he says. But for his sake, don't mock or make fun of his speech. When I was a young dad, I broke my leg in a bicycle accident and was in a full leg cast for more than a year. When my little son asked in a concerned voice, "Yeg hawt?" *(translation: leg hurt?)*, I simply replied, "Yes, honey, leg hurt." It was absolutely the wrong time for even a gentle correction of the mispronunciation. Be sensitive to your child's needs and feelings.

- **Use appropriately simple and useful words.** When you talk with your baby and encourage him to speak, use words that reflect his interest and that he has the ability to say at this early age. Remember that words formed by a CV sound such as *me* (the consonant sound *mmmm* and the vowel sound *eeeee*) or CVCV sounds like *dada* and *mama* are the easiest for him now. Longer CV combinations, such as *banana* and *pajama*, will most likely be shortened as *nana* and *jamee*, respectively. (Check Appendix C for words that will be easy for your baby at this stage.)

- **Imitate wordlike vocalizations.** Your baby will still be making lots of wordlike sounds. No child wakes up one morning and starts speaking in real words exclusively. Parrot his "almost-words" when you can and make a game of it. It adds your seal of approval to his linguistic attempts and lets him know that his sounds are so worthy that even Mom likes to say them.

- **Use your child's name when referring to him.** There are two schools of thought regarding the use of pronouns with babies. One believes that you should use the word *you* when speaking to your baby about himself, and *me* or *I* when referring to yourself. The other feels you should use proper names—Timmy, when talking to Timmy about himself, and Mommy or Daddy when referring to yourself. I belong to the latter group—I believe in using proper names.

  I feel that *you* and *me* can be very confusing to very young children. Think about those two words a minute. First, *you* is the listener, of which there can be one or many, and *I* or *me* is the speaker—two words for the same person. Second, both roles change with each speaker. It's tough for a young child to keep track of who's who. A name, on the other hand, refers to a specific person and is consistent in all contexts. The rationale for not using a name is that you are referring to the child as you might refer to a third person—someone outside the conversation. Some think that could be confusing. I don't. At this stage of the game, I suggest that you opt for the specificity of your child's name. Truly, the choice is yours,

SHARED COMMUNICATION TIPS AND REMINDERS

but trust me, if you follow my advice and consistently use your child's name, he won't be confused in the least. An example for you:

ADULT: Ali push car.
CHILD: Push.
ADULT: Yes, push car. Oops! Ali drop car. (Pause) Where car?
CHILD: Car.
ADULT: Yes, Ali find car.
CHILD: (Moves car) Up!
ADULT: Car up. Car go up. Ali push car up.

- **Encourage your baby to initiate communication.** We adults often forget that children need to start up conversations, too. We tend to fall into question-and-answer mode—we ask, they answer. But children will take the first step in communications—especially with a little clever manipulation of their environment on our part. Doing things like sealing tasty treats or fun toys in clear plastic containers, or putting tempting objects just out of his reach while he's watching you will definitely elicit some verbal response. Another idea: You and your mate (or a friend or older child) could take turns rolling a ball or pushing a toy back and forth with your baby, and occasionally "forget" his turn. That's almost always a surefire conversation starter, as is a leaky cup, or temporarily holding back on an expected snack. In our little realm, even mild protest is counted as initiating communication.

- **Respond appropriately.** When your little one attempts communication, respond immediately if possible. Confirm his "talk" by repeating it, expanding it, or commenting. Try to incorporate his words in your response. If, for example, your baby sees a bird flying by the window and says, "Birdie" (or, more likely, "Bawdy"), you could:

CONFIRM: Yes, birdie.
EXPAND: Yes, bird fly.
COMMENT: Yes, birds live in our tree.

A fourth alternative combines all three. Encourage your baby to expand upon his own word. When he says "Bird," reply with something like, "Yes, bird go up . . . (Pause) . . . Say 'Bird go.' " In this kind of interaction, be sure to use words that he already knows. We don't want to frustrate him by demanding tough new words or a long sentence. If he attempts communication only to have you demand an encore performance that's beyond his abilities, he'll be less likely to start a conversation next time around.

- **Take advantage of pointing and vocalizing.** When your child points to something, immediately say the word for what it is and talk about it. Most children will point to things that attract their interest and attention, especially things that are new, different, or changing. So, should you and your tot come back from an outing to find that Fido has trashed the house, think of the newly arranged decor as a fabulous opportunity for conversation rather than a minor catastrophe.

- **Sing at bedtime.** Try variations on "Hush Little Baby." It's a wonderful quiet way to use language to soothe your child.

Month Ten

A lot of your baby's gestures are now accompanied by sounds—saying "Bye" as he waves being the most popular. His vocalizations sound more like actual talking as he perfects your intonational patterns. He's paying more attention now, and is better at finding a hidden or missing object—he looks in the last place he saw it. He's also using things for their intended purposes, since he can now remember not just the object itself but its use, too! He may even try to put on a shoe, hat, or sunglasses. This is a big change over just randomly playing with toys and treating each one the same. He's building those pathways in his brain. He's off and . . . well, crawling.

● ■ ▲

MILESTONE WATCHLIST:
Ten-Month-Old

Does your child . . .

❑ Say "Uh-oh" appropriately?

❑ String together four or more syllables with adult-like intonation?

❑ Gesture and vocalize his intentions?

❑ Imitate sounds, such as coughs, sneezes, or tongue clicks?

❑ Vocalize to call others?

❑ Imitate facial expressions?

❑ Imitate gestures?

❑ Use his voice to get attention?

❑ Wave and say "Bye-bye"?

❑ Hand you requested objects?

❑ Pay attention to both a person speaking and an object simultaneously?

❑ Look at a person who calls his name?

❑ Crawl?

❑ Sit unsupported for a long time while playing with toys?

❑ Try to "help" with routines like dressing or bathing?

❑ Pull himself up to a stand?

❑ Imitate adult actions like waving?

SHARED COMMUNICATION ACTIVITIES: MONTH TEN

Even as we add new exercises this month, continue having fun with the ones from the last two months, especially those that combine music and movement, encourage word imitation, and connect words to pictures. Your baby can still use the practice, and it's fascinating as a parent to see the qualitative changes in his abilities.

Communication ◆

Pick 'n' choose. This is a more advanced version of the *option* exercise ("The choice is yours") we did when your baby was eight months old. Now that your tot's on the verge of talking, instead of just presenting visual choices, we're adding names to the objects presented—a big developmental difference. You can let him make decisions when it comes to toys, snack items, dinner food, clothing—any baby thing will work. For best results, hold up each item and look at it as you name it. Ask "What want? Want ducky? (Look at it and pause) or froggy?" (Look at it.) If he takes both, don't resist, but hold them farther apart next time. To up the ante you could place a highly desirable item next to a lackluster one, say, a cookie next to a sock, and ask "What want?" Now his choice will have real consequences. Of course, have a nice chat about his selection. Choice-making is an *anytime activity*—do it whenever it seems natural and integral to the situation.

Follow the leader. Your baby's already doing things like clapping and waving when you do; now it's time to encourage him to add vocal imitations to the physical ones. The trick? Real action. Even the most reticent tot can be enticed to mimic your sounds when you add irresistible action into the mix. At the playground, sit on a slide or swing, set your little one on your lap, and say, "Wheeeeeeeeeee!" as you head down the chute or shoot up toward the sky together. (Don't forget to hold on to him!) Inspire him to "Wheeeeeeeee!" right along with you. Once he's got the sound and action thing together, try to get him to imitate your nonverbal sounds in other situations like saying "Mmmmmmm" as you both pretend to eat. If your baby seems resistant to these sound-action combos, use our old strategy of imitating him first. Just do whatever he's doing. After a few times, he won't know who's copying whom. After a short time, begin with your own sound again. This time he should chime in.

Every once in a while, you might find an opportunity to follow your baby's lead in this sound imitation game. One of my granddaughter's favorite things at this age was being bounced on a knee, and for some reason she loved making noises while being bounced—her sounds came out as *Uh-uh-uh-uh-uh!* She thought it was beyond hysterical when I *Uh-uh-uh-uh*-ed her right back. You've never seen such laughter! And to think we actually discovered this feel-good "game" quite by accident. You might, too.

Gimme, gimme. Your child has about thirty thousand to sixty thousand words to learn by adulthood—but not to worry. We can give him an excellent head start. When you see your baby play with something or examine an object as he starts to explore his environment, name the objects one at a time. Forget exotic appliances (cappucino maker) or tools (skill saw) and stick with common, everyday things found in his environment that he's familiar with, such as toys, clothing, or animals. After you've told him the words for various items and thoroughly explored them with him, hold up two objects for him—say a hat and cup, and ask him to give you one of them by name—"Give Mommy cup." (Or "Show me cup" or "Touch cup.") This is a good check to see if he's learned the name, and it takes advantage of your baby's growing penchant for passing objects back and forth.

Don't expect Junior to learn a name for something after hearing it only once. He'll need to hear a word repeatedly, as well as touch, taste, smell, feel, and see the object several times before he makes the connection. If he hands you the wrong object in this activity, gently tell him the name again and give it another shot. If he always picks the same object, it could be because he finds that one the most interesting. Try again with objects he'll find equally appealing. Make this a game, *not a drill*. Again, a do-anywhere activity.

Is there a doctor in the house? At about this time, your baby will become a little actor and pretend to cough, hiccup, or sneeze. Although these are not speech sounds per se, they're natural ways to make noises, and children find them tremendously amusing—especially when you act surprised or shocked or overly concerned for his health. Play along, or even mimic his pretend disorders. Keep it light and fun—maybe something like this:

CHILD: (Accidental or pretend burp)
ADULT: (Startles and looks at child) Ah! What that? (Pause, chuckle) Did you burp?
CHILD: (Makes noise)
ADULT: Oh! Stedman burp. Something in tummy. (Pause) Where tummy? (Puts mouth on Stedman's belly) Ptheb! (Raspberries on skin)
CHILD: (Giggles and giggles)
ADULT: Ooooo. Something silly in your tummy.

Spill the beans. If you or your child spills something by accident—which is sure to happen—simply comment, "Uh-oh!" It's an easy utterance for a child to imitate and the situation in which it's used is very specific, making it a perfect learning opportunity. Naturally, we don't want him dumping everything, especially food, but you can practice the *"Uh-oh!" response* by letting him knock over containers of non-messy items or block towers. Act surprised when the objects fall; ham it up. Give your little terminator a turn—babies adore knocking things over.

More vocalizations, please. While your baby continues to make gestures to get your attention, he should also be adding sounds now—an attention-getting shriek or an insistent squeal when he wants you to do something. Respond to his gestures *only* when they're accompanied by one of these kinds of sounds, or a word or wordlike noise. We're upping the ante again by making your tot's soundmaking more important in communication. If he makes a gesture out of your direct line of sight, just ignore it for a few seconds to give him a chance to attract your attention with a sound. If after ten seconds or so he doesn't come up with some sort of vocalization, reply to his gesture by reproducing it and talking about it. If he still refuses to make a sound, save the lesson for another time and respond to his gesture by giving him whatever he needs—along with plenty of TLC.

Cognitive Development ◆

No slacker, this stacker. As we briefly discussed, babies nearing their first birthday love to pile up things and topple them over. Now it's time to add a fresh dimension and variety to the activity with new and different shapes, colors, and sizes. In addition to stimulating motor maturity, stacking is an important cognitive skill that includes making a plan and executing it. You'll find lots of different kinds of stacking toys in toy stores, even some with brightly colored plastic rings and a stave for stacking, but household items can work just as well. Small, empty boxes are perfect for stacking. Boxes of differing sizes present a real mental challenge, especially if your little architect tries to put the smallest ones on the bottom.

Push, pull, lever, and switch. Last month, we attached a ribbon to an interesting object so your baby could get the desired object by pulling the ribbon toward him—a great way to learn about cause and effect. Commercial toys with switches and levers that cause bells to sound or animal figures to appear add a novelty to cause-and-effect training and make it much more interesting for your inquisitive tot. Some of the ones I find especially well-designed are included in the resources listed in Appendix E.

Hearing Stimulation ◆

Listening continues to be an important skill, especially as your baby readies himself for his first words. Remember, listening is active; hearing is passive, so encourage your baby to listen by providing interesting sound experiences. Words aren't the only noises; learning to listen is very inclusive. Bring his attention to barks, beeps, roars, tweets, purrs, music . . . you name it.

Music, please. Recorded music is extremely popular with this age group. Choose albums with easy songs in which the words are simple, well articulated, easy to understand, and the lyric lines are repeated often—but don't play it too loud. These factors raise the chances considerably that your little music lover will get involved and want to participate. A simple beat and a solo performer is often enough to keep a tot's interest. The first time you play the music, say the words along with the singer to make the words easier for your little one to understand. Later, as you listen together, add some little action like clapping, or sing a word or phrase at specific points in the song. Your tyke will learn to anticipate and become animated just before your solo part, and may even join in. "Dance" together or clap hands. This mom and her "party animal" know how to get down!

> ADULT: I'm a little teapot . . . yes, clap hands with Mommy.
> CHILD: (Claps)
> ADULT: Here is my handle . . . Where's handle?
> CHILD: (Imitates Mom's hands)
> ADULT: Yes . . . and here is my spout. Marcy do spout.
> CHILD: (Mimics)
> ADULT: La-la la-la la la la-la la! (Moves with hand still placed for teapot song) Dance!
> CHILD: (Moves in high chair)
> ADULT: Um-hm! Tip me over and pour me out! (Bends at the waist)
> CHILD: (Sways side to side)
> ADULT: Yeahhh! Marcy help Mommy sing.

By the way, don't assume that your tot will automatically take to *your* favorite artists—they may be an acquired taste. Play a few different selections and see which one your baby seems to like. If you're shopping for new CDs, listen to them before buying if possible (many stores have accommodations for this). I've included recommendations from several of my music-savvy ten-month-old friends in Appendix E.

Bring in da noise. Continue to call your baby's attention to noises around the house. When you hear a sound, tell him what it is, and talk about it. The tweak this month is that now your baby is old enough to expand the discussion into related areas. In the following conversational snippet, for instance, you can see that the mom has not only called her baby's attention to the sound of their pooch, but also introduced the concept of in

and out and the physical sensation of cold, *and* invited her tot to participate in the action as well—all in a context that makes perfect baby sense.

> ADULT: (Noise) Ooops! What's that? (Pause) Doggie. (Barks again) Doggie
> bark.
> CHILD: (Looks)
> ADULT: Doggie want in. Doggie cold. (Turns toward door) Help Mommy
> open door? (Picks up child and opens door) Okay. Doggie in. (Pause;
> lowers child to pat dog) Doggie cold.

Should you call your dog by his name instead of referring to him as
doggie as this mom does? Well, you could. It's a judgment call. *Dog* or
doggie is relatively easy for most children to say, so they're very likely to
use the word when they start to talk. If your pet's name has lots of consonants, especially *r, l,* or *th,* or has consonants next to each other, as in
Stripper or *Thumper,* it will be very difficult for your toddler to say. In
that case, *doggie* or *dog* would definitely be the better choice. Another
consideration: The generic *doggie* or *dog* can also be used to refer to more
animals than the name of one particular pooch, which gives your child
more flexibility to use the word. So all in all, you're probably better off
starting out with *doggie* or *dog*—or *kitty* or *cat,* if your pet is of the feline
persuasion.

Visual Stimulation ◆
More mirror play. For some reason babies—and alas, some adults—never
lose their fascination with mirrors. You can use it to your teaching advantage. Since Junior can now wave, clap, and copycat some of your other
movements, let's see if he can do it while looking in the mirror. This requires a little more cognitive skill, so it's a bit more challenging for him.
Hold him in your arms like you usually do, stand in front of a big dresser
mirror or full-length wall mirror, then make funny faces in the mirror (our
standard wiggly brows, waggly nose, eyelash batting, rubber rotary mouth
will do). See if he follows suit. Chat about what you're seeing and doing.
Do a little copycatting yourself. If your baby puts his arms in the air, do the
same, and then encourage him to follow your actions. Add actions of your

own—shrug your shoulders, wave, or sway side to side. Put on some music and dance together in front of the mirror, too. This can all be wonderfully entertaining as well as an excellent way to enhance imitation.

Sensory Stimulation ◆
How stimulating! Continue to play with toys of all different textures, shapes, sizes, and colors. This kind of sensory input is just as important now as in past months; perhaps even more so now. Our senses tell us about the world and our place in it. Your baby will soon be describing that world in words, and will talk about what he knows; you need to give him lots of experiences to talk about. Try playing with things like textured blocks of varying colors; plush teddy bears, dogs, and dolls in bright outfits; spongy balls of differing size and color; multicolored cellophane; shiny or vivid pieces of fabric; or colorful stacking rings. As you can see, you don't need fancy commercial items for this exercise. Everyday household objects, like colored dish sponges or empty plastic containers, will do the trick. As always, talk about your play as you go. Even ordinary things will take on more meaning for your baby when he experiences them physically *and* verbally. He'll understand function better when he hears the word for a certain object at the same time he watches it being used.

At this point though, your little one is not fully able to understand real distinctions of color and shape, so limit your chat to simple descriptions like *big, little, soft, hard, fuzzy,* and the like, and save phrases like *red sphere* and *lime green isosceles triangle* for his later years. Although young children are very capable of *discriminating* between different colors and find bright colors extremely attractive, they're not good at remembering the names. So for now, I'd stay away from color names—they're rarely among children's first descriptive words.

Motor Development ◆
Oops, gutter ball. Now that your baby can sit unsupported for long periods and has full, free use of his hands, ball rolling is a natural. So let's make it a little more of a challenge. Roll a beach ball or any other kind of large, soft ball to your baby like you normally would, but for this exer-

cise, roll it a little off to the side so it just misses him, or very lightly so it doesn't quite reach him. Encourage him to give chase. Most likely, he'll be crawling, so go easy, and definitely avoid hard rubber balls, golf balls, baseballs, or other coated balls. They tend to roll too far, are difficult for your budding athlete to hold, get lost under furniture, and have the potential to cause injury. Whew! Needless to say, talk as you roll. Suitable words for this game are *push, ball, me, uh-oh!, go,* and the like. Let's give a listen to a dad playing with his son:

> ADULT: (Sitting facing child at a distance of five to six feet) Daddy push ball.
> CHILD: (Ball goes to child; he holds it)
> ADULT: Push ball to Daddy. (Pause) Push ball.
> CHILD: (Pushes ball) Baw!
> ADULT: Ball! Harry push ball.
> CHILD: Baw!
> ADULT: Yes, ball. Daddy push ball. (Pushes ball to side of child) Uh-oh! Ball go bye-bye. Harry get ball. (Pause) Get ball, Harry.
> CHILD: (Crawls after ball)
> ADULT: Where ball? (Pause) Harry get ball! Good, Harry. (Pause) What do?
> CHILD: (Rolls ball, squeals)
> ADULT: Harry push ball.

Copycat games. At this age, you can take full advantage of your baby's ability and desire to imitate. We've talked about imitation a lot, but now the range of copycat behaviors you and your baby can share expands. They go from whole body movements—rolling across the floor together (you go first)—to facial exaggerations and sticking out your tongue. See if you can get your little tyke to imitate mouth movements like licking, making raspberries, kissing, and blowing horns or whistles. And of course, don't forget to keep up classic imitation games like clapping, peek-a-boo, "This little piggy," patty cake, "So big," and "Ahhh-boo."

You'd be surprised how much motor, mental, and talking stimulation goes on in these kind of activities. Beyond the obvious muscle movement development, your little one is perfecting his planning and movement control—both important cognitive skills. Imitation helps develop sequential memory and establishes the notion of using other people as teachers. Finally, if you can get your baby to replicate your mouth movements, you are right on the edge of his mimicking your sounds. And word imitation is just a blink away.

Let him help. Your baby has more motor skills than before and a small but growing sense of independence. So it's a good idea to let him take more responsibility for dressing, undressing, and feeding if he shows an inclination. Your little guy may be a long way from tying his shoes or cutting his own steak, but he still has some impressive skills. Typically, a ten-month-old can take off his hat, mittens, shoes, and socks; pull on a loose shirt or sweater after being helped with arm and head insertion; smooth the diaper tab; and eat with his fingers and an infant spoon. Remember to stay nearby and monitor his behavior. He may want to do it himself, but he'll still appreciate your help. A good rule of thumb is to work together, letting him take charge when he can.

Baby obstacle course. Obstacle courses can be fun, challenging, and are great for growing little muscles. Use big pillows and chair cushions. Put your baby on one side of a big pillow as you sit on the other, and encourage him to come to you. He might go over or around. Try a simple maze, but don't make it too complicated. Stay at floor level—and have fun.

Month Eleven

Your baby understands even more of the words he hears every day now, and is continuing to learn about problem solving. His ever-increasing abilities to anticipate outcomes and hunt for missing items are developing in parallel to his language abilities. Now he'll anticipate your spoken response, and later hunt for the right word for a specific situation. He's also responding strongly to simple color pictures now and, more important, taking some meaning from them. Children are not born with the ability to interpret pictures, and unlike adults, who take it for granted that a picture of a car is just that, babies have to learn to decipher the images . . . and your little guy is gearing up to do just that.

● ■ ▲

MILESTONE WATCHLIST:
Eleven-Month-Old

Does your child . . .

❑ Use meaningful words that you understand? Not all children will begin this early, but you may hear "Mama," "Dada," or "Me" used appropriately.

❑ Imitate nonspeech sounds?

❑ Imitate speech and gestures?

❑ Point when you ask, "Where's X?"

❑ Perform a routine activity when requested?

❑ Initiate "Peek-a-boo" and "So big?"

SHARED COMMUNICATION ACTIVITIES: MONTH ELEVEN

Communication ◆

"Where's X?" Although you've searched for objects with your baby before, we're now going to *ask him* to find them. The teaching emphasis shifts from finding objects to *responding to your question*. The "X" can be any baby-friendly object or person that interests your child. In this exercise, your tot will be learning to follow directions, take turns, and to identify objects and people by name. There are several variations—"Touch X," "Find X," "Where's X?" and "Show me X"—and they're all pretty simple.

"Touch X" is better for objects close by—just put several objects in front of your baby and ask him to touch a specific one. (Some babies respond better to "Give me X.") "Where's X?" "Find X," or "Show me X" can be used for people or things farther away since pointing in the right direction constitutes an astute answer. When your child touches or points, give him an enthusiastic, "Yes, there's X." If he doesn't touch or point, set an example for him; point and say, "There's X." Either way, have a nice conversation about the object or person pointed to. Keep your words simple; no fair asking, "Where's the triple fudge parfait with crème brulee sauce and whipped cream topping?"

Use it or lose it. As you play with your baby, chat about how the toys and objects are *used*. His early definitions will be based in part on the function of things. As he begins to talk, he may name a particular food or actually tell you how it's used. When you offer him a banana, for instance, he's just as likely to say "eat" as " 'nana." So give him some fuel for this language engine. There are lots of simple use or action words, such as *push, pull, roll, drink, wash, fall,* and the like. Our mantra: Talk as you "do." Let's eavesdrop on a play scene that incorporates the idea:

ADULT: Mommy push car. (Pause) Car go bye-bye.
CHILD: Bye.
ADULT: Yes, go bye-bye. (Pause) Car on road. Go fast.
CHILD: (Crawls over)
ADULT: Cindy want car?
CHILD: (Takes car; pushes)
ADULT: Cindy drive car. Cindy go bye-bye in car.

Easy does it. Up to this point, we've encouraged your baby to replicate your actions and sounds because young children learn much of their talking by imitating those around them. Now we make a qualitative leap. Try to get your little one to imitate *very simple words*. Remember the building blocks: CV or VC syllable words, such as *hi, go, out, eat, up, toy, see, ma, da [dad], hi, me, tea, shoe, bye, ear,* etc. are the easiest for eleven-month-olds. (Check extended list in Appendix C.) Also at this age, words only make sense in the appropriate context. Although your tot might say "Toy" immediately after you do, it won't help his comprehension unless a toy is nearby and visible. Asking him to say "Toy" when there's not one around will only confuse him.

Cognitive Development ◆
Far afield. Within reason, let your baby expand his exploration to include new items, within the house and yard. Exploring is the way in

which we find out about our world. Baby-proof the environment first, and then let him look under tables and into boxes, give him permission to open baby-friendly drawers or cupboards, let him taste new varieties of fruits and vegetables, and let him touch different texture surfaces. If you provide a simple running commentary it's even better. Give him new words to match the new experiences (don't ask him to say them yet). Your input will definitely help him process the information and understand his experiences as they broaden his worldview.

Hearing Stimulation ◆

Work it on out. Babies love music for its rhythmic, repetitive beat and the shared interactions associated with it. Continue to play music, but this month ask for a little more sound and action participation from your baby as you inspire him to dance with your own movements. Snuggle him up in your arms and turn and gyrate to the beat; hold his little hands as he stands and sways gently with you; or encourage him to move his upper body as he sits in his high chair or infant seat.

There are lots of repetitive actions he can do at this age that will help keep the dancing interesting, such as hand clapping or waving motions, body swaying or turning, and head nodding, turning, or shaking. When you do these kinds of movements at specific points in the music, your little one will begin to anticipate the action and join in. Then, if you add a little vocalization to the exercise, such as saying a word or sound in unison at a certain part of the song, you've got an activity that stimulates four important developmental areas—motor (dance movements), cognitive (the anticipation), hearing (the music), and verbal (communication). And there's another big bonus: Music is as beneficial to you as it is to your baby. It can soothe your frayed nerves, calm your mind, and lift your spirits—all very necessary for a new parent. Go with your favorite music—if you're inspired, your baby will be, too.

Visual Stimulation ◆

Kid, meet book. As you know, it's never too early to begin sharing books with your baby. Hopefully, you've already been "reading" and enjoying picture books together—which for the most part has meant looking at simple, colorful pictures of a single object while you said the word for it.

Now you can move on to bright, interactive picture books that contain pictures of *more than one object,* and that may even have textures like fake fur or spongy material added to enhance your little reader's sensory experience. Books about animals and transportation—trains, cars, planes, boats, etc.—are big hits at this age.

Although this is your child's first real introduction to the nature of reading, you don't have to actually read yet. Feel free to make up your own story as you go along, using the pictures as a guide; just keep it simple. It's really more about the concept of reading and using the book as an interactive tool. The pictures serve as a vehicle for introducing language into conversation. Have a little chat about what you see on the page and, of course, make it fun; this is not a school lesson. Your interaction could go something like this:

ADULT: Where farmer? (Pause) There farmer.
CHILD: (Points) Ah-er.
ADULT: Yes, farmer. Farmer on tractor.
CHILD: (Points again) Ah-er.
ADULT: Yes. Farmer on tractor. What see? (Pause) See piggy?
CHILD: (Points)
ADULT: Good! Piggy. (Pause) Pig in mud. Pig like mud.

Limit your "literary" sessions to about five to ten minutes. Your baby's attention span is still on the short side. If he wants to continue, of course, stick to it. Every tot is unique and will have slightly different wants and needs. Hold off a few months before introducing books with moving parts like pull-tabs since at this age they're likely to result in torn pages, and avoid books with pictures of angry or scary faces that might frighten your baby. (See Appendix E for names of terrific books for this age group.)

Sensory Stimulation ◆

Bubbles doubles. Have a bubble-blowing fest! Bubbles fascinate young children and are terrific fun for them. They also make for a developmental stimulation quartet—visual, motor, cognitive, and sensory. Your little one probably won't have the breath control to blow bubbles himself yet, so help him out by getting up close and blowing with him, then hold his hand while you wand bubbles together. As always, accompany the fun with words: *wet, up, go, big,* and *all gone* are naturals for this situation. Chances are he'll be more interested in watching the bubbles—and tasting them—than blowing. One tiny taste won't hurt, but watch it after that if you don't want a sick little papoose on your hands. You can find "bubble stuff" at most toy stores, or you can make your own solution simply by mixing the following:

> *1 cup water*
> *¼ cup dishwashing liquid*
> *1 teaspoon sugar (The sugar helps form a better, longer lasting surface on each bubble. Who would have guessed?)*

Motor Development ◆

Meatball catch. At this age, your little tyke will begin to throw objects— like plates of spaghetti, toys, silverware, clothing, you name it; nothing is off limits as far as he's concerned. It's a new skill and he'll work hard to perfect it. The reason throwing is such a big deal is because he's learning how to let go—how to release an object when he wants to. He's also learning to coordinate hand and arm movements, although his aim will still need lots of work. For now, his throw will be very primitive and in- clude only his arm and hand, not his shoulder and the rest of his body, but you have to start somewhere . . . and this is a momentous beginning!

To give him plenty of practice (and maybe save you cleaning up some of that spaghetti), encourage him to throw soft objects like stuffed ani- mals to you, then retrieve them and give them back to him, while talking about what you're doing. Say, "Throw teddy, Mommy." Then, "Good throw, Sammy. (Pause) Sammy strong!" He'll sit and repeatedly toss you things for minutes on end. Forget about throwing anything back to him— his catching ability is still a few months down the line. Meanwhile, his tossing and your retrieving is a great activity for instilling the idea of tak- ing turns, practicing language and motor skills—and all that bending and stooping is a great little workout for you!

Fill and empty again and again and . . . Dumping and filling, filling and dumping—it's fascinating business, at least for an eleven-month-old. A pail, shovel, and sand are the obvious way to go, but your baby's enjoyment will be enhanced and his hearing stimulated when you add noise to activity. Dropping clothespins or wooden blocks into a coffee can or cardboard oatmeal canister, then dumping them out, and refilling (ad infinitum) is just the ticket. Such a lovely sound! (Make sure that the container has no sharp edges.) This also presents an excellent opportunity to use words like *in, out, over, can,* and *on,* as well the names of the items dropped and dumped. Make a big fuss when the objects make a loud noise. Knowing that you enjoy the cacophony as much as he does makes it even more fun for him.

"Do as I do." This is the perfect time to incorporate the classic "Do As I'm Doing," song into your baby activity repertoire. In this simple version, say with pleasing lilt in your voice, "Do as I do, follow, follow me, do as I do, follow, follow me (Pause), X." Insert some physical action in the place of the X. The action can be anything that you know your baby can do, such as *clap hands, hit table, shake head, touch nose, pull ear,* or *make funny face.* You get the picture. The idea is to get your baby to physically imitate you. The lyric makes the whole process into a special game. After a few run-throughs, your little one will be anticipating your command with glee. Remember, the activity is "Do as I do," not "Do as I say." That means you have to demonstrate each action for him—don't expect him to be able to follow spoken commands. Make it fun. Babies love seeing their mommies and daddies act silly. Here's an example to get you going:

ADULT: (While clapping) Do as I do, follow, follow me, do as I do, follow, follow me . . . Shake arms! (Flaps arms and makes a funny face)
CHILD: (Flaps arms)
ADULT: Good! (Laughing) Fly like a bird! Fly!
CHILD: (Flaps arms more; squeals)
ADULT: Yes, shake arms.

For variation—"Do as I do," Part II—say what the action is as you do it, then when your baby begins to mimic your action, say "Stop!"as you come to a standstill. If, for example, the action is *kick leg,* kick your leg

repeatedly and say, "Kick leg." When your baby begins, say, "Stop."
Then repeat the sequence. Let's try it with another action:

> ADULT: (Shaking head) Shake head!
> CHILD: (Shakes head) Ahhhhhhh!
> ADULT: Kristen shake head. Make noise. Ahhhhhh? Stop! (Stops movement
> and noisemaking)
> CHILD: (Child stops)
> ADULT: (Looks shocked) Kristen stop.
> CHILD: (Giggles)

Peek-a-boo and So big. Peek-a-boo and the So bigs may sound like a rock
band, but they're favorite kiddie games for this age group. Although
you've played these before, your baby is more mature now and can fully
participate and do his part. With Peek-a-boo, take turns covering your
faces and surprising each other by removing your hands and revealing
your face. Add a little snuggle or tickle when you show your face to your
baby. With So big, you raise your child's arms as you declare "You are
sooooooooooooooo big!" He'll catch on quickly and get ready for his part
by raising his arms over his head.

Month-Twelve

*This is an exciting time! Your little one has already said his first word, or
will any minute. Encourage him to talk but don't put too much pressure
on him. There will be times when he would prefer to be silent, even when
he can say the word that you're asking him to say. He'll be especially resistant if the word is out of context. After all, why say "Cookie" when
you're in the bathtub? For a word to make sense to him, he needs to hear
it and use it in the context in which the word usually appears. Short, appropriate, and consistent names for objects, actions, places, and people
are more important now than ever. He's becoming more mobile as his
motor skills continue to develop, and his repertoire of possible activities
is expanding greatly. He'll soon be talking AND walking. If he's not
walking already, he'll at least be cruising—helping himself stand by using
furniture as he cautiously moves about—while holding on for dear life.*

● ■ ▲

MILESTONE WATCHLIST:
Twelve-Month-Old

Does your child . . .

❑ Babble in monologues when alone?

❑ Listen when others talk?

❑ Respond verbally when you ask him to say something?

❑ Repeat sounds or gestures when you laugh?

❑ Say one or more words consistently?

❑ "Talk" throughout the day to persons and objects?

❑ Vocalize to songs and rhythm play?

❑ Try to follow simple directions?

❑ Identify one or two body parts by name?

❑ Cruise (walking around while holding on to furniture)?

❑ Stand alone?

❑ Drink from a glass, with help?

❑ Respond physically to most requests?

SHARED COMMUNICATION ACTIVITIES: MONTH TWELVE

Communication ◆

Dress-up. While changing outfits isn't very high on the scale of twelve-month-olds' interests, they do love playing dress-up with different hats. So gather up all your different-colored visors, baseball caps, and winter head warmers, and mine your mom's and grandmother's closet for old, seldom-used chapeaus. Put the call out to friends, too. Once you've assembled your collection, you're ready to start having fun. Put on different toppers for your budding style guru, then wave and say, "Hello," changing your voice and taking on a new persona with each hat change. Then let him take a turn choosing hats and trying them on. Play by a mirror so he can look at himself if he's interested. It's a super game that can be played repeatedly, and while you're having fun, your little one is learning about pretend play and symbolism, as well as social skills. Keep the camera close at hand for this one—you're in for some priceless Kodak moments.

Original bedtime stories. Children love to hear about their own lives. Create very simple stories with your baby as the main protagonist. Incorporate familiar environments and routines, and tell tales about recent things that your baby's experienced. These stories can become more elaborate as he matures. Here's an example of one that's perfectly suited for him at this stage.

> ADULT: Mommy and Jack go store. Buy bananas. Did they buy bananas?
> CHILD: Yes. (Or shakes head)
> ADULT: Yes. And monkeys?
> CHILD: (Shakes head yes)
> ADULT: Monkeys? You're silly! Monkeys?
> CHILD: No!
> ADULT: Right. No monkeys at store. Buy milk?
> CHILD: Yes.
> ADULT: They buy bananas and milk. For monkey?

You get the idea. The story is interactive and allows your baby to participate. You could use a book with relevant pictures—say, a store or a banana in this case—to serve as an introduction and help set the scene, but stick to events that your child knows.

Say "X." Now that your little one is beginning to use single words, you can ask him to say particular words—"*Say X.*" He'll be overjoyed at being able to please you, and it will be thrilling for you to hear him say words. Keep your requests in check, though, since even the most patient child will get tired of it after a couple of encores. Don't overdo it. A few other reminders:

■ Ask him to say words only in contexts where the words are appropriate, so that the word makes sense to him.

■ Only request words that refer to things that are visually or audibly present. Although your baby's ability to extract words from his memory is rapidly expanding, he still needs a sight, sound, or other sensation to help him connect to the word in his memory.

■ Pick words that he has already said, or that contain sounds you know he can say.

■ Respond in a conversational way. If your baby repeats your word *Car*, for instance, say something like, "Yes, car go fast."

■ Vary the way you make your request. Instead of always asking him to "Say X," try "Tell me X" or say the word then, "What's this?" as in "Teddy, what's this?" You can also have an older child or other adult mimic words after you say them without your requesting it. Look at the other person as he speaks, then look at Junior—maybe, just maybe, he'll say the word, too. But remember that your baby still has limited short-term memory and will likely remember only the last two words of any given sentence, so if you want him to say a particular word, make sure you put that word at the end of the sentence.

■ Only ask for one word at any given time. Don't ask him to "Say X and X."

■ Keep it fun!

A body of words. Explore your bodies with words. We've done this exercise before, but in this advanced version, we want to supply the words for all the easy-to-say, obvious body parts, and encourage your baby to repeat the words after you. Remember that your baby can't see his own face, so let him look into a mirror, or use your face when you point out and name the parts. Many facial features and body parts are easy for a twelve-month-old to say—*eye, nose, tongue, tummy, hand, toe, foot, knee, neck, ear, arm, finger, cheek,* and *chin,* for example—so don't get academic here. *Gluteus maximus* is out, and muscle groups, bones, or internal organs are against the rules.

Cognitive Development ◆

Pretend food. This little game nurtures a brand-new cognitive skill that your baby is just beginning to grasp. He's now gaining the ability to represent one thing with another, albeit still in a limited way. You'll see it in his play as he moves toy cars and dolls around in realistic ways or does things like use paper for a doll's blanket. Using one item to represent another like this is called *symbolic play,* and it's a big step toward learning language since it relies on a similar concept. Words, after all, are essentially a representation of something.

One fun way to encourage symbolic play is to have a feast with pretend food (and it's a perfect diet if you're counting calories!). You can use toy "chinaware" or any old plastic dishes, cups, or bowls you have around. Variations are as limitless as your imaginary menus. Here's a mom sharing a delicious pretend breakfast:

MOM: Seth make food? (Pause) For Mommy?
CHILD: (Smiles and hands bowl)
MOM: Oh, my favorite! Oatmeal. Mmmmm! (Pause) Seth eat? (Pause) Seth eat.
CHILD: (Takes a pretend mouthful; smiles and makes sound)
MOM: Yes, good oatmeal. Want more.
CHILD: Maw!
MOM: Yes, more. More juice, too.
CHILD: Doose! (Pretends to give juice)
MOM: More juice. (Pause) Mmmmmmm! Juice. Where Mommy's oatmeal?

The old shell game. At this stage in your baby's cognitive development, he should already be able to find objects that he's watched you hide, and recognize them when he finds them. This variation on the old shell game fine-tunes that skill. Hide a tasty morsel of food under a paper or plastic cup—use clear plastic until he gets the idea—and ask him to find it.

Now you can also ask him to find things that he didn't see you hide. This is a new skill, so make it easy for him at first. Hiding an electronic or wind-up noisemaking toy works great, since it continues to make noise as your little sleuth searches, providing a little friendly assistance as well as hearing stimulation. You could also conceal these prehidden items under a thin cloth at first, so that he can discern the shape of the object and find it easily. Hiding things in boxes and other difficult areas will come later—no jumping the gun.

Exploring beyond home base. It's time for your little intrepid explorer to expand his horizons further. Take your baby to a petting zoo or airport. Let him experience people and places in all their varied forms. Talk as you travel, introducing him to new words for things and giving him simple explanations about what they are.

Hearing Stimulation ◆
More music. Your baby's love of music continues. Try playing anything from Mozart to Bossa Nova to The Beatles to Britney Spears. Take clues from your little one—at this stage you should be able to tell from his smiles—or lack thereof—whether he prefers the Fab Four to a Brazilian beat. There's also lots of baby music available on the market these days—much more than when my kids were little. (Check Appendix E for a list of my favorites.)

Another way to go is to sing your own renditions of popular baby songs and personalize them for your baby—and, of course, have him join in. Repeat the words over and over again so your little one can learn them with the music. "Mary Had a Little Lamb," for example could be modified into something like this:

Adam is a big, big boy
Oh, so big
Oh, so big
Adam is a big, big boy
In his new, red coat

or

Little Martha
Sing and dance

Sing and dance
Sing and dance
Little Martha
Sing and dance
With her mommy now.

You won't win a Grammy, but you'll probably get some baby giggles and maybe a big wet baby kiss—and that's tons better, if you ask me.

Visual Stimulation ◆

More and more books. From here on your baby will become increasingly interested in children's books. Now that he's almost speaking and has the basic concept of books and pictures, you can add more to his experience with additional interaction and lots of give-and-take conversations. Use books as a vehicle to share topics suggested by the pictures. Now you can move beyond questions like "What's this?" and expand into comments, and even broach subjects that are related but not part of the book. In the following scenario, for example, the mom has used the picture of a dog in the book to talk to her child about the family's dog.

> ADULT: I see something. What that? (Points to book)
> CHILD: Doggie.
> ADULT: Yes, that dog. Antwon have dog.
> CHILD: (Points) Dog.
> ADULT: Yes, Antwon's dog. Dog's name is . . . (Wait for him to say it if he can)
> CHILD: Dog!

Don't worry about the book's plot at this point. The goal is to use the pictures to gain, hold, and focus your child's attention so you can share communication. One caution . . . he may want to help turn the pages, and he has a strong grip at this age, so board books are still best. (See Appendix E for some of my hands-down favorites.)

Sensory Stimulation ◆

Rub-a-dub-dub. Baths are as comforting and relaxing for children as they are for adults, making them a great place for babies to explore and learn. Play and talk with your tot about things that float—and things that don't—and discuss the things he feels and sees as you introduce him to easy bathtime words like *wet, soap, bubble, splash, wash, hair,* and *tub.* There are some wonderfully innovative tub toys on the market these days. Mega Bloks Block Boat, for instance, includes eighteen bright colorful blocks, a little floatable captain, a dinghy, a bubble-making smokestack, *and* a tow-ring that doubles as a bubble-blowing ring! Think of the conversation opportunities there! As you play, push the toys under the water and play "All gone," then let them bob to the surface and search together for the soap—a variation on finding hidden objects. Here's one mom who's managed to squeeze in lots of language with only a bar of soap and a rubber ducky as props.

> ADULT: Oops! Where soap? (Pause) Soap under water.
> CHILD: Soap.
> ADULT: Help Mommy find soap. (Pause) Find soap.
> CHILD: (Finds it) Soap! (Holds it with both hands)
> ADULT: Yes, soap. Amare find soap.
> CHILD: (Drops soap) Uh-oh!
> ADULT: Oops! Soap in water again. Soap all gone. Now where soap? (Reaches for toy) Here ducky! (Squeaks it) Duck stay on top.
> CHILD: Duck. (Squeak, squeak)
> ADULT: Amare play with duck. (Pause) Mommy find soap.

It's a good idea to arm yourself with a net storage bag that allows for air circulation and keeps wet tub toys from growing the dreaded "green fuzzies." And remember never to leave your child unattended in the tub.

Motor Stimulation ◆

Tune-up fine motor skills. As your baby matures, fine motor development in his hands and fingers become increasingly important. At this age, he'll most likely become fascinated by toys with small switches, dials, and slides that he can move and manipulate. Bead frame toys, such as Pathfinder Rollercoaster by Anatex Enterprises, are also big hits with

Shared Communication Activities:
Months 10, 11, and 12

MONTHLY ACTIVITIES

Age (Mos.)	Communication	Cognitive Development	Hearing Stimulation
10	▲ Pick 'n' choose ▲ Follow the leader ▲ Gimme, gimme ▲ Is there a doctor in the house? ▲ Spill the beans ▲ More vocalizations, please	▲ No slacker, this stacker ▲ Push, pull, lever, and switch	▲ Music, please ▲ Bring in da noise
11	▲ "Where's X?" ▲ Use it or lose it ▲ Easy does it	▲ Far afield	▲ Work it on out
12	▲ Dress-up ▲ Original bedtime stories ▲ "Say X" ▲ A body of words	▲ Pretend food ▲ The old shell game ▲ Exploring beyond home base	▲ More music

Shared Communication Reminders
- Be a good role model
- Don't interrupt
- Expand your baby's world
- Don't expect your tot to get it right each time
- Try not to be critical of your baby's speech
- Use appropriate, simple, and useful words

Visual Stimulation	Sensory Stimulation	Motor Development
▲ More mirror play	▲ How stimulating!	▲ Oops, gutter ball
		▲ Copycat games
		▲ Let him help
		▲ Baby obstacle course
▲ Kid, meet book	▲ Bubbles doubles	▲ Meatball catch
		▲ Fill and empty again and again and . . .
		▲ "Do as I do"
		▲ Peek-a-boo and So big
▲ More and more books	▲ Rub-a-dub-dub	▲ Tune up fine motor skills

- Imitate wordlike vocalizations
- Use your child's name when referring to him
- Encourage your baby to initiate communication
- Respond appropriately
- Take advantage of pointing and vocalizing
- Sing at bedtime

the twelve-month-old set. They come in all shapes and sizes, but all are essentially brightly colored wooden beads that slide up, down, and around gently bent and twisted pieces of colored aluminum tubing. The tubing, which is often in the shape of an animal, is mounted to a wooden base for stability. Your tot gets to move the beads along the tubing and when he let's go the beads take off sliding down and around on their own—sort of like a miniature roller coaster. The toys are brilliant for stimulating eye-hand coordination, as well as spatial insight, concentration, observation of colors and shapes, and even hearing stimulation as the beads bang together. They also provide opportunity for new vocabulary words within your communication. All in all a winner, and available at all toy stores.

CHAPTER TEN

Months 13, 14, and 15

Now We're Talking!

Progress Report

MOTOR

ALTHOUGH your baby's overall growth rate is slowing down, she's still growing in leaps and bounds—especially developmentally. Her walking, while still adorably wobbly, is progressing nicely. It'll take her quite a few months and lots of determination to perfect it—tricky maneuvers like starting, stopping, and cornering require lots of practice. Like an airplane pilot who needs some serious time in the cockpit to perfect his flying skills, your little one needs some concentrated "ground hours" to fine-tune her walking skills. But that won't stop her from indulging in some serious baby locomotion. By fifteen months, she'll be experimenting with running, and then . . . look out! My sons were fifteen months old when my daughter was born, and if you think one nimble-footed toddler is a handful, try dealing with two of them and a newborn at the same time. Chaos is *not* an understatement. Thank heavens for that twin stroller!

Unless you too have twins, most of your baby's play and exploration will be solitary and nonsocial. When she plays near other young children, she'll usually play side-by-side without a lot of interaction (called *parallel play*). She'll still love playing with you, though, not just because you're special, but because she knows something of your behavior and can anticipate what you'll do. She doesn't know that about other children—they're less predictable.

As her grasp becomes more coordinated, your cutie will use her hands more for touching, pushing, pulling, and lifting, and, as a consequence, bring fewer things to her mouth for exploration—happy days! She'll roll, push, and even kick a ball, although the kick will be more like walking into it, and she'll be able to throw better, too. She may not be Little League material yet, but by fifteen months she'll have a lovely, if primitive, whole-arm toss. Her aim, need I say, still has a long way to go. Even more important than her burgeoning athletic skills, your baby now possesses the ability to use *tools*. Not dad's table saw, obviously, but tools that are *extensions of herself*—like using yardsticks or broom handles to snag unreachable objects. Nothing will be safe! A year ago, "out of sight" meant "out of mind." Not anymore. Now, she'll fish that ball from under the sofa with any "tool" she can find.

COGNITION

With her increased memory, your baby will be able to transfer learning between different situations more easily—if she learns that flicking a switch turns on the light, she'll try using a switch to activate other things, too. By fifteen months, she'll be able to plan new strategies by combining ideas from previous encounters instead of going through physical trial and errors. Faced with the challenge of getting items from a container, for instance, she'll actually think and consider the best way to do it, rather than just going at it randomly. Gradually, over the next year, she'll gain the ability to concentrate on two things simultaneously. She'll also be able to anticipate movement. When she sees something, like a rolling ball, for instance, she'll be able to predict where it will go. Add this to her rudimentary knowledge of time and order gleaned from daily routines, and you have a formidable little problem solver. Now that she can walk and investigate, she'll explore her world more actively and, with your help, learn new names for all the new and wonderful things she encounters as she goes.

COMMUNICATION

As her self-awareness increases and she realizes she has the ability to influence others, your little one will make more of a play for the spotlight. She may yell or scream for attention, and assert herself by going against your wishes. It won't be as bad as the dreaded "terrible twos," but you'll notice the difference in her behavior. She'll dawdle when you need her to hurry, rush off when you want her to stay, and "No" will become a favorite word. Her growing sense of self will also be reflected in her notion of possession. Everything will become *mine*. Fortunately, "no" and "mine" aren't the only words she'll acquire.

During the first few months after she begins talking, your baby's vocabulary will grow slowly. Her speech will consist mostly of single words or words that are mixed in with jargon (those intonation patterns that seem like speech but really aren't), and when she tries to repeat adult phrases like *all gone* and *go up* they might come out as single words. Your toddler will have her own personal dictionary that reflects her environment, but since your baby's experiences with her surroundings are so much more limited than yours, her definition of things will be considerably more limited as well. The most common word categories for one-year-olds are names of family members (including herself), animal names (and the sounds they make), body and facial parts, clothes, common objects such as *cup*, toys, action words, descriptors such as *big*, feelings such as *tired* or *hungry*, and greetings.

Don't expect perfect pronunciation yet—remember, the words your toddler chooses to say reflect the sounds and syllables she can easily produce. The easiest speech sounds for her now are consonants that are formed in the back and front of the mouth—*g, k, h*, and *b, p, w, m*—and most vowels. Some consonants like *l, r*, and *th* will still be a bit difficult, and consonant blends, such as *sl, bl, br, str*, and *tr* will take a few years to master. So go slow and easy. Just supply words for all the new things and actions she experiences and let her pick and choose which ones she wants to imitate. Even when she does mimic a word she still may need to hear it repeatedly over time before she adds meaning to it and makes it her own. The way you use a new word and what you say about it helps your little budding linguist form a meaning. When she talks, she'll use words in a familiar context with only partial understanding. Meanings form slowly from repeated exposure.

SHARED COMMUNICATION TIPS AND REMINDERS

- **Continue to encourage talking and comprehension.** Now that your tot understands much of what you say, real, albeit limited, dialogues are more possible. Talk about what will happen in the immediate future, as well as what's happening now. Discuss things in your immediate environment that she can see, feel, smell, and hear; tell her what you're doing as you do it; and expand upon her words. Remember to speak slowly, clearly, and simply. At this point you understand more of your toddler's words than any other family member or friend. Use that knowledge to its best advantage—talk with your baby in caring, real, and meaningful ways.

- **Treat your child as a participant and conversational partner,** not just an observer. Take turns—always give her a chance to talk after you say something. Allow her a chance to be in a real conversation, and even if you don't understand much of what she says, respond to what you think she's trying to tell you. Don't stop an interaction to correct pronunciation or grammar; just provide a model based on what she said and move on, as in this example:

  CHILD: Mommy doe. (Rhymes with hoe)
  ADULT: Yes, mommy **go.** Mommy **go** work.
  CHILD: Doe car.
  ADULT: Um-hm, mommy **go** in car. **Go** work in car.

- **Teach by imitation.** Teach your tot new words by saying them and asking her to say them after you. Don't overdo it—just a few times per request. Try to pick words that incorporate sounds she already makes and be sure these words are relevant to your immediate surroundings, lest she get confused or overwhelmed. A few easy words for one-year-olds: *baby, bye-bye, cookie, doggie, bed, juice,* and the like. (Check Appendix C for more baby-friendly words.)

- **Play show-me-how games.** Expand your baby's action verb vocabulary by having her act out the actions named. Use verbs like *dance, drink, eat, jump, read, run, sit,* and *sleep.* This activity guarantees lots of laughs and chuckles—have fun!

- **Pull toys out, name them, then play.** Pulling toys or other objects out of a chest or a bag one at a time is a terrific way to introduce new items, since it adds elements of surprise and theatrics to the event. Be sure to say the name for each item *several times* as you introduce it, and to use the objects in their intended way. An example:

  ADULT: (Pulling toy out of bag) What's this? (Pause) It's a top.
  CHILD: Top.
  ADULT: Top! Watch. (Operates top) Top spin. (Pause) Top go round.
  CHILD: Go.
  ADULT: Yeah, top go. Uh-oh! All done. (Pause) Top done. No more spin. (Pause)
  CHILD: Go.
  ADULT: Okay. Let Mommy help.

- **Bring out your baby's inner decorator.** Pictures are increasingly important and encourage interest in books. Give your tot a space of her own to decorate. Stick some Velcro on the back of small reinforced pictures and let her arrange them to her liking on a Velcro strip affixed to a piece of bright cloth or board in her room. Or she could "hang" her art on a metal surface with big fridge magnets. Chat about the pictures, and help her update the art gallery regularly.

- **Participate in shared reading.** Your toddler is now beginning to relate to the two-dimensional world of books. Talk about the pictures in a way that helps her connect the images to the things in the environment they represent. Picking books that depict familiar, everyday events and objects will help her relate and aid her comprehension.

Month Thirteen

By now your little one most likely has a favorite few words that she says regularly, like Mama, Dada, and doggie, and understands a lot more words than she's able to say. Many of her words are probably still mixed with jargon (those charming, meaningless baby sounds with adult inflection) and gestures, such as reaching for a cookie as she says the word for it. As her language and cognitive abilities improve, your thirteen-month-old is taking even a greater interest in books, physical problem solving, and play, and is starting to feel more like a real participant in the family. Although our activities focus on play and learning, don't forget essentials like rolling, hugging, and cuddling together. We all need that!

● ■ ▲

MILESTONE WATCHLIST:
Thirteen-Month-Old

Does your child . . .

❑ Say five or more single words?

❑ Use vocalizations and words more during interactions?

❑ Tell what she wants by verbalizing, vocalizing, pointing, and gesturing?

❑ Hand objects to you when you ask for them?

❑ Understand approximately ten words?

❑ Help with dressing or bathing by holding out her foot or arm?

❑ Look at pictures in books and help turn the pages?

❑ Imitate other children physically and vocally?

❑ Understand words and phrases when gestures are used?

❑ Walk without assistance?

SHARED COMMUNICATION ACTIVITIES: MONTH THIRTEEN

Communication ◆

Phone call for you. Telephones are super-appealing to children at many ages—this one especially. Your tot has been patiently watching you on the phone for months; now let's give her a chance. Although it's a stretch to expect her to talk to someone she can't see, your little one might be lured into phone chat if she can see the other person. So have your spouse or partner talk on the cell phone or an extension of your landline while your tot uses another phone in the same room. With the additional input of see-ing *as well as* hearing her conversational partner, your baby may just start chattering away. If she does, have her phone partner slowly slip around the corner and out of sight, and see if your little chatterbox continues.

Dress for success. Continue to play dress-up with hats, but now add other accessories like gloves, scarves, or maybe even a big glittery brooch into the mix (no sharp edges, please). Try to include various interesting tex-tures—velvet, fleece, silk, chenille, corduroy, and others. Dress-up is not just for girls, by the way; boys find it great fun, too. New clothes signal a new persona and can lead to interesting pretend games. You or your tot could put on gardening gloves and a big sunhat like Grandma wears, then get down on your knees and make believe you're pulling weeds just like she does. Or you could be Grandpa golfing, or Auntie Jane cooking, or big brother driving the car—you get the idea. Imitating each other in front of a mirror adds another dimension.

Peek-a-boo family. Learning family and pet names is important, especially for later sentence building. Glue family photos on foam or sturdy paper plates. (You can get color Xeroxes made for about a dollar if you want to save your originals. Of course, digital images are easy and inexpensive to print.) Use the photos in creative ways to elicit language from your child. Play peek-a-boo with the photo-plates or, after showing your baby a quick flash of the photo, flip it around to the blank side and ask who's on the other side. Get excited when you see who it is—"Oh look! It's Aunt Matilda!"

Director on the set! Now that your baby is using more language and under-stands more, you can use directions to help her complete routine tasks like dressing and eating. Here, for example, is a dad helping his budding fashionista get her ensemble together for her morning outing:

ADULT: Let's get dressed. Where sock? (Pause) Find sock.
CHILD: Sock! (Picks up sock)
ADULT: Yes (Big smiles), Emme find sock. Sock on.
CHILD: Sock! (Tries to put sock on foot)
ADULT: Um-hm, sock on. (Pause) Put toe in. (Pause) Daddy help?
CHILD: Hep.
ADULT: Okay, sweetie, Daddy help. (Places Emme's toes in sock) Pull sock on. (Pause) Pull on. (Pause) Good girl!

Don't be too bossy—remember it's no fun being told exactly what to do every time. Work with your little one and allow her to do what she can with your very gentle guidance and direction.

Be "en-CHANTING." Turn whatever you're doing into a song. African mothers do it in the form of a chant, and it's an excellent way for babies to hear a word over and over in the appropriate situation. I've suggested similar activities before, but now *context and real words are key*. Now it's important for your toddler to hear repetitions of words in relevant situations. Try adapting some of these classic children tunes:

"Are you sleeping? (Frere Jacques)"
"Here We Go 'round the Mulberry Bush"
"London Bridge"
"Mary Had a Little Lamb"
"Row, Row, Row Your Boat"
"This Is the Way We Wash Our Clothes"
"To Market, To Market"
"Twinkle, Twinkle, Little Star"

Let's try one. First choose an activity—let's say bathtime. Now choose a song—how about "Mary Had a Little Lamb." The song might go something like this:

Daddy washing Kelly's face,
Kelly's face, Kelly's face,
Daddy washing Kelly's face,
Now Kelly's face is clean.

I'm sure you get the idea. This is a great way to introduce new words and phrases, and to let your toddler hear them over and over again without boring or overwhelming her. Repetition is critical for learning—but this makes it fun and easy. My daughter, Jessica, sang constantly with my granddaughter Cassidy when she was a baby. Now at four, Cassidy serenades her mom during their morning snuggles. Jessica said she was almost in tears one morning when Cassidy's song was all about how much she loved her "very special mommy." So start singing—with those potential rewards in store, it's worth every off-key note.

Cognitive Development ◆

Explore more. Continue to help your baby with her exploration of new and different situations that challenge her understanding and problem-solving ability, such as opening containers, finding surprises under furniture, and looking into storage closets. Don't be afraid to tell her what's off limits. Sure, we want her to grow cognitively, but we also want to keep her safe. Never leave your toddler alone outside, and child-proof the house:

- Remove any harmful substances from your house or put them in *locked* cabinets. There's nothing a thirteen-month-old likes better than pulling everything out of cupboards and drawers.

- Don't leave matches or lighters around.

- Put your antique origami collection out of reach.

- Make sure that toys are age-appropriate and don't have small parts, which can cause choking.

- Block stairs and open windows with safety gates, and put covers on electrical outlets.

As your toddler explores, give her the appropriate words for all the various new things she sees and hears. Be consistent in your names and descriptions. Visit previously unexplored venues like a marina, the farmer's market, your neighborhood park, a petting zoo, or a flower shop. You can boost your tot's interest and learning by reading a book together that centers on the location or its attractions before or after you go.

Hearing Stimulation ◆
Sound off! The world is a great classroom for sounds as well as sights. As you venture farther from home with your toddler, make sure that you name noises that she hears, such as chirping birds, barking dogs, slamming doors, rumbling trucks, rustling leaves, howling wind, and whirring appliances. You'd be surprised how much more you hear, too, when you're really listening for things to share with your little companion. When you have the capacity to turn noises on or off, like you can with your Cuisinart, vacuum cleaner, or hair dryer, tell your toddler what she's about to hear just *before* you turn the appliance on. That gives her a chance to anticipate the sound so she won't be startled, and helps grow those important cognitive pathways.

Visual Stimulation ◆
Pop-goes-the-whatever. Pop-ups and other kinds of toys that surprise (not frighten) are fun and excellent for visual memory at this age. Aside from the visual stimulation, they help your baby learn to anticipate, plan, and problem solve. A few of the better pop-up toys are listed in the resources in Appendix E for you. But of course, you can also pop-up your own creations—puppets, dolls, or any visually interesting objects. Ask your tot, "Where's Elmo?" and when she guesses, have Elmo pop up and play. (You can substitute any fun or lovable toy or object for Elmo.)

Sensory Stimulation ◆
Edible finger paints. Let me get the disclaimer out of the way right up front. This activity may sound odd, but it's really fun. Toddlers love it, and it's a sensory bonanza. The activity? Finger painting with different flavors of yogurt! The different flavors vary just enough in color to make for some . . . well, *interesting* art, and the licking of fingers in-between is always a big hit.

Plus, you can have some scintillating conversations about the aesthetics, the tastes and the textures, and there's no end to new descriptive words: *yummy, gooey, sticky, smooth, icky, tasty, slippery,* just to name a few. It's not even as messy as it sounds. Get the smallest size yogurt containers—you'll only need a scoop or two from each one for "painting" (save the rest for snacks); and for your canvas you can tape a big piece of paper to the table, high chair, or floor. Just toss it in the trash when you're done. (Oh, and keep a roll of paper towels nearby.) Also, make sure that in the future your toddler doesn't confuse other *nonedible* finger paints with these tasty yogurt ones. As a good general rule, always keep all bona fide paints out of reach.

Motor Development ◆

Muscling in. Now that your baby is up and running (so to speak), you'll want her play box to include lots of toys that require different muscle movements. There's an infinite variety of push and pull, sorting and nesting, building (and destructing), and rolling push-and-go toys, like lawn mowers, wagons, vacuum cleaners, and vehicles. The toys are ideal for gross and fine motor development, and the variety gives you plenty to talk about. And don't forget good old standbys like big balls and small plastic bats.

The new and improved pots 'n' pans band. Reintroduce this dubious musical treat if it's been neglected for a few months. You won't believe how your child's motor skills have improved. This activity is not suggested for the morning after a big cocktail party. If you've never had the pleasure of hearing a kiddie kitchen band, get out the pots and pans (or better yet, let your toddler pull them out—she'll love that!), select a few wooden or metal spoons, and let your thirteen-month-old go to town. It's terrific exercise for muscle control. Put a towel over the pots before the "music" begins if you have sensitive ears.

Step lightly. Your toddler may be cruising around, but she has a lot to learn before she becomes a proficient walker. You can aid this development by helping her practice turning and stepping over *small* obstacles like a wooden spoon or hose. No hurdle jumping, please. Keep the obstacles close to the ground and hold your tot's hand. Make it a game and have fun. For a twist, show her how to do it and then pretend to trip and fall down and have a big laugh about it—"Whoops! Mommy fall down!" That way, when she trips up—which she inevitably will—it won't seem like a big deal. After all, even Mommy falls.

Month Fourteen

By now, your toddler has most certainly discovered the glory of the word "No!" She understands it and has, in all probability, tried it out more than a few times. Other simple, but happily less irksome, one-syllable words also fill her small, constantly growing vocabulary. Your little miss now understands simple questions like "What's that?" and "Where's X?" which paves the way for more word games, sets an example for initiating conversation, and presents more opportunities for dialogue. Her walking also continues to mature, and may take ever increasing amounts of her energy, sometimes to the detriment of talking. It's difficult to perfect more than one skill at a time, so be patient and continue being a good conversational partner. Before long, she'll try to walk, talk, and explore objects all at the same time!

● ■ ▲

MILESTONE WATCHLIST:
Fourteen-Month-Old

Does your child . . .

❑ Shake her head *yes* and *no*?

❑ Imitate some animal sounds?

❑ Imitate most one-syllable words?

❑ Comprehend simple questions? At this age most children understand *what* and *where* questions.

❑ Enjoy acting out routines from home, such as housework?

❑ Explore physically?

SHARED COMMUNICATION ACTIVITIES: MONTH FOURTEEN

Communication ◆

Starring teddy. Your tot's favorite teddy bear is now ready for primetime. Here he gets to strut his stuff as he performs pretend actions that you and your little one sing about. Use the melody from the old song "The Bear Went over the Mountain" (it's the same tune as "He's a Jolly Good Fellow") to sing about Teddy's activities—any happenings familiar to your little one has lyric potential. The teddy bear:

Brushes his/her teeth

Takes a bath

Cooks his/her dinner

Goes for a walk

Sleeps in his/her bed

Washes his/her dishes

Puts his/her clothes on (Puts on his/her . . .)

Eats his/her . . .

Watches TV

Combs his/her fur

Have you ever seen? Your child already has a growing sense of silliness and, like other toddlers, probably loves animals. This little activity, based on the song "Have You Ever Seen a Lassie," nurtures them both. The lyrics of the original song, which is about a young Scottish girl, are:

Have you ever seen a lassie, a lassie, a lassie.
Have you ever seen a lassie go this way and that?

Here are our variations. Take your pick—or make up your own.

Did you ever see a kitty sleeping in a hat?
Did you ever hear a doggie barking like a cat?
Did you ever kiss a fishy while bathing in the tub?
Did you ever hug your mommy when her eyes are closed? (Close your eyes
  and wait for the hug!)

Sing the last line as a question, and talk about how deliciously silly the words are. If you don't know the "Lassie" tune, substitute "Twinkle, Twinkle, Little Star." It will work just as brilliantly with just a little creative modification on your part.

"That's negative, sir." Right about now, as we discussed, you'll be getting a lot of "No's" from your tyke—either verbally or with a head shake. That's okay, it's perfectly normal as she starts to assert her independence. The trick is not to take these negatives personally, but simply respond to them as serious communication attempts. Here's a dad who's got the right idea:

> DAD: Here's your juice, sweetie.
> CHILD: No!
> DAD: No juice?
> CHILD: No!
> DAD: Okay. No juice. Daddy drink juice. Mmmmmm, good.
> CHILD: No!
> DAD: No juice for Daddy?
> CHILD: (Shakes head no)
> DAD: Hannah want juice?
> CHILD: (Reaches for juice)
> DAD: Yes, Hannah want juice.

If ploys like this don't work and you still get constant negative responses, offer choices. Instead of asking questions like "Do you want juice?" to which you'll get a resounding *"NO!"* ask "Do you want juice or milk?" and hold them both out for her to choose. If she refuses both, then simply move on to the next activity. I believe in real consequences. A consequence of saying "No" to *everything* is that you don't get *anything*. It's also a good idea to have one of your older children or your partner set a good example. Ask them if they want something, and when they say "Yes" reward them with some yummy treat.

Grunts, growls, and assorted moos. Whenever you and your baby are reading or playing with toy animals, be sure to include the appropriate proper animal noises. Ask your tot, "What does a cow say?" or "A doggie says . . . ?" (Await a response.) Obviously, your little animal lover can't ask these questions of you yet, so consider her pointing to the pictures or toys as a cue to start meowing, barking, mooing, ribitting, tweeting, or any other relevant sound. Be theatrical and entertaining. You may not win a Tony, but your audience will be more appreciative than any Broadway play–loving crowd.

What and where? Now is the perfect time to start asking *what-* and *where-* type questions. Your toddler should understand both, and you're teaching her about names of things and locations, two categories of words that will be useful to her later when she's able to speak in longer phrases. Since she's going to try to repeat the name of whatever object you ask for, make sure you request things with names that your toddler can pronounce. It might go something like this:

ADULT: Where ball?
CHILD: Ball!
ADULT: Um-hm. Where ball?
CHILD: (Reaches into box where ball is not) In.
ADULT: I don't think . . .
CHILD: (Pulls out doll)
ADULT: Not ball. What that?
CHILD: Baby.
ADULT: Yes, baby! (Pause) Oh, Audra hug baby.

Also encourage your little one to ask *what* and *where* questions herself by showing her various objects or by hiding things. Let's change the previous situation just slightly.

ADULT: See ball? (Looks around)
CHILD: Ball!
ADULT: Um-hm. Mommy can't find ball. Audra find ball?
CHILD: Where?
ADULT: Where ball? (Pause) Audra look in box.

CHILD: (Pulls out funny stuffed animal)
ADULT: Not ball.
CHILD: What?
ADULT: Funny doggie.

Notice that Mom pretended not to know where the ball was so Audra had to ask the location. If Audra hadn't asked, Mom could have had the dog ask the question and Mom answer with the *wrong* location. There's a good chance Audra would have followed suit and asked again.

Cognitive Development ◆

Lend a hand. Everybody should pull some of the weight in a family. If not, Mom usually ends up doing it all. So let your toddler help with routine chores, too. Cooking, cleaning, washing dishes, folding laundry, and gardening are all naturals. Helping out is a bonding experience for you both, good practice for her, and at the same time makes her feel like a bona fide member of the family. But it's even more than that. Her participation now boosts her ability to later interpret and tell stories— an important precursor to reading. How? Well, as your toddler participates in various activities, she's building a storehouse of knowledge about everyday events and occurrences; a sequential memory, if you will, which are the scripts and core of stories. To tell a story about making dinner, for instance, she has to know how it happens step by step. When she begins school, all the "scripts" about various household happenings will help her understand stories that she reads and help her compose her own. So while washing dishes might be a big drag for your teenage daughter, it's a cognitive and language development aid for your toddler.

Hearing Stimulation ◆

Are you listening? Some of the listening activities that we've been doing over the last few months take on a new dimension and have an even greater impact on your toddler's language development now that she has the cognitive ability to store more words and images in her memory. Here are some of the ones that will be tremendously effective in boosting her vocabulary and language growth this month:

- During meals, dressing, play, or bathing, provide simple directions that your toddler can easily follow—"Drink juice," "Put arm in sleeve," "Turn big dial," "Give Mommy froggy."

- Allow your tot to eavesdrop on the phone and encourage her to say "Hi" and "Bye" to Grandma, Auntie Jane, and the rest of your clan.

- Play "Hide-and-seek" so that your tot has to follow your voice to find you.

- Hide a squeaky toy like a rubber ducky within easy reach, squeeze it, act surprised at the noise, and ask your tot, "*Where's ducky?*" (Electronically activated toys that can be operated from afar are even better.) Talk about the toy *and the hunt* as you and your child search.

- Add this new one to the collection: Sing the following song to the tune of "Muffin Man" and have your tot respond "Yes" as she points, or "No" with a shake of her head.

I can see a great big truck,
A great big truck,
A great big truck,
Does Allie see a great big truck?
Can you show me where? (Allie says "yes" and points)
There it is!

Yes, Allie sees a great big truck,
A great big truck,
A great big truck,
Allie sees a great big truck?
The truck is over there! (Mom and Allie point together)

Every once in awhile name something totally absurd—"I can see an elephant"—so your child can say *"No!"* and you both have a good laugh.

Visual Stimulation ◆
Reading solo. By now, your toddler can look at books all by herself for short periods of time—for at least three or four minutes! These short periods alone should be encouraged since they foster appreciation of books and

nurture literacy skills. For now, stick to brightly colored picture books with limited text. If your little one looks up from her book and seems to want reassurance, feel free to comment from your chair as she "reads."

> ADULT: Oh! I see funny elephant!
> CHILD: (Points to monkey)
> ADULT: Is that elephant? (Pause) That monkey. I still see elephant. Elephant dancing.
> CHILD: (Points to camel)
> ADULT: Are you being silly? That camel.
> CHILD: (Giggling, points to giraffe)
> ADULT: That not elephant! That giraffe. No elephant.
> CHILD: Efat! (Points to elephant)
> ADULT: Yes, elephant! You are such a big girl.

At only fourteen months, your little reader will still do best with books that have tear-resistant cardboard or hefty double-ply paper pages. Some toddlers will insist on books with thin paper pages like the ones their older siblings have. If your gal is of that ilk, give it a try, but set some limits and let her know that when it comes to "big girl books" you'll be the lead page-turner—"This big girl book! Read together. Help Mommy turn pages." If page-turning becomes a serious issue, check used bookstores, yard sales, or library sales for old books that can be sacrificed to the cause—we certainly don't want to let page-turning squabbles spoil the reading experience.

Sensory Stimulation ◆

Such good taste! I've suggested sensory stimulation activities before, but now we're ready to add real language and a lot more variety. It's time for a tasting party! This special event is in perfect keeping with your fourteen-month-old's increasing ability to chew foods of differing textures. Describe the tastes and name the goodies as you both sample the "cuisine." Tasting possibilities include raisins and other dried but not hard fruit (no banana chips); juices; pieces of crackers, pretzels, or cookies; small pieces of baloney, chicken nuggets, or hotdogs; canned fruit or small peeled pieces of apples, pears, peaches, or plums; dry cereal; small chunks of cheese; fruit bars; and the like. Contrast the flavors for maximum enjoyment and learning. Let's crash an eating party where all the treats are under paper napkins.

ADULT: Now which one?

CHILD: Dat. (Points)

ADULT: Ohhhhhhhhhh! What's that? (Lifts napkin)

CHILD: Apple. Eat.

ADULT: Yes. Let's eat apple. (Pause) What next?

CHILD: Rayshu.

ADULT: Raisins? Remember where?

CHILD: Rayshu. (Points)

ADULT: Let's see. (Lifts napkin) It's cracker.

CHILD: No. Rayshu.

ADULT: You're right. Raisin! I can't fool you. Taste.

To make this an even more language-enriching activity, snuggle up with your little one and read *The Very Hungry Caterpillar,* by Eric Carle, before or after your party. It's a wonderful tale of a lovable caterpillar's last eating binge before he metamorphoses into a beautiful butterfly, and, as a bonus, the story introduces many of the fruits you may have served at your buffet—or are about to.

Motor Development ◆

Crawl spaces. Toddlers are constantly in motion, and yours, no doubt, will be raring to experiment with locomotion—walking, running, climbing, crawling . . . you name it, she'll try it. These types of exploratory activities are excellent for her overall development of strength and control, so let her at it—but remember to always keep an eye on her since her zeal greatly surpasses her capabilities. Take her to the playground often, especially if it has a toddler section with tunnels and bridges for walking and climbing. Also, if possible, buy a large, plastic, children's crawl space plus slide. All toy stores have them—and I've seen great deals on used ones. My neighbor found one in a thrift store that her daughter used for over three years as it morphed into a house and finally an imaginary castle. You can also make your own homespun tunnels from old boxes by taping them together with duct or masking tape. Check packing boxes for sharp staples, though, and make sure you remove them before your baby gets moving. Think of all the possibilities for language with *in, on, up, down, go, run, slide, box* . . . and on and on.

Two for one. Your toddler now has the ability to respond to two-part verbal requests such as "Touch nose, then touch ear." But because she may not be quite able to remember both parts of the request, help her out. Do the actions first and then ask her to follow. It's like a mini-imitation game. Here's a game already in progress . . .

> ADULT: (Pats head, then knee) Pat head, pat knee.
> CHILD: (Pats head; looks at adult)
> ADULT: Um-hm, go ahead.
> CHILD: (Pats knee)
> ADULT: Yes, pat head, pat knee. Linda so big! (Pause) Let's try another one. . . . Touch nose and touch tummy.
> CHILD: (Touches nose and knee; giggles)
> ADULT: Linda silly? (Points to child's knee) Is that tummy?
> CHILD: No.
> ADULT: Where knee?

Make this fun. Within a month or two, at the most, she'll be able to follow two-step commands without your actions to imitate.

Month Fifteen

This month, your little whirlwind may be using gestures and words together as a way of expanding her communication. To let you know that Fido's having a munch, for instance, she might say "doggie," followed by the sign for eat. Most children don't combine two words in their speech for another three months or so, but you may hear a word said twice in sequence—doggie doggie, or in combination with another sound—doggie-wah or beba-doggie. Your tot can now use one object to represent another as she plays—say putting a sock on her doll's head in place of a hat, and pictures are now another part of her mental concept of familiar things, as their two-dimensional representational images are stored with all the other information in her memory.

● ■ ▲

MILESTONE WATCHLIST:
Fifteen-Month-Old

Does your child . . .

❑ Gesture and verbalize simultaneously or in sequence?

❑ Say ten or more single words?

❑ Identify three or more body parts by name?

❑ Use single words within jargon?

❑ "Sing" independently?

❑ Understand the names of many common objects?

❑ Respond to two-step commands?

❑ Use objects symbolically, creatively, or for a nonintended purpose? This can be a close call. Random actions don't count. Using a shoe as a doll's car or a small bottle as a cell phone is the kind of thing we're looking for.

❑ Point to pictures of things when they're named.

❑ Help turn pages—often more than one at a time—when you share a book?

❑ Scribble with crayons or markers?

SHARED COMMUNICATION ACTIVITIES: MONTH FIFTEEN

Communication ◆

Emotional puppets or dolls. By this age, children understand limited emotions such as sad, hungry, and tired. As you and your little one play with dolls and puppets, talk about how they *feel,* as well as how they look and act. Make facial expressions yourself—act happy, sad, frightened, or surprised, and mimic your tot when she expresses emotions. To show you how it works, here's a mom and her daughter playing with a despondent puppet.

CHILD: (Drops puppet) Uh-oh. Fall.

ADULT: Oh, puppet fall. Poor puppet. (Pause) Puppet sad.

CHILD: (Picks up puppet) Sad.

ADULT: Yes, puppet sad. (Pause) Puppet cry.

CHILD: Sad.

ADULT: Yes, sad, Mommy sad, too. See mommy's sad face. Nicole make sad face.

CHILD: (Frowns)

ADULT: Oh, such a sad face. Nicole sad, too.

Look for books that include photographs of different emotions on people's faces too. *Everybody Has Feelings*, by Charles Avery, is a good choice. It's a wonderful photographic essay on children's moods that features pictures of a wide range of emotions (along with simple prose in English and Spanish). As you and your toddler go through books like this, talk about the feelings of the children pictured, but keep it simple—*sad* or *unhappy* is appropriate; *clinically depressed* is over the top.

Finger plays. Finger plays are those very simple rhyming songs that you act out with your hands. They're great fun for kids—toddlers are enthralled by them. Aside from providing excellent language learning opportunities, they're brilliant little exercises for their burgeoning fine motor skills. You can do them anytime and anywhere, and there's an endless variety of them—one is just as good as the next. Some popular classics include "Where Is Thumbkin," "Eensy Weensy Spider," and "Patty Cake." (Make sure to try some from my collection of favorites in Appendix B.) Even if your tot can't quite use her fingers independently enough yet for some of the games, or has trouble remembering the names, she'll still have a ball trying. The important thing is that she's participating in a communication activity that's fun. And trust me, she'll soon surprise you with just how much of the song she's learned.

The mom and tot in the following example have played "Eensy Weensy Spider" many times. Note how the mom gently helps her child along.

MOM: (Moving hands up together, fingers spread, alternating pinky to thumb on opposite hands . . . as a spider might crawl) Eeensy Weensy Spider went. . . . Where?

CHILD: Up!

MOM: Yes! . . . up the water spout. (Hands come down, then off to the side) Down came the rain and washed the spider . . .

CHILD: Out!

MOM: Good! Out. Out came the sun and dried the rain away (Hands open, palms up). And the Eeensy Weensy who?

CHILD: Pi-a

MOM: Yep, spider. And the Eeensy Weensy Spider went . . .

CHILD: Up!

MOM: Um-hm. Up again to play.

Now it's your turn. Give it try. Have fun!

This is the way. We've sung songs before as a fun way to introduce your baby to new words relating to people, things, actions, and locations. Now, at fifteen months, she's ready to join in—to a degree, anyway. One song she'll find hard to resist is "This Is the Way," which you sing to the tune of "Here We Go 'round the Mulberry Bush." After you sing *"This is the way we,"* you fill in the action, like this:

> *This is the way we drink our juice (or Eda drinks her juice)*
> *Drink our juice*
> *Drink our juice*
> *This is the way we drink our juice*
> *In the kitchen with Daddy (any variation will do).*

Any familiar objects and actions can be transformed to song lyrics: This is the way we . . . *eat our cake, comb our hair, wash our face, sing a song, ride a bike, drive a car, bake the cake,* and so on. After you've sung the song a few times, invite your little rising star to join in. Try following this example to get her started:

ADULT: This is the way Eda drink her juice. Drink her juice. Drink her . . .
(Pause)
CHILD: Juice!
ADULT: Yes! This is the way Eda drink her . . . (Pause)
CHILD: Juice!
ADULT: Um-hm. In her brand-new high chair.

A variation on the theme, sung to the tune of "London Bridge Is Falling Down," goes something like this:

> Adam's riding in the car
> In the car
> In the car
> Adam's riding in the car
> Going to his daycare.

A few other lyric possibility include, *riding on a bike, driving in the car, riding in the plane (bus, boat), living in the house, eating at the table, sitting in the chair,* and the like.

You can also try the "Who is" variation on the variation, still to the tune of "London Bridge," in which you end with a question to coax a reply, like this:

> Who is eating in her chair?
> In her chair
> In her chair
> Who is eating in her chair?
> Is it my sweetie, Lourdes?

Cognitive Development ◆

Wrong move. Now that your moppet has the ability to anticipate familiar games and routines, she'll begin to understand when you deliberately make a mistake—and if you add a little theatricality to the "mistakes," she'll probably find them quite hilarious. So show her a good time and act in unusual and unexpected ways—eat from her spoon instead of feeding her, put her hat on your own head before you leave the house, gargle with your juice, or pretend to fall down. React as if totally surprised. Your only limitation is how silly you want to be—turn it into a goof-fest. Talk about your "mistake" afterwards . . . and enjoy all the giggles you get from your comic routines. Here's an example to get you started:

> ADULT: Daddy put Theo in tub. (Lifts child)
> CHILD: Awk! (Becomes very active)
> ADULT: What? Theo bath. In tub. (Keeps moving child up and down over tub)
> CHILD: Wawa!
> ADULT: Yes, in water? (Pause) Daddy forgot something? (Pause)
> CHILD: Wawa.
> ADULT: I see water. (Moves child toward water)
> CHILD: No. Socks.
> ADULT: Oh, Daddy forgot clothes. Take off clothes?
> CHILD: (Giggles, kicks feet)
> ADULT: Socks off. In tub. (Lifts child again)
> CHILD: More.
> ADULT: More clothes off? Oh, no!

Hearing Stimulation ◆

"What do you hear?" You've talked about natural sounds with your baby before—dogs barking, birds chirping, car horns honking, and so on, but now you can begin to ask her to identify them for *you*. Record environmental sounds on a tape recorder, buy some sound effects CDs or tapes, or take advantage of sounds as they occur naturally. Ask "What's that?" or "What did you hear?" If your little one doesn't seem to know the answer, help her out. Tell her what made the sound and describe it if it's visible: "Oh, Robyn hear that cricket? Look how small. Funny legs." If the sound reoccurs, remind her of the name again. Keep in mind the difficulty of the word you're asking for. If she makes a reasonable attempt, respond positively. For example:

> ADULT: What did you hear?
> CHILD: Kuck.
> ADULT: Yes, truck. Big truck.

CHILD: Kuck.
ADULT: Where is truck?

Visual Stimulation ◆

Fitting in. Right about this time, your toddler is gaining the ability to solve problems involving shapes. You can nurture this new skill with problem-solving toys that call for your tot to match certain shaped blocks to similarly shaped holes. First Shape Fitter by Plan Toy, for instance, features colorful chunky square, circular, and triangular blocks than fit perfectly into cut-outs in a wooden tray. (See Appendix E for more ideas.) With any of these toys, your tot will need some help in the beginning. You might need to move the container, for instance, so that the appropriate hole is perfectly positioned to receive whatever block shape she's holding. Just keep it simple—deal with one shape at a time, and make your verbal directions very easy for her to understand. "Manipulate the sphere into the circular cavity" is a no-no! This is more what we're looking for:

ADULT: Put block in. (Pause) Block in.
CHILD: Bok.
ADULT: Um-hm, block. Oops, try another one. (Pause) Other hole.
CHILD: Bok!
ADULT: That's right. Turn block. (Pause) Let Mommy help.
CHILD: In.
ADULT: Push. (Pause) Push block in. You did it! Block in!

Sensory Stimulation ◆

Birthington's washday. Water play is always a kiddie favorite, but at this age, spreading liquids around is pure heaven! Combine that with two other fifteen-month-old favorites—helping you and emulating everything you do—and you've got an exercise that guarantees satisfaction. This one is great to do while you're bathing your tot or playing outside on a nice day. Fill a bucket with warm water, give her a nice soft sponge, and ask her, "What should we clean?" Then let her use the sponge to wash different objects. The warm water, suds, and soft-textured sponge provide a nice sensory experience along with large muscle activity. As always, talk about the activity as you do it. It might go something like this:

ADULT: What wash?

CHILD: Caw!

ADULT: Wash car?

CHILD: Caw!

ADULT: Okay. Wash car. (Pause) Jolie put sponge in water.

CHILD: (Pulls sponge out of bucket and toddles to car . . . dripping all the way) Caw!

ADULT: Wash car. Jolie wash car wheel. Wash wheel.

CHILD: Weew!

ADULT: Yes, wheel. Oops, Jolie drop sponge. Jolie sit on sponge . . .

Blender drinks. Fruits offer a huge variety of tastes and textures for your tot's developing palate. Plus, they're wonderfully aromatic, terrifically healthy, and make for some, uh, juicy conversation. So crank up the blender or juicer and make some sensational mixed fruit drinks with your child. Blend to taste; no recipe needed!

ADULT: Nora help Mommy? Make juice?

CHILD: Doos!

ADULT: Juice. First, banana. Where banana?

CHILD: (Points)

ADULT: Okay, banana. Oh, smell banana. (Pause) Mmmm, good! Taste banana?

CHILD: Nana!

ADULT: Taste banana. Here's some. (Pause) Mmmmm. (Pause) Mommy took off peel. Here, Nora. Put banana in. (Pause) Banana in blender.

CHILD: Nana.

ADULT: Banana in. What else?

CHILD: (Points to peach)

ADULT: Peach. Want peach? . . .

Edible dough play. Playing with dough—patting, rolling, pulling, and kneading—is excellent sensory stimulation, and ideal for strengthening little hand and arm muscles. It's also great fun for toddlers. They adore spreading around soft textures, and it's a brilliant way to keep their hands busy for a substantial amount of time—that's anything more than two minutes by the baby clock, as attention spans are very short at this age. To get this going, all you need is the dough, a plastic bowl, a spoon, and plastic cookie cutters. Your little chef can use all these utensils at this age—with your help, of course. Set her up in her high chair for this one; we don't need dust bunnies in the mix.

Dr. Bob's Divine Edible Dough Recipe
1 cup smooth peanut butter*
1 cup honey
1½ cups powdered milk
*Subsitute soy butter or another nut butter (available at natural food
    stores) if you're at all concerned about peanut allergies.

Place peanut butter, honey, and powdered milk in a plastic bowl and stir until thoroughly mixed and smooth. Then simply dump it out and play! Roll it into ball together, make snakes and worms, and flatten it and use cookie cutters . . . and don't forget to take a nibble, too.

Motor Stimulation ◆
Simon Says. Simon Says is the classic children's game where you instruct a child to do a specific action, like dance or sit down. The only time the child is supposed to act out the action is when it's preceded by the words Simon Says. So every once in a while you issue an instruction without saying Simon Says. Many times the child will forget the rule and do the action anyway. Then everybody laughs about it and has good time. It's a great combined motor and language activity. Your tot is obviously not old enough yet to understand that she's not supposed to move unless you say "Simon Says," so for now just say "Simon Says" all the time. That makes it more of a "Do as I say" game. A few age-appropriate actions that Simon could suggest are:

brush teeth, clap hands, close X, color X, comb/brush hair, come here,
dance, drink X, drop X, eat X, give X, go to X, hold hands, hold X, hug X,
jump, kick ball, kiss X, lie down, look at X, look in X, open X, pick up X,
point to X, pour X, push/pull X, put X in, put on X, read book, roll ball,
run, sit down, stand up, stop/go, take X, throw ball, tickle X, touch X,

turn around, and turn on X (child toy). With specific toys, you could say listen radio, mow/cut grass, sweep floor, vacuum rug, and wash dishes.

Be sure to allow your toddler a turn at being Simon. Children love to tell adults what to do for a change—a penchant that unfortunately resurfaces in their teen years.

Move over, Picasso. Toddlers adore scribbling with a crayon or washable, nontoxic marker. It's also wonderful for fine motor and small muscle development, and Grandma will be thrilled to receive an original work of art in the mail—who wouldn't? Be sure to supervise your budding artist closely. Use big fat crayons rather than small crayon pieces, and hold on to any marker caps that could inadvertently be ingested. She'll only need one or two crayons at a time—more could overwhelm her, and it's a good idea to tape the paper to the floor with masking tape so it doesn't move around too much as she creates her masterpiece. Masterpiece, I should mention, is a relative term here. Don't get your expectations up. Fifteen-month-old art isn't exactly representational—if there's any recognizable object on the paper it's pure luck. At this point, your little artist's work will be more in keeping with the abstract expressionist school; more Jackson Pollack than Rembrandt. You have about two years to wait for a picture that even vaguely resembles anything in the real world. But art is still art, and beauty is in the eye of the beholder.

Shared Communication Activities:
Months 13, 14, and 15

MONTHLY ACTIVITIES

Age (Mos.)	Communication	Cognitive Development	Hearing Stimulation
13	▲ Phone call for you ▲ Dress for success ▲ Peek-a-boo family ▲ Director on the set! ▲ Be "en-CHANTING"	▲ Explore more	▲ Sound off!
14	▲ Starring teddy ▲ Have you ever seen? ▲ "That's negative, sir" ▲ Grunts, growls, and assorted moos ▲ What and where?	▲ Lend a hand	▲ Are you listening?
15	▲ Emotional puppets or dolls ▲ Finger plays ▲ This is the way	▲ Wrong move	▲ "What do you hear?"

Shared Communication Reminders
- Continue to encourage talking and comprehending
- Treat your child as a participant and conversational partner
- Teach by imitation
- Play "Show-me-how" games

Visual Stimulation	Sensory Stimulation	Motor Development
▲ Pop-goes-the-whatever	▲ Edible finger paints	▲ Muscling in
		▲ Pots 'n' pans band
		▲ Step lightly
▲ Reading solo	▲ Such good taste!	▲ Crawl spaces
		▲ Two for one
▲ Fitting in	▲ Birthington's washday	▲ Simon Says
	▲ Blender drinks	▲ Move over, Picasso
	▲ Edible dough play	

- Pull toys out, name them, then play
- Bring out your baby's inner decorator
- Participate in shared reading

CHAPTER ELEVEN

Months 16, 17, and 18

Single Words to Word Combinations

Progress Report

WE'RE on the cusp of another exciting and significant change in your child's language. He's ready to being combining words. You'll soon be hearing things like "More cookie" and "Throw ball." As he gears up for that milestone, he may repeat the same word—"Kitty, kitty," or combine real words with meaningless sounds, such as "Mommy beda" and "Daddy beda." These are early attempts to transition between single words and two-word phrases. When you hear those "almost-words," try to determine what they mean, then provide a more mature example of what you think your tot's trying to say. Try to include at least part of what he said in your response. For example, if your little fledgling communicator says, "Mommy beda," you might answer, "Um-hm, Mommy eat. Mommy eat soup." He'll almost certainly be talking about something within the context of your current surroundings, so take your cues from the context. He's still concentrating on expanding his vocabulary, but he understands a lot more words than he can say.

Now that Junior is more mobile, he'll be even more curious and eager to explore than ever—and he won't be satisfied if he can't reach something. Remember, he's a little tool-user now and will be able to figure out clever ways of using one object to obtain another. Don't be surprised if you see him try to push a footstool over to the table so he can climb up to investigate the tabletop. Be sure to keep potentially harmful items—anything sharp, very small, poisonous, etc.—well out of his reach or, better yet, safely locked away.

By now, your little one will be looking at your face for longer periods of time when you talk together. Books will hold his attention longer, too, as they become increasingly important in his world. Continue reading together and discussing the pictures as you go—we want those little ears perked up and listening! Junior still has lots to learn from all the sights and sounds around him as well, so keep up your informative commentaries as you share walks and outings. Since he'll talk about what he knows, all this sensory input will pay off in spades when he begins talking in earnest. A warning that bears repeating: Right about this age, your little pitcher is growing big ears, so remember to watch what you say around the little guy. He'll very quickly pick up words he hears often. When my twin sons were sixteen months old and my mother came up to help with our newborn daughter, she repeatedly shouted "scat" at the uncouth neighborhood dogs hounding our un-spayed female mutt. It only took a few days for "scat" to become the twins' favorite and most frequently used word. They especially liked to direct their "scats" at their brand-new baby sister.

Toys are increasingly important now as your child is maturing—favorites around this age are giant snap beads or rings, balls, and blocks—while building with blocks is fun, knocking them all down is a blast! Push and pull toys will vie for a position on his top-ten toy list as his mobility increases and he begins to master walking and running. Your interaction in his play is still terribly important. Introduce each toy, share some time playing, and then let him have some alone time with the toy if he wants. Feel your way into his play slowly and be flexible if he signals an interest in another toy or another way of playing. Parents sometimes insist on their own choices or their playing styles. Don't—it's not necessary. Meet your child halfway.

SHARED COMMUNICATION TIPS . . . AND REMINDERS

- **Model two-word phrases.** As your toddler moves into word combinations, you can help by talking in two-word phrases as you describe events and talk about emotions and actions. As always, the phrases should be in context and be relevant to whatever's happening at the time. Repeat yourself so that your toddler has a couple of chances to hear the word combination, and vary your language slightly. Don't worry about asking Junior to repeat your words—he will soon enough. There's a vast variety of two-word combinations that your tot will be able to understand, including noun-verb combos like *Mommy cook* or *fish swim*; verb-noun variations, such as *push car* or *kiss Mommy*; and adjective-noun pairings like *big cookie* and *more juice*. (Check the full list of possibilities in Appendix D.)

- **Name it.** Continue to provide words for all the things that are of interest to your child, especially when he asks, "Wassat?" But don't stop here. Explore the object with him and talk about it.

- **Sing "favorite" songs.** Many children's songs, such as "Ring Around the Rosy" can be adapted to allow your tot to fill in the missing word— "All fall . . . down." With this song, children love being able to command adults to fall. So take a dive when your baby says "down." While you're on the floor, you could follow with, "Now what?" to encourage him to say *"Up!"* Then you get up and start to sing again. This is a good little workout—for both of you.

- **Go on treasure hunts.** On a walk, collect "treasures" along the way, such as stones, leaves, twigs, flowers, or other nature items—most children are fascinated by small things in nature. Talk about each one as you add it to your collection. Later, use the items to remind your toddler of the treasure hunt and share a nice conversation about it.

- **Gesture less.** Your child is relying more on words to communicate and no longer needs extensive signing or gesturing—especially for the words he understands and can say on his own. Continue to gesture or sign for the words your toddler can't say if it seems natural to you. Don't fret if he continues to sign and talk; he'll quit when signs no longer serve a function for him. If he's only signing, try to get him to combine the sign with a word (the sign for *more* with the word *juice*, for example). Show him several times how to combine the two and see what happens.

- **More is more.** When serving Junior a snack, only give him a small amount and see if he'll request more. If he does, give it to him, along with lots of praise for asking. If he seems to want more but doesn't ask you, ask him what he wants. If he still doesn't respond, ask him to "Say 'more.'" Needless to say, keep all this in perspective. There's a point when he'll have had his fill of whatever he's been munching—we're trying to encourage your tot to talk, not bulk him up.

Month Sixteen

A lot of Junior's efforts this month go into learning to concentrate on two things at once—first two actions, then two words. Encourage play that combines dual activities like dancing while clapping, swinging while singing, pushing the ball while talking, and so on. As your tot becomes better able to focus on these activities in meaningful ways, you can provide additional sensory experiences. His interest in books, rhymes, and songs continues to grow, and can be enhanced by putting new actions to familiar songs or adding pictures to a music activity. With more talking comes more demands. Now "More!" is almost as popular as "No!" and "Wassat?" is a constant refrain.

MILESTONE WATCHLIST:
Sixteen-Month-Old

Does your child . . .

❑ Ask "What that?" (Variants include "What?" "Tha?" "Dat?" and "Wassat?")

❑ Request "More?"

❑ Consistently respond by pointing to the right body parts, especially facial ones, when you name them? (Common body parts include mouth, ear, nose, hand, foot, fingers, and toes.)

❑ Retrieve objects requested by name, not gestures?

❑ Listen as rhymes and songs are repeated a few times?

❑ Try to throw or catch a ball?

❑ Pull a toy as he walks?

SHARED COMMUNICATION ACTIVITIES: MONTH SIXTEEN

Communications ◆

A duck goes . . . quack! Incorporate environmental noises into your play with your tot. Encourage him to imitate noises that he hears—animal noises, car horns, sneezing, coughing, airplanes, trains, the lot. Mimicry requires careful listening, which stimulates hearing discrimination, and provides more information for forming definitions of things. Make this fun! More enjoyment makes for better learning.

"Touch and talk" toys. There are some wonderful educational toys on the market that work on the touch and talk model—that is, they sound off at the touch of a button, the pull of a string, the flip of a lever, or the wind of a handle. The best ones for language growth have a voice describing a picture, since they provide a context for the words and sentences your tot

hears. Talking toys that just chatter away are rather ineffective learning tools. It's very hard for toddlers to connect meaning or make sense of words they hear out of context. It's still a bit early for toys that ask children to identify colors, shapes, numbers, and letters—so hold off on those. (See Appendix E for recommendations.)

"Show me how." This is another fun exercise that can be played anywhere, and helps your child work on his verbal memory. Ask your child to show you how to do something—"Show me how you X." But now, expand on the action verbs your little one already knows by including longer, more specific directions. Instead of just "Show me how you brush," for instance, extend to "Show me how you brush your teeth." Or "Show me how you . . . eat ice cream cone," or ". . . ride bike." If your child is already using a few action words, let him be the one to give you a command—it will probably just be one word like "Dance!" Then it would be your turn to act out the action—lucky you! It can be fun and turns it into a real game. You could also have another adult or older sibling help out by having them say "Show me how you . . ." and having your toddler name the action.

Name that body part. When getting your little one bathed or dressed or just being quiet together, help him strengthen his word memory by having him name body parts as you point to them. With his increasing memory for words, he'll now be able to make the shift from imitating what you say to naming things on his own. If he doesn't seem to know what to do, show how it works first. Point to the body part, name it, then look at him and point again. If this doesn't work, try a fill-in-the-blank approach: "This is Mommy's _____" or "This is _____." This activity is a more mature variation of one we've used before. Here your toddler is *saying the names without hearing them first*. It may not seem like a big stride to you, but trust me; it's a huge change in his abilities.

Cognitive Development ◆
I can't find you. So far, we've always asked your toddler to find something or someone. Let's turn the tables. Here we add some surprise, help him begin to understand rule-following behavior, and give him a big dose of hugs and snuggles—all in one activity. Have him hide; then say, "Where

are you?" He probably won't grasp the rules, so you might have him hide with an adult or older child (in a very safe place). Make this game real. He'll get so excited that he may even jump out of hiding. Act surprised and give him a big hug when you "find" him.

If it ain't broke . . . At this age, your baby has begun to develop an expectation that objects like machines and wind-up or electronic toys operate in a certain way. He anticipates that action and is surprised when it doesn't happen. Fortunately, for our training, wind-up toys run down and electronic toys can be stopped by flipping a switch. When that happens, your toddler will need to ask you for help restarting the toy—excellent for our purposes since it encourages him to initiate verbal communication. So every now and then, when you and your tot are playing with one of these kinds of toys, allow it to stop for whatever reason. Your little mechanic will shake it, poke it, examine it . . . and eventually ask for your assistance. In a slight variation on the theme, you could put a nonoperational toy in front of your toddler and await his request for action. He may say *help, on, go,* or name the toy. Any of these might be accompanied by handing the toy to you. If he doesn't ask for help, play dumb and say, "What want?" (or "What Ramona want?").

Hearing Stimulation ◆
Find the noisy animal. Your child can now search for you and for objects without seeing them hidden beforehand. Take advantage of this to have some fun. Hide and make animal noises as your child tries to find you. Bark, meow, or moo. When he finds you, pretend to be the animal in question. Ask him to join you in barking, mooing, or croaking.

Visual Stimulation ◆
My scrapbook. Scrapbooks are tons of fun. Make one especially for your toddler and fill it with favorite objects, colorful pictures, and all kinds of photographs. While books are always good for visual stimulation, there's nothing better than your very own personalized editions—and it's something he'll especially treasure when he's a parent himself. (My daughter cherishes hers to this day.)

Scrapbooks can be a wonderful source of conversation between you and your little one, especially before bed or during a quiet sharing time.

Potential scrapbook items include family photos (the best!), leaves or flowers collected together on nature outings, a favorite texture—like that piece of velvet from Granny's old hat–pictures of favorite book characters or animals, and any other items suitable for gluing down that have special meaning to your toddler. Even if you're not crazy about your child's favorite item—like that old red sock—include it anyway; the book's for him, and you're just the facilitator here. Aesthetics—as we understand them, anyway—are a secondary consideration in this activity. Obviously, bulky objects like an old teddy or a big rock are not scrapbook-friendly. If your little one really wants to include something like that, you might suggest a very special box—a "scrapbox!"—which you could decorate together, maybe even with teddy mounted on top. Or see how your little collector feels about putting a *photo* of the beloved object in the scrapbook rather than the object itself. Or take it a step further and suggest a photo of the little guy holding the object—that would be a tough one to refuse. You can buy basic scrapbooks with heavy paper pages at craft stores like Michael's or Jo-Ann Fabrics. Glue pictures and lightweight flat items to the pages with non-toxic glue sticks; use tape if they need additional support.

Sensory Stimulation ◆

Bubbles everywhere. Although we did this at eleven months, it will be like a totally new experience to your more mature toddler—he's gained so many new cognitive and physical skills these last five months. At this age, bubble blowing is an endless source of wonder. It's also loads of fun, an excellent exercise for breath control, provides visual and tactile stimulation, offers plenty of opportunity for running around and making noise, is very inexpensive—and gives you lots to talk about. It is, in short, an overall, guaranteed winner! Your toddler may still lack the breath control needed to blow. Show him how to do it by blowing on his arm. If needed, get next to him and help him blow the bubbles. He'll really be excited when he blows his own first bubble—and, of course, he gets to chase them too, making this a terrific two-for-one activity. Try different kinds of bubble blowers for variety and to hold your toddler's interest, and remember to explore all the language learning opportunities. Talk about the different kinds of bubbles, bursting them, and how they feel.

Motor Development ◆

Build 'em high. Stacking blocks, boxes, and rings is still a totally enjoyable activity for most toddlers, and an excellent way to strengthen fine motor muscles in the hands and fingers. Of course, knocking over the stack is the most fun of all. At this age, your child will be experimenting with kicking, although it will look more like he's walking into whatever he's targeting. Let him decimate his precariously balanced tower with those "powerful kicks" if he's so inclined. You won't need to use soft blocks anymore, although cardboard is better than wood since he can throw—take it from one who knows, wooden blocks can really hurt!

Pour, pour me. Pouring things from one container to another is still a fascinating and wondrous thing for your toddler, so let him play with containers and water in the tub or at the sink. Combine his penchant for pouring with his inclination to imitate your everyday actions, and a little dishwashing game is a natural. Toss a sponge and some plastic dishes into the bathtub with him and let him go to town. It may be the last time he'll volunteer to do dishes until he's well into his twenties! As Mother's little helper washes, talk to him about his actions. Phrases like *wash cup, pour water,* or *find bowl* are perfect. You could also pretend to make dinner by filling cups and bowls from other containers ("Let's put the soup in Daddy's bowl, and fill this cup with juice . . . and . . ."). Filling and, of course, dumping, are viable, fun activities this month, too—and toy dump trucks should prove a big hit.

Push me, pull me. Push and pull toys are excellent for strengthening your toddler's muscles for walking. Mental development also comes into play as he navigates his way around the household or outdoor obstacles. Encourage him to participate in familiar activities by using his child-size vacuum cleaner, lawn mower, or baby stroller. Many large supermarkets also have toddler shopping carts for the little "shopper-in-training." If he's "training" in a crowded store, make sure you run interference for him.

Month Seventeen

Unless your child is a true exception to the rule, he's now totally enamored of his own ability to say "No!" and delights in tossing it around to test his boundaries and display his growing independence. You'll hear it a lot for the next few months as you feed, dress, and bathe him—no situation is off-limits as far as your little naysayer is concerned. Other popular one-syllable words include the more benign "Hi" and "Bye," and the ever popular "Mine." At this age, most children don't use possessive pronouns (his, hers, yours, etc.) or possessives (Daddy's). They note possession by saying "Mine"—which is why you hear it so much—or the name of an object's owner—"Mommy car" rather than "Mommy's car." As Junior's communication skills blossom, so does his motor development. He may even try to climb the stairs alone. Get that gate put up at the top of the stairs to protect your intrepid explorer.

● ■ ▲

MILESTONE WATCHLIST:
Seventeen-Month-Old

Does your child . . .

❏ Use the owner's name to show possession?

❏ Say "No" consistently and meaningfully?

❏ Say "Hi" and "Bye" (or other similar words) appropriately?

❏ Repeat single words in a conversation?

❏ Request assistance from adults?

❏ Try to influence the behavior of others?

❏ Feed himself (complete with spills)?

❏ Walk up stairs with one hand held by adult?

SHARED COMMUNICATION ACTIVITIES: MONTH SEVENTEEN

Communication ◆

Decorator sandwiches. Cut bread into hearts, animal shapes, or circles using a cookie cutter. Then, after you and your tot spread peanut butter, marshmallow fluff, or jam on each shape, make faces with raisins, craisins (dried cranberries), chocolate chips, or peanuts. A note of caution: Some children have severe peanut allergies. Soy butter and soy nuts are great substitutes. Try for facial expressions that represent different emotions. For a happy face, for instance, arrange the raisins or chips in a U-shape; for a sad face, turn the U upside down. Talk about the "artistic process" and about the emotions shown on the sandwich faces. This is a particularly fun activity since you get to eat your artwork. It's also good and messy—so schedule in some clean-up time. Here's one little sandwich shop hard at work:

> ADULT: Let's cut a round one. (Pause) Make a happy face!
> CHILD: Wown. Happy.
> ADULT: Round and happy. Yes! A round and happy face. Push down.
> CHILD: (Pushes cookie cutter down; makes grunting noise)
> ADULT: Hard bread. Rachel push hard. (Pause; separates pieces) There's round one. (Pause) Make face?
> CHILD: (Shakes head up and down) Face.
> ADULT: Okay. Need some peanut butter. (Pause) Rachel put on peanut butter. Mommy hold.
> CHILD: Mommy. (Attempts to spread)
> ADULT: More on Mommy than on the bread. (Laughs, pauses) Good job! Now what?
> CHILD: (Points)
> ADULT: Raisins!
> CHILD: Wasee.
> ADULT: Yes, raisins.

Funny voices. We've been using funny-sounding voices from the beginning to keep your baby's interest. Now let's give him a chance to actually create funny-sounding voices himself. If he thought making funny noises was fun, wait till he tries this. Show him how to talk through a paper towel tube or a hose, and then take turns doing it with him. When he speaks into the tube, act like you're really impressed and give him lots of praise. Use different voices yourself to make it even more interesting. If you have a small, portable tape recorder, try taping your "tube-talk" and playing it back—it should give you both a good laugh. Although we've done similar soundmaking activities, adding speech changes the quality of the learning experience and raises word awareness.

Who owns it? Pile up some things that clearly belong to certain people—Dad's comb, Mom's brush, Fido's leash, brother's baseball glove, articles of your tot's clothing—then hold up one at a time, and say, "Whose is this?" Your toddler will catch on quickly. This is a more advanced version of the "What's this?" name game. By asking for the owner instead of the name of the object, we're preparing your tyke for two-word phrases that express ownership, such as *John's bike* and *Mommy's keys*.

Mary had a little car. Let's relieve Mary of her little lamb and try some variations that express possession. Substitute other people for Mary, as in the following:

> *Big brother has a two-wheel bike*
> *Sister has a little cat*
> *Mommy has an SUV*

For obvious reasons, I'd avoid verses such as *Grandma has a new face-lift*, even though they are tantalizing. Pick items and people that your tot knows, and possessions that won't get you into trouble if sung for the wrong audience.

Help me, Mommy! Most of us think that we have to ensure our children's success at everything they do all the time. But while success builds positive self-worth, asking for assistance every now and then builds humility. So encourage your child to ask for assistance (*Mommy help, Daddy do, Help, Open*) by presenting challenges that will require help. Last month we foiled him with inoperative electronic toys; this month, let's try things like difficult buttons and jars that won't open—actually, the possibilities are endless. You'll get guaranteed results if the objects presented are toddler-desirable and visible, say a green and red rubber froggy or a tempting cookie in a clear, unbreakable jar. Those would entice any-body—anybody under two years old, anyway. If your child fusses or whines rather than asking for help, be positive and use the phrase you want him to say, as in, "Oh, Mommy help. Jar stuck. Mommy open. Now jar open." Once opened, chat about the newly recovered prized object.

Cognitive Development ◆

Teddy, kick up your heels! In this activity, your toddler learns about fol-lowing directions, as you give him instructions for certain actions during your play together—"Brush the doll's hair," for instance; or *in* and *out* variations—"Put teddy <u>in</u> the box," or "Put hat <u>on</u> Teddy's head." If you're really feeling creative, make up little rhymes for action routines and have your child manipulate the toy to do them, as in this example:

> *Teddy kicks his leg up,*
> *Then he brings it down.*
> *Teddy puts his arm up,*
> *Then he turns around.*
> *Teddy brings his arms down,*
> *Then jumps into the air.*
> *When Teddy comes back down,*
> *You hug the little bear.*

Recite your rhyme slowly and help your tot follow the directions. Praise him as he completes each step. Gradually lengthen the rhyme re-peated between pauses. Don't expect your little one to remember more than two directions in a sequence.

Hearing Stimulation ◆

Find that song. This game can be played with a tape recorder and empha-sizes *listening to words*. Turn on a tape recorder with one of your tod-dler's favorite songs, and hide the machine. Now ask him to find his song. As you search, sing the song together. We've played this game before with noisemaking toys, but now we're adding singing to help your tot focus on words. Now that he's more mature, and you'll be helping him on the hunt, the hiding places can be trickier to find than before. Talk while you investigate:

> ADULT: I hear "London Bridge falling down, falling down." Where is it? (Pause) Nicolas looking in kitchen. (Pause) No music. I hear music. (Pause) Sing. (Pause) Yeah, London Bridge is falling down. Nicolas go in living room. Look under sofa. No. Music louder. Yes, in sofa. Music under pillow. Nicolas find music. Sing with Mommy.

Visual Stimulation ◆

Chalk it up to fun. Big and little kids alike love to draw on sidewalks with chalk—and it gives your little one a new venue for his artistic expression. If it's too cold for outdoor art now, just wait a few months—this is one activity that will take your toddler years to outgrow. For variety, try precutting some easy shapes from cardboard and help your child trace them on the sidewalk. Be sure to talk about your drawings as you play.

Sensory Stimulation ◆

A body of painting. Some children love messy projects, and others hate them. As an aware parent, you'll soon be able to intuit your child's inclinations. If he's not too fastidious, he'll love body painting or printing—on both of you! My granddaughter used to think it was hilarious to paint my face and watch my shocked expression when I looked at her handiwork in the mirror. All you need for this fun adventure is paint, a soft brush or two for painting, and an ordinary dish sponge for printing (a new, clean one, please). Cut the sponge into small interesting shapes, dip into the paint, and press against the body. Fun! You'll definitely want to use specially designed, washable body paint for this, which is available in all toy stores. It's always a good idea to double-check for washability before you get in too deep—a little experiment on your arm should do it. I've personally found red coloring to be a bit resistant to an easy wash. There are also some soap-based body paints that are like thick, colored shower gel and are perfect for painting tiled tub walls and bodies with rainbows of color—those are very easy to wash off.

Motor Development ◆

Name that action. When you're at the playground or outside, let your toddler go, but follow close behind. This is the perfect time to name large motor actions. He'll probably know *run* and *throw,* so find new actions to name—*chase, bend, pick up, climb,* and the like. Also, take advantage of your tot's anticipation as you get ready for your outing. Talk about what *will happen* in the park—"We'll swing on swing, and slide down slide, and climb on jungle gym . . ." And in the car on the way home, chat about *what you did* while you were there—"It was fun sliding down slide!" Talking about things before, during, and after they happen is wonderful for cognitive growth and gives language learning a real boost. Remember to keep your utterances simple. You might ask "What doing?" for action words he knows, but don't overdo it. Even though these are in effect little language lessons, we still want it to be fun!

Keep 'em singin'. Songs that allow pretend play are terrific fun at this age and can be a very effective way to connect language to various movements. Pretend to be an animal ("Old MacDonald") or thing ("I'm a Little Teapot"), or to do an action described in a song ("This is the Way"). You can raise the fun quotient in this last song with water activities— "This is the way we splash the water . . ." Lots of hoots and hollers are guaranteed with that one. Other possibilities: "This is the way we paint the walls (with water); wash our feet, and squeeze the sponge."

Even songs like "Frere Jacques" ("Are You Sleeping?") can be modified into an action song. Try this variation to that classic tune:

I am running
I am running
Yes, I am
Yes, I am
Running with my two feet
Running with my two feet
Here I go
Here I go

Naturally, you'll want to move your feet like you're running. "I am smelling, with my nose," could work to the tune too—just pretend to sniff around. If you did it while you were cooking and there were wonderful aromas permeating the room, it would make even more sense to your little one.

Feeding myself. Let your child feed himself—within reason, of course. It's actually excellent motor skill practice. Sure it will be a little messy, but there's nothing wrong with a little mess now and then and besides, it's actually fairly easy to clean up. By this age, he should be able to use a spoon and child's cup on his own, but eating with fingers is absolutely fine— even spaghetti can be finger food, and half an ear of corn, even with most of the kernels gone, can be particularly enticing.

Upstairs, downstairs. Hold your tot's hand as he walks up the stairs— which he'll be dying to do. He'll cleverly ascend, leading with the same foot on each step, which is easier than climbing with alternative legs like we adults do. Getting down, though, is not so easy—he's much better at going up the stairs. When he's ready for the descent, make sure he kneels and goes backwards, and stay close by to lend a hand. Don't let him do it on his own! For some idea of how it might feel for a toddler to come down stairs like we do—and how dangerous it can be—try going down two steps at a time. Hold on to the railing as you experiment. Don't forget to put up the stair gate for your little wanderer.

Month Eighteen

Your little one is probably speaking at least ten words clearly now— maybe more. But the really big advance this month is that he's also able to link two words together. While the combo might sound almost like a rudimentary sentence, there's a good chance it's actually two separate words, as in "Mommy" and "Eat." In a month or so that will morph into a real sentence . . . "Mommy eat." To understand the difference, say "Black" and "Board" (two words) and "Blackboard" (one word). He's now also comfortably into fine-motor play, easily scribbling with

*crayons, stringing blocks, and doing simple wooden puzzles. And this
month, as pictures seem even more fascinating, books are king.*

● ■ ▲

MILESTONE WATCHLIST:
Eighteen-Month-Old

Does your child . . .

❏ Follow two-step commands with the same object (e.g., "Hug doll," then "Feed doll")?

❏ Understand about fifty single words?

❏ Say twenty or more single words?

❏ Protest with words, especially "NO!"?

❏ Use consonants *g, k, b, p, m, w, t, d, n,* and *h*?

❏ Talk more and rely on gestures less?

❏ Enjoy messy activities such as finger painting and "decorating with food?"

❏ Occasionally put two words together?

❏ Seldom fall while walking?

❏ Walk while trying to kick a ball?

SHARED COMMUNICATION ACTIVITIES: MONTH EIGHTEEN

Communication ◆

Talking to Thumbkin. Draw a happy face on Junior's thumb with a washable marker. While you work around the house or while driving the car, ask "Thumbkin" simple questions that can be answered with *yes* or *no* or a single word. Your child can either verbally reply for his little thumblike friend or just have Thumbkin move his head (which, of course, is the thumb) for yes/no responses. This is a fun variation on question-answer conversations and helps stimulate imagination.

"I see X." Encourage your little one to describe his world and to use location *names*. When looking out the window with him, say, "Mommy looking out window. What Mommy see? I see . . ." (Or substitute your child's name: "Johnny looking out window," etc.) At the end, pause and let your tot fill in the blank as he tells you what he sees—"Kitty!" Then ask, "Where?" Hopefully, he'll reply with the name of the location—"Fence!" If he points instead, name the location for him and ask "Where?" again. After he names the location, talk about what he's seen—"Yes, cat fence; cat on fence."

One of the two-word phrases he'll say in a month or two will most likely be a person, thing, or action followed by its location, as in *Mommy car, Doggie bed,* or *Throw me.* Those might not sound like locations to you, but most young children have difficulty with the prepositions *(in, on, to)* needed to turn these kinds of phrases into ones that indicate place *(Mommy in car, Doggie on bed,* and *Throw to me). Here* and *there* aren't that easy for them yet either, which is why most toddlers prefer to name the site.

"Hi, neighbors!" Here we combine pretend play with talking. While outside, "introduce" your toddler to inanimate objects, like this:

> Hello tree. I'm Mommy. This is Jimmie. Jimmie, say "Hello tree."

When Jimmie "talks" to the tree (or other objects), reply with a funny tree-like voice, "Hello, Jimmie." Continue on and introduce other objects. This type of pretend play is fun in a playground or park and can be easily extended into longer conversations . . . and it stimulates his cognitive growth. You'll probably just want to ignore the strange looks you get from other adults.

Cognitive Development ◆
This, then this. This activity introduces imitation play with two actions in a sequence, and is a wonderful way to increase your tot's short-term

memory. As you say certain action words and do the appropriate actions, see if you get your toddler to imitate you. Try, for example, *clap hands, then touch head.* As he becomes better at remembering sequences, drop your actions and just use words to direct him. Don't expect him to get it right away; this is a skill that he'll acquire gradually over the next few months—this is just a start.

Hearing Stimulation ◆
All stop! This is a way to introduce new words and to check on your child's understanding at the same time. Ask him to suggest an action:

> ADULT: What do?
> CHILD: Jump!

Or you suggest an action that may be a new word:

> ADULT: We can jump. What do you want to do?

As you and your child perform the action, both of you say the word over and over—"Jump! Jump! Jump!" Then suddenly shout "Stop!" All movement ceases, and you begin again with a new action.

Visual Stimulation ◆
"Tell me about this one." Try to get your toddler to describe pictures in his favorite book. Although he will most likely label rather than describe, you can help pave the way from one to the other. For example, if your little one says the words *Pooh* and *house,* you might respond, "Yes, that's Pooh's house," or "Um-hum, Pooh in house." Use your child's words to describe the picture as you help him build toward two-word phrases. Here's another example of how it's done:

> ADULT: What see?
> CHILD: (Points)
> ADULT: Um-hm, tell Mommy.
> CHILD: Hawsie.
> ADULT: Horsey. More?

CHILD: Boy.
ADULT: Yes, boy on horse. (Pause) And I see . . .
CHILD: Hat.
ADULT: Yes, the boy's hat. Boy lost hat.
CHILD: Hat.
ADULT: Boy on horse lost hat.

This is a great teaching moment. You've got him! He's interested in the picture and in what he just said, so you can use both to expand his language.

Sensory Stimulation ◆

Dough play. Playing with dough is a wonderfully flexible activity that continues to be viable since its benefits grow right along with your child. It's actually an ideal form of play throughout the preschool years. We first talked about dough play when your baby was six months old. The goal then was to give him a chance to squish and feel the dough. Now we're going to use it to tune-up his fine-motor skills as he spreads and rolls the dough. (There's still lots of sensory stimulation from the feel, smell, and color of the dough, too.) You can play with your child side by side, or keep an eye on him from close by. Try this new recipe. It's safe if eaten (but isn't meant to be), and is good for about a week if kept in the fridge—discard before then if it becomes dirty. If it's too stiff and needs to be thinned, add a bit more water or a few drops of food coloring.

Dr. Bob's Dough Play Me Recipe

1 cup flour
1 tbsp. oil
1 cup water
¼ cup salt
1 tbsp. cream of tartar

Mix all ingredients in a bowl and stir until blended smoothly.

Shared Communication Activities:
Months 16, 17, and 18

MONTHLY ACTIVITIES

Age (Mos.)	Communication	Cognitive Development	Hearing Stimulation
16	▲ A duck goes . . . Quack! ▲ "Touch and talk" toys ▲ "Show me how" ▲ Name that body part	▲ I can't find you ▲ If it ain't broke . . .	▲ Find the noisy animal
17	▲ Decorator sandwiches ▲ Funny voices ▲ Who owns it? ▲ Mary had a little car ▲ Help me, Mommy!	▲ Teddy, kick up your heels	▲ Find that song
18	▲ Talking to Thumbkin ▲ "I see X" ▲ "Hi neighbors!"	▲ This, then this	▲ All stop!

Shared Communication Reminders
- Model two-word phrases
- Name it
- Sing "favorite" songs

Visual Stimulation	Sensory Stimulation	Motor Development
▴ My scrapbook	▴ Bubbles everywhere	▴ Build 'em high ▴ Pour, pour me ▴ Push me, pull me
▴ Chalk it up to fun	▴ A body of painting	▴ Name that action ▴ Keep 'em singin' ▴ Feeding myself ▴ Upstairs, downstairs
▴ "Tell me about this one"	▴ Dough play	▴ What are you kicking about? ▴ More filling and dumping

- Go on a treasure hunt
- Gesture less
- More is more

Motor Development ◆

What are you kicking about? Your toddler can run and kick now. Although it's not quite like an adult kick, it is wonderfully amusing to watch, great exercise for his growing muscles, and excellent coordination practice. Soccer, here we come! Use a large, colorful, lightweight beach ball and run around with him as you take turns kicking the ball. Take it easy; tiny little kicks on your part will do the trick. Talk about what's going on as you go—like this:

> ADULT: Jess is going to kick.
> CHILD: Kick.
> ADULT: Yes, big kick. Going for a goal! Kick again.
> CHILD: 'gain.
> ADULT: Kick again. Daddy catch Jess. Daddy chase.
> CHILD: (Squeals and runs)
> ADULT: Silly! Jess forgot to kick. Daddy kick.
> CHILD: Me.
> ADULT: Okay, to Jess.

More filling and dumping. Eighteen-month-olds have a ball filling, pouring, dumping, and mixing—and uncooked rice or dried beans is the perfect stuff for the job. It pours and dumps like a dream, is reusable and readily available, and the price is right. You can often find discounted open packages in the grocery store, or pick up a ten-pound bag of basmati rice. It usually runs between $5 and $10 and often comes in a zipped burlap bag that's perfect for storage—one of the best deals going.

For kiddie dumping and pouring, set your toddler up with any kind of plastic containers—colorful baby cups, children's beach buckets, and even some of your old measuring cups or Tupperware containers will do the trick. (Pick some up from the thrift store if you don't have any. Just be sure to wash thoroughly before using.) Your tot can use plastic spoons to fill small containers, smaller cups to fill larger tubs or buckets, and larger tubs to pour into smaller ones. You could also furnish a plastic plate or two and let him spoon out rice as he serves a pretend meal. This activity offers lots of variety, will keep your little dumpster very busy, and is great for coordination. Supervision is needed, though, since the rice grains are small and could cause choking if ingested—and be sure to store the rice in an inaccessible place. This gets messy; so if you play indoors, spread out a large cloth or plastic sheet first.

CHAPTER TWELVE

Months 19 through 24

Multiword Phrases—and Another Birthday!

Progress Report

NOW we're really rocking! By nineteen months, your child will be able to walk backwards—should she be so inclined—and to stop her forward motion smoothly without falling down. Give her six more months and she'll walk on her tiptoes, stand on one foot (with assistance), and jump with both feet! For now, she'll be a whirlwind of motion as she begins to combine movements such as throwing and running. She'll use objects more for their intended function, and play with toys imaginatively and more appropriately—feeding a doll with a spoon, for instance. The real change is that her play is *more purposeful and less random* than it's ever been. Instead of just spinning a toy car's wheels aimlessly, she may be doing it in an attempt to *fix* a damaged tire.

By the time she's two years old, your tot will be able to predict routine behaviors and find familiar objects in their usual locations. Household routines like washing dishes and cleaning will show up in her play, and she'll be raring to help you in your everyday chores. She'll have the reading routine down pat, too, and will "read" books all by herself. Although the tearing-pages stage should be long past, cardboard pages will still be easier for her to turn and are generally more toddler-friendly.

She's about to make another incredible leap in her expressive language, too. During this period, as your little one's vocabulary continues to increase, she'll begin to combine more words. Her combinations will no longer be random, but rather will follow predictable word order patterns based on adult language—"Daddy eat" and "Eat 'nana," for example. Within a few months, she'll give you "Daddy eat 'nana" or even "Daddy eating 'nana." Once she crosses into word combining, she'll begin to make rapid changes in her language that reflect her ability to remember several things at once. At times she'll seem totally absorbed in speech and language play. Before she falls asleep at night she may repeat various word combinations and play with words—and even laugh at some of her own more creative attempts. Although it took her a year to get to her first word, and six more months to corral two-word combinations, it will take her only three to four months to start combining four and five words and to add word endings, such as *-ing* and *-s*. By the time she's two years old, her expressive vocabulary will be between 150 and 300 words.

As her language increases over these next few months, you'll find her using much less jargon and babbling, although you'll still hear some occasionally—she might try to talk as fast as you and produce a jumble. Or she may say words a few times in a row as she tries to compose an idea, as in "I want . . . I want . . . I want chips." Be patient. Don't rush her. And please, please don't make fun of her attempts. Her sound repertoire won't increase much during this time period—but she's got a nice little collection of sounds already. Most likely she can at least pronounce *m, n, p, b, h, w, g, k, d,* and *t* sounds along with vowels, as in *keep, up, body, boot, coat.* Her word categories will include action words (*go, walk*), physical states (*tired, hungry*), body parts, descriptors (*big, little, hot, dirty, yukky*), facial expressions (*happy, sad*), farm and zoo animals and pets (*doggie, kitty*), food, location prepositions (*in, on*), numbers (with little concept beyond *one* and *more* than one), some nursery rhymes and songs, people in the community, relatives (*Gran'pa Bob*), rooms and furniture (*potty*), self-help, TV and video/DVD characters, and vehicles (*car*). That's a lot for a little gal!

Her use of language will show great versatility, too. She'll be able to command, request, ask, answer, reply, comment, declare, name, exclaim, protest, call, greet, and demand, to name a few. Not bad!—although the demand part might take its toll. It was just around this time that my granddaughter picked up the charming habit of saying things like "Eat now!" or "Juice now!" She was a real little tyrant for a few months. If your little one slips into despot mode, just wait it out. This, too, shall pass.

SHARED COMMUNICATION TIPS AND REMINDERS

- **Keep setting good language examples.** Respond to your toddler's talking by expanding what she says into longer, more mature sentences. Don't correct her, and do keep it positive. The trick is to stay a step or two ahead of her. Use short adult sentences—five or six words maximum—when you talk with her. At this stage of development, she should be able to understand them, but remember, she's only beginning to combine words and still has very limited working memory. That means she can only hold a few items in her head for a very short time as she tries to decipher the words and grammar to determine what you mean. A few examples:

CHILD: Horsey run.
ADULT: Yes, the horse is running. Horse run fast.

CHILD: Want juice.
ADULT: Um-hm, Tandy want juice. Okay, here's more juice.

CHILD: No bye-bye.
ADULT: Daddy no go bye-bye. No, not today. No work.

Unfortunately, while expanding is a great teaching technique, it doesn't advance the conversation. *So don't overuse it.* And always follow it with a comment as in the above the examples, to help keep the conversation going.

- **Take advantage of ALL language opportunities.** Aside from your everyday conversations, give your tot directions to follow and continue to read books together—you'll be getting a lot more feedback from your shared, interactive reading now. Continue to chat about pictures as you go through a book, but now ask her to tell a familiar story or to finish a favorite story using the pictures as a guide.

SHARED COMMUNICATION TIPS AND REMINDERS

- **Have real conversations.** Your child is beginning to combine words, and this is a very important step toward acquiring language. So now it's more important than ever to have real conversations with her. Talk about what you both are doing, comment on sounds you hear, and ask questions and answer hers with enthusiasm. Reply to her attempts to communicate and comment on what she says. Her practice and participation in real conversations is the key to her becoming a good communicator.

- **Sing social songs in which your child can participate.** Pick simple, repetitive songs or make up your own about everyday activities. Old standards include "Good Morning to You," "I'm a Little Teapot," "The Muffin Man," "The Wheels on the Bus," "If You're Happy and You Know It," and the like. It's great fun to modify the words.

- **Be silly.** Children love to correct adults. Call things by the wrong name. At first your child will probably be reticent to correct you, so ask, "Is that right?" or "Is that your nose?" when it's really her ear. Here's a mom giving her tot plenty to correct:

ADULT: Mommy wash your toe. (Pause) Is this toe?
CHILD: (Shakes head side to side)
ADULT: No! That ear. Now, Mommy wash other toe.
CHILD: No! Ear.
ADULT: How silly! Yes, Mommy wash . . .
CHILD: Ear.
ADULT: Um-hm, that ear. (Pause) Now, Mommy wash hand.
CHILD: That nose!
ADULT: Oh, no! Mommy made another mistake. What's that?
CHILD: That nose.

Note how the mom sets up the expectation that she's going to say the wrong word in the last part of the sentence each time, and gives her tot a good example to follow—*That + X*. This is great teaching—and makes for good laughs. Add to the fun by making silly faces when you "flub up." She'll love it.

- **Provide opportunities for language growth.** Your tot can do much more than give you words for things. Encourage her to stretch her uses of language—give her chances to make requests, ask questions, and describe things. Instead of anticipating *all* her needs *all* the time, let her ask for things occasionally. Instead of supplying the name for every object that she doesn't know, let her ask sometimes. She may need a few hints to get her motivated. A few ideas: To encourage her to ask someone else for help, try asking her questions like "How can you get help?" "How can we get someone to help?" "What should you do?" or "Who can help?" Here's how it works:

  ADULT: What want?
  CHILD: Cookie.
  ADULT: Want cookie. I'm busy. Who can help?
  CHILD: Daddy.
  ADULT: Yes. Ask Daddy to help.
  CHILD: (Goes to daddy) Daddy help. Want cookie.

To encourage her to ask for the names of things, try phrases like "Ask Daddy," "Who knows the name?" or "How can you ask?"

  CHILD: Want!
  ADULT: Want what?
  CHILD: That.
  ADULT: What is that?
  CHILD: That.
  ADULT: How can you ask?
  CHILD: Wassat?

And to encourage her to describe something, try "Tell me about this," "What can you tell me about this?" or "Tell me more."

> ADULT: Here's an interesting picture. (Pause) I see lots of things. (Points) Tell me about this.
> CHILD: Boy. Swing. Boy fall. Down. Hurt.
> ADULT: Um-hm. And over here. Tell me more.
> CHILD: More boy. Bike. Go fast.

Months Nineteen and Twenty

As your child's vocabulary increases, her repertoire of two-word phrases continues to grow. She chatters throughout the day during regular routines and when she's playing—even by herself. Continue to provide a variety of listening activities, including tapes and CDs with songs and stories, toy telephones, and talking toys—she needs your input. Cognition and language continue to develop in unison and remain equally important— an advance in one is reflected in the other. Motor skills are rapidly increasing, and will be for some time—and at this stage they provide lots of potential for shared communication. There's lots to talk about now that your tot knows how to run, jump, climb stairs, throw and kick balls, color, roll clay, pinch, pick up, or squeeze things . . . whew!

● ■ ▲

MILESTONE WATCHLIST:
Nineteen- and Twenty-Month-Olds

Does your child . . .

❑ **Imitate two- to three-word utterances?**

❑ **Combine two words occasionally?**

❑ **Use words during pretend play?**

● ■ ▲

MILESTONE WATCHLIST:
Ninteen- and Twenty-Month-Olds

Does your child . . .

❏ Understand and respond to verbal commands, such as *stop that, sit down,* and *come here?*

❏ Imitate environmental noises, such as dogs barking or car horns?

❏ Have twenty or more words in her vocabulary?

❏ Use *mine, me,* and *you?*

❏ Enjoy games in which she names things?

❏ Talk for many different purposes, such as asking questions ("Horsey?" "Where Mommy?"), answering questions, greeting, and demanding?

❏ Pretend to "dance?"

SHARED COMMUNICATION ACTIVITIES:
MONTHS NINETEEN AND TWENTY

Communication ◆

"My day" book. Take photos of your sweetie during the day. Then put them together in a book. Talk about the photos as you look through the book together, and have her tell you the story of "My day."

This one's ON you. At this age, children love to open drawers, boxes, or other containers and put things in, so it's not surprising that your little one will begin to use the words *in* and *on*. Give her a little practice by directing her to put her teddy *in* or *on* various things. Pick a location that's very obvious at first, where there can be no confusion whether *in* or *on* is the correct word. "Put the teddy *in* the box" is a good starter, for instance, since teddy couldn't be put *on* a lidless container (with the opening facing up anyway). "Put the teddy *on* the table" is another good one, since putting him *in* the table would require Matrix training. As your tot understands the commands better, you can add more items and make the choices less obvious. For example, a box with the opening to the side can be used for either *on* or *in*. You can add a little tune to reinforce the word learning. Here, for instance, teddy enters the box to the tune of "London Bridge."

> Put your teddy **in** the box
> **In** the box
> **In** the box
> Put your teddy **in** the box
> All day long.

Spin and talk. Let's put a new "spin" on an old activity, naming pictures. Mount pictures on a "Lazy Susan," help your toddler spin it, then name and talk about the picture that lands the closest to her. Encourage her to name objects and people in the picture and describe what's going on. Try to get her to remember events related to the photos. After you've been through all the pictures, exchange them for some new ones and begin again. If this exercise just becomes a naming drill, close it down and move on to something else. Ideally, the pictures should become the focus of communication.

Oh where, oh where . . . This game uses variations on the song, "Oh where, oh where has my little dog gone?" Hide an object (or even yourself). Then ask your mini-sleuth to find it (or you) while you sing your personalized song—which might go something like this:

> Oh where, oh where is rubber duck?
> Oh where, oh where is the duck?
> Mommy and Suzie look under the bed
> Oh where, oh where is the duck?

This can be played endlessly. The only limit is your imagination. Items don't even have to be hidden. Try it while sorting laundry (*Oh where, oh where is little red sock?*) or standing before a closet or drawer full of clothes *(Oh where, oh where is Suzie's dress?)* To reinforce the *"where is"* idea, snuggle up with your tot and read *Where's Spot* by Eric Hill together. It's a wonderfully illustrated, interactive little book with colorful flaps that your cutie can lift up as she helps you search for the mischievous pup.

"What would you like?" While your toddler still has a year or so before she'll be able to pretend to be other people, and she'll need to mature socially before she'll have the ability to make voice changes to take on the role of Mommy, Daddy, or baby, she can pretend to be doing things now. So have make-believe dinners, tea parties, picnics, and shopping expeditions. Take a drive in an imaginary car. And have a lovely conversation about the events—the make-believe cows you see out the car window as you drive, the ants at the picnic—be creative and make it fun. You could even ask your little one to serve as the "go-between" for you and teddy. Ask her—"Please ask teddy what she wants to eat" or "Ask teddy what she wants from market." This type of play is not only fun, but is extremely important for your tot's cognitive growth, since imagining and pretending stretches her language.

Cognitive Development ◆
Sort and match. Your child is beginning to notice similarities between objects that are not exactly alike. Let's encourage this problem-solving skill. When you're doing laundry, ask your little one to help you match colored socks and sort clothes. See if she can pick her clothes out of the basket, and maybe Mommy's, too. There are some terrific sorting games in toy stores, such as matching animals in a Noah's Ark, but the possibilities for sorting and matching of objects in your toddler's everyday world are infinite. She could match spoons to spoons in the silverware drawer, sort fruits while helping you make fruit salad, put away certain kinds of toys or groceries, match the same size leaves or find flowers that look the same on nature outings, or sort—and eat—different kinds of finger foods.

Mail call! Your toddler's already interested in books and reading; this simple ploy helps her gain even more understanding about the role of printed matter—it helps her connect the dots. When the mail arrives, call out "Mail is here," and allow her to open junk mail while you open the other mail. If you're anything like me, there will be a certain perverse thrill in seeing all that junk mail being torn apart by a toddler—a nice little bonus. You can also compose a letter to Granny or Gran'pa and have your child add a drawing or stickers. You'll still have to write the message, though. I promised you progress—not miracles!

Hearing Stimulation ◆

Dances with scarves. Toddlers love to dance with scarves—both boys and girls. There's something about the flow of the material moving gently behind them that seems to enchant them. Give your little miss a few of your old scarves and let her show her stuff. It's a fun way to dance with lots of movement (even though it sounds like a striptease). Use slow music so you can relax and enjoy the movement. Join in—it's a great stress reliever.

Visual Stimulation ◆

Shine, little flashlight. Sit in the middle of a semi-darkened room with your child. Shine a flashlight on various objects and talk about them. Or you could use a variation on the song "This Little Light of Mine." It might go something like this:

> *This flashlight of mine, shine, shine, shine.*
> *This flashlight of mine, shine, shine, shine.*
> *This flashlight of mine, shine, shine, shine.*
> *Shine on the <u>flowers</u> all the time. (Shine light on flowers)*

For a twist on the game, you can sit in front of a mirror and highlight parts of her body with the flashlight and name each one together. Show your little one a few optical tricks, like all the kinds of shadow faces that can be created with the light from various angles. Discuss what you see, and keep this scenario laid-back and fun—you don't want to scare her.

Sensory Stimulation ◆

Pass on something nice. Your child can express emotions and knows that a caress means love. Sit with her and other children or your partner. Take turns initiating an action like a hug and passing it around the circle. Possible other feel-good actions include a snuggle, touch, pat, kiss, butterfly kiss (brush the other person's cheek with a blinking eyelash), rub, tickle, gentle word, and so on. This exercise can be really sweet and tender and leave you all with some really nice memories. One book that would fit nicely into warm togetherness activity is Charlotte Zolotow's *Some Things Go Together*. It's a wonderfully illustrated rhyming story about how things are linked together—"Peace with a dove/home with love. Sand with the sea/you with me." Both the words and pictures foster feelings of familial love that will stay with you a nice long time.

Fed up. In this little game you and your toddler take turns feeding each other, but the person being fed has his or her eyes closed or covered and has to guess what the food is. When you're the one who's blindfolded, make wildly absurd guesses that your child will find hilarious. She'll correct you, especially if you pretend not to be able to guess the real food name. This one guarantees loads of laughs. Suggested taste-treats include yogurt, raisins, various fruits, oatmeal, peanut butter (assuming no peanut allergies), lemonade, chocolate, cheese, pudding, Jell-O, marshmallow fluff, jellies, and the like. This could get messy, so cover up or wear your old sweats.

Special cards. Create cards together for special occasions or for special people. You can paint, trace shapes, scribble, or glue on pictures, decorate with washable magic markers, or use stickers, which are much less messy and are bound to be just as appreciated by Aunt Madge. Get creative and talk about Aunt Madge (or whatever special person) and the kind of things she likes, as well as what you're doing. You might even have Aunt Madge's picture nearby or call her on the phone while you're creating. Aside from your standard toddler artist tools (crayons, markers, washable nontoxic glue or glue sticks, etc.), all you really need is sturdy paper for the card itself. If you really want to get fancy, you can glue on buttons ("Red ones—Aunt Madge's favorite color!"), yarn, or even small pieces of foam packing material. Make sure to pre-cut any pictures or small pieces of paper you plan to glue on. Your tot's fine-motor abilities are not yet up to the task, and we don't want to frustrate her. This should be a closely supervised activity. Don't leave your little artist alone with a glue bottle or other art supplies—especially if you're using small objects that could cause choking.

No-bake cookies. Making bakeless cookies can be terrific fun, provide lots of sensory stimulation, and maybe even offer a hint of nutrition. There are numerous recipes available, but here's one of my favorites. It includes peanut butter, so use a soy substitute if there's any chance your toddler is allergic to peanuts.

Bob's Blissful Bakeless Cookies
¾ *cup peanut butter*
½ *cup honey*
¾ *cup dry oatmeal*
¼ *cup graham cracker crumbs (more if cookies are too moist)*
1 *tsp vanilla extract*
¼ *cup raisins*

Put all ingredients in a bowl and have your little sous-chef help stir until smooth. Then have her help roll the mixture into balls. Place in fridge for an hour or so to help cookies solidify. Have a fabulous tasting party.

For variations, substitute cereal crumbs—the stuff in the bottom of the box that no one will eat—for the graham cracker crumbs; try small pieces of other dried fruit in lieu of raisins; or add a pinch of cinnamon.

Motor Development ◆
Sliding. An indoor slide (with soft landing) or a slide-climber combo is a perfect contraption for a nineteen- or twenty-month-old toddler. Aside from stimulating her large-motor development, it can be used for all sorts of imaginary play: hiding from the scary dragon (or her favorite dreaded animal), playing house, cave exploration, chasing sisters or brothers, crawling like a cat or dog . . . you name it. There are some wonderful commercial products on the market. (See recommendations in Appendix E.) But you can also take advantage of slides at your local

playgrounds. Hold your baby as you slide down together, or let her go down alone as you stand *very* closely by, ready to support her as she climbs up and catch her at the bottom (playground slides can be a little high off the ground at the bottom). Only let her slide if she seems to enjoy it. If she's at all scared, forget it for now and try it again in another couple of months.

Animal moves. Take turns pretending to be various animals by moving around like they do. This will probably be more of a challenge for you than your uninhibited toddler, but just get in touch with your inner animal and go for it! Critter action possibilities include getting down on all fours like a dog (don't forget to wag your tail), duck waddling, frog jumping, kangaroo hopping, chicken scratching, crab walking, stiff-legged elephant walking, ostrich strutting, and the ever-popular seal flapping. My granddaughter loved pretending to fly like a bird—especially at the beach. She'd run with the shore birds, her arms back like wings. It was adorable (said her doting grandfather). Be sure to include sounds in your imitations—no sense just going halfway here.

Squirrel away. At this stage, your child will be into special places and "nesting." She'll love to have her own little areas where she can squirrel things away, and she'll most certainly have her favorite blankets and things that she'll drag everywhere. Combine that with her continuing interest in building with blocks, and homemade "caves" and simple mazes are a natural. Get some large foam or inflatable blocks in a toy stores and let her build herself a little hideaway. (Yes, she will definitely need a little help from you—and you might possibly need some reinforcing duct tape.) If you want to save yourself a few bucks, just hang an extra-big tablecloth or a sheet over a table for an instant tent-cave. Obviously, it doesn't need to be very large for your little camper, but if you're planning to join her at any point (which you inevitably will, since toddlers this age usually want to be in physical contact with you at all times), think dining room table tent as opposed to one made from the side table. Whichever, let your tot stash away her favorite objects and play in her own little world . . . for a little while, at least.

Months Twenty-One and Twenty-Two

Your child is now a real conversational partner who upholds her end of any discussion—simple ones anyway. Your chats are even more frequent than before, and your little linguist may be stringing together three-word phrases. They'll typically be modified versions of previous two-word combinations. Although her "sentences" are getting longer, she still has a long way to go. We're still in the "doggie drink water" period, so don't expect "The dog is drinking water from his bowl." But you can expect lots of variety in form and use, such as "No go ni-night!" "What Mommy do?" "Gimme more cookie!" "Baby fall down," and "Me throw Daddy?" Expect to be flooded with requests for book sharing, too. Don't be surprised if she asks for the same books over and over and never seems to tire of her favorites. Continue to use the pictures in an interactive way—talk about them and pose questions based on their content. If your tot wants to tell you stories from some of her favorite books instead of hearing your version, encourage it! It's an excellent way for her to grow her language.

● ■ ▲

MILESTONE WATCHLIST:
Twenty-One- and Twenty-Two-Month-Olds

Does your child . . .

❑ Mix words and jargon?

❑ Engage in dialogue with adults?

❑ Enjoy simple stories?

❑ Point to appropriate pictures when named?

❑ Turn book pages one at a time?

❑ Understand *he, she,* and *it?*

SHARED COMMUNICATION ACTIVITIES:
MONTHS TWENTY-ONE AND TWENTY-TWO

Communication ◆

Jazzed up "Old MacDonald." So are you bored yet with "Old MacDonald" and his tiresome, predictable farm? If so, it's time to try some variations. Maybe he has a plane that goes *zoom, zoom, zoom*; a tractor that *rhhumm rhummm, rhhummms*; a teakettle that goes, *eeeee, eeeee, eeeeeee*; a cow who thinks she's a cat and goes, *meow, meow, meow*; or a fly swatter that goes *whoosh, whoosh, whoosh*. I'm betting that you can be even more creative than that—so have a go at it. While we're at it, "Mary Had a Little Lamb" could use a makeover, too. Substitute your child's name for Mary's and come up with something new for those dreary lambs. Maybe something like:

> *Josie had a teddy bear, teddy bear, teddy bear*
> *Josie had a teddy bear*
> *And he went Grrrrrrrrrr all night.*

Or maybe:

> *Jamal had a great big tryke, great big tryke, great big tryke*
> *Jamal had a great big tryke, and he went really fast.*

You get the idea. Personalize it and give Mary a rest.

Ins and outs. Have your child move brightly colored objects *in* and *out* of containers, grocery bags, toy chests, and the like. This is the next stage of the *in* and *on* exercises we did last month. Here we're adding another preposition, *out*, and reinforcing the two your tot recently learned. Be sure to talk about *in, out,* and *on*—animals can go in and out of the barn, people in and out of the house, cars in and out of the garage, trains in and out of the tunnel . . . your options are limitless.

Let it blow! Blowing requires muscular strength, the ability to create a pressure and release it, and breath control—all important for speech. So let's strengthen your tot's speech abilities by engaging her in some blowing activities. A few possibilities: blowing bubbles through a straw in clean bathtub water or in a cup of liquid, inflating a collapsed paper bag, and blowing feathers, leaves, dandelion or milkweed fluff, and other lightweight things.

Cognitive Development ◆

Sink or swim in the tub. Use bathtime as an opportunity for learning about water. Show your child—in the form of play—that some objects disappear *below* the water and others stay *on top*. Talk about *heavy* and *light, float, sink, go down, stay up, on top,* and *in water*. This will come in very handy when it's time to venture to the beach or frolic in a swimming pool—she'll have plenty to say about it!

Match pictures. Although matching pictures seems like a visual exercise, this fun activity moves beyond simple visual stimulation and into cognition. It helps your toddler learn the skills that that allow her to interpret two-dimensional images and match things that are called by the same name but are not identical—say, a sports car and a station wagon, as both are cars but very different. All we're going to do here is cut a variety of different kinds of pictures from a magazine and help your toddler match them up. Start with different versions of the same thing, such as two different cars, hats, or dolls. In a few months, you can match things that go together as naturally as a horse and carriage: gloves and hands, hats and heads, shoes and feet, and glasses and eyes. Keep it very simple and explain why certain things are similar or go together, for example:

ADULT: What's this?
CHILD: Shoes!
ADULT: Yes, shoe. Shoe on foot. I see another shoe.
CHILD: (Looking at pictures)
ADULT: Let's see. Another shoe over here?
CHILD: Nudder shoe.
ADULT: Yes. You found Daddy's shoe. Here's . . .
CHILD: Mommy shoe.
ADULT: Um-hm. Two shoes. Daddy's shoe. Mommy's shoe.

Hearing Stimulation ◆

Look! Books! Your child is now capable of following and remembering a simple, *very simple,* plot. So if you haven't begun to do so already, start moving away from all-picture books and toward books with very simple stories. The books should still have lots of pictures, since they'll still be the most interesting part to your toddler, but now story counts, too. (Check Appendix E for a list of guaranteed tot-pleasers.)

Visual Stimulation ◆

Simply puzzling. Your toddler will love the challenge of simple, easy-to-handle wood-block puzzles now. Aside from helping her understand abstract shapes and problem solve, puzzles are wonderful for development of fine motor coordination and cognitive skills. Puzzles also provide the bonus of a series of little victories—what better feeling than having each little piece fit perfectly in its place—and she did it! Talk about the picture being constructed and give simple, concise, and consistent instructions. Just a suggestion: Your tot may be able to hold the puzzle pieces better if you buy the kind with handles on each piece. *Lights, Camera, Interaction* makes several wooden puzzles with large wooden knobs that are perfectly suited for tiny hands. My favorite for simplicity is the brightly colored Geometric Shapes Jumbo Knob puzzle, although there are several others with animals and vehicles that are pretty terrific, too.

Sensory Stimulation ◆

Rip 'em up, tear 'em up. This activity stimulates vision, hearing, and movement all in one . . . and it's perfect for little hands. Get out your old T-shirts—the ones ready for the rag pile . . . then let your little terminator tear them to shreds! It's a marvelous, powerful feeling to be able to rip up paper or thin fabric. You may have to start the tear for your child, but then stand back—she'll love the sound. The resultant cloth rags can be used for cleaning the house or washing the car—or for more fun. Long, thin pieces of material can be used as scarves for dancing (dance of the seven rags?)—or to make magic wands. Wands are easy. Just roll a few pieces of newspaper together, beginning at the top edge of a page and rolling down to form a cylinder about two feet in length. Tape it together, then glue torn T-shirt streamers to the end and voilà!—an awesome wand!

To make it more magical, paint it with some bright glitter paint. Play some music—I'd recommend something like "Puff the Magic Dragon." Dance to the music while waving the wands. Nothing beats a little magic wand dancing . . . if you ask me.

What a ripoff! Another fun "ripping up" treat is unwrapping gifts. For a child, unwrapping is often more of a treat than the actual gift. Wrap up some objects from around the house—a kid's book, clothes to share, fruit or a juice box, for instance, in the Sunday funnies (for a touch of festive color), and rip away together.

Finger paint the town. Washable, nontoxic finger paints are fun and very sensual. Use traditional paper or buy bathtub finger paints for the tile and tub. If you go the traditional route, spread big sheets of paper out on a table, tape it down, and let her go to town. Show her how to make spirals, circles, or lines. Then have her "sign" it with a handprint. Be sure to keep some of this "art." It'll be great fun to look back on it together in a few years—and that handprint will seem so tiny! Body painting is an option, too.

And you thought the other activities were messy! This game is not for the squeamish! And the timing has to be right—only do it when you have lots of time, you and your tot are both in a fun, relaxed mood, and—most importantly—it's almost time for a bath. Ready? Get in front of a mirror and decorate each other with edible materials, such as whipped cream, raisins, pudding, yogurt, and peanut butter. Yes, it's incredibly messy, but it's fun, too! Think of the pleasure involved in licking your own whipped cream or peanut butter moustache! Of course, you'll want to have some fun conversations while you decorate and taste—a perfect time to name face parts. (Again . . . forget the peanut butter if there's any chance your child may be allergic.)

Motor Development ◆

Jump, jump, jump. Now that your toddler has mastered walking—more or less—she'll find jumping extraordinarily interesting and endlessly entertaining. Since this is an important developmental step and there's no getting around it, let's make it as safe as possible. Be very firm about where and when jumping is allowed and hold her hand. A bed, old mattress, or kiddie gym mat is ideal for jumping. No trampolines at this age, please, unless you hold both her hands and she jumps very lightly with you. She'll still lose her balance easily, so be sure to supervise her closely. You could also let her jump off a very low footstool into a pile of pillows or a sofa cushion— heaven for a toddler! Naturally, talking about the activity as it occurs is part of the package—try making up a story about jumping. Here's one idea:

ADULT: (As child is jumping) Sophie jump. (Pause) Sophie jump up . . . down. Up . . . down. (Pause) Sophie is the biggest jumper. (Pause) Biggest jumper in the world! (Pause) She jumped over a . . . teddy bear. Oops, on the teddy bear. She jumped over some string (lying on the mat).

CHILD: Dump up!

ADULT: Yes, Sophie jumped up . . . down. She jumps everywhere! Even to Gran'ma's house!

CHILD: Gahma!

ADULT: Yes, Gran'ma and to school. Jump to school.

If you're feeling energetic and need a little workout yourself, you could play "Stop" where you both jump until one of you suddenly says "Stop" or "Stop jumping."

To the park. Community parks often have elaborate playgrounds that can offer hours of climbing, sliding, crawling, digging, and running. Many parks also come with imaginative structures to use as a fortress or a house with bridges and towers, and some even offer water play. Use your imagination and play along with your child. Stones can become pretend food; tunnels can be places to explore; and slides can offer an escape from a big but not too smart, very unthreatening, pretend "monster." Playgrounds are ideal places to combine words with actions, such as "Mommy slide down", "Sally swing fast", "Mommy push me", "Boy run in", and the like.

A magnetic personality. Your child has the fine motor skills now to handle some small objects, and refrigerator magnets offer her plenty of opportunity to exercise this new ability. Plus, toddlers love the way magnets seem to magically cling to a metal surface. Put five or six colorful magnets shaped like fruit, animals, people, or other familiar things on the bottom of the fridge or on a cookie sheet and let your toddler have at it. Show her how to slide them around, pull them off, and put them back on. She'll thoroughly enjoy it and it will keep her busy for—well, minutes at a time. After playing, leave them low on the fridge door so she can access them easily whenever she wants—when she feels the magnetic pull, as it were. Although you'll find alphabet letter magnets in the toy stores, too, it's best to resist the urge to teach spelling at this stage. Our goal is fine-motor manipulation here, not reading or spelling—yet, anyway. We still have a while before that happens. The most you'd want to do now is show her letters that make up her name. But believe me, she has no idea yet that letters represent sounds—that's a very complex notion.

Spin city. At about this age, many children develop a love of spinning and seem to do it endlessly. Nobody's quite sure why this happens. One theory is that it stimulates the balance mechanism at a time when the child is developing balance for locomotion. But whatever the case, limited spinning can strengthen coordination and balance, and can be added to your dance routines. Although your little one has the ability to spin herself around, she may become dizzy easily, so stay nearby—as both dancing partner and catcher. Remember to do any "dancing" in a nice safe space with nothing breakable or sharp around, and preferably on a carpeted floor.

Months Twenty-Three and Twenty-Four

As your toddler approaches her second birthday, language and cognition continue to run along on parallel developmental tracts. Language blends even more smoothly with cognition now and is becoming the inner voice of most of her thoughts. Language also now forms the basis for a lot of her cognitive organization—the word categories that affect thought. Your child may now be gracing you with four-word phrases and words ending in "ing" and the plural "s." Since she's still not quite two years old, she's not talking like an adult, but her language is so much fun, and so adorable, does it really matter? Her fascination with books continues, and now she's able to follow very simple story lines— although she still enjoys books with pictures for naming. She might enjoy picture cards, too, but only use them interactively as a basis for communication—if you have pictures of food, for example, set them around the house and play supermarket. But no drills please; that's not shared communication.

MILESTONE WATCHLIST:
Twenty-Three- and Twenty-Four-Month Olds

Does your child . . .

❑ **Refer to herself by name?**

❑ **Use some pronouns, such as *me, you, mine, he, she,* and *it?***

❑ **Understand new words quickly?**

❑ **Relate personal experiences?**

❑ **Use four-word phrases occasionally?**

❑ **Understand simple sentences?**

❑ **Scribble with a crayon or pencil?**

❑ **Draw in a circular motion if shown?**

SHARED COMMUNICATION ACTIVITIES:
MONTHS TWENTY-THREE AND TWENTY-FOUR

Communication ◆

Pass it on. When you're talking with a relative or good friend on the phone, have your toddler talk into the receiver to pass along a very short message, or at least have her say "Hi" or "Bye." Just a quick little chat with someone she can't actually see will strengthen your little one's communication and cognitive skills and stimulate her long-term memory, since she has to reach into her databank to find the identity of her conversational partner. It will also tone up her auditory sequential memory as she tries to remember the message you've asked her to relay. Try to keep your message short and sweet—"Tell Nana, see you soon"—since at this age your tot can't remember phrases of more than three or four words.

The ever-popular body tracing. This exercise combines visual two-dimensional memory with listening memory, and is a terrific way to help your toddler remember the names of different body parts. Have your tot lie down on a large piece of paper while you trace her body shape with a crayon or marker. When that's done, ask her to name the parts of her body that are evident in the tracing (arms, legs, hands, head, etc.), and help her find the corresponding parts on the tracing. Color the parts on the tracing together. If you want to take it a step further, trace individual parts in more detail, such as a foot with all the toes, color it, cut it out, then match it to the whole body tracing.

Knock, knock. Who's there? We've played *knock, knock* before, but now that your toddler is more mature, she can be a much more active participant. In this new and improved game, each of you gets to portray someone else, which adds to the fun while increasing the communication possibilities. Both of you can put on funny hats and silly clothes or manipulate dolls and puppets, and take turns knocking at the door. First, one of you knocks, and when the door is answered, the conversation begins. Your child will love being the one who knocks first, so sit on the other side and make a big show of it when you see who's there. Once you've greeted each other, hug, cuddle, kiss, have a conversation. Then start again with a fresh knock and a new persona. Hey, I think I hear someone knocking now . . .

ADULT: Who's there?
CHILD: Mommy knock door.
ADULT: (Opens door) Oh, it is Mommy. What a beautiful hat.
CHILD: Big hat.
ADULT: (Laughing) Yes, and you look so good in a ball cap!
CHILD: Mommy dress on.

ADULT: Are you going to Gran'ma's? Dresses and ball caps are so lovely.
CHILD: Go Gra'ma's now.
ADULT: Okay. Bye. Drive safely.

One story building. In a very limited fashion, your child can now begin to tell you stories, so let's encourage it. Storytelling, after all, is one of the foundations of good conversational skills. Don't expect plots, character development, or even imaginative or pretend stories yet. Your little one's stories will be more about the things that make an impression on her; objects and events and people that are outside the realm of her everyday routines. A trip to the zoo with all the new and amazing animals would be a great subject for a toddler story. A fast-food restaurant or a trip to the beach or library can make for good stories, too. She won't relate the day's events in sequence, as you might expect. The tale will be more stream-of-consciousness—she'll just tell you things as they pop into her head. Encourage her with your positive responses and total interest: "Wow! What happened next?" or "How nice! Tell me more."

Cognitive Development ◆
Not-so-instant replay. Talk to your toddler about things she has recently experienced, even if the events are relatively mundane like going to the park or picking up her sister Sheila at soccer practice. By "telling" these stories together, you're helping your child relate to events thematically, which is a precursor to later storytelling and understanding and an important part of talking and preliteracy. One of the best ways to help your child tell stories is to start by setting the stage for her: "Who went to the doctor?" or "Where did we meet Gran'ma?" Then move her along with leading questions, very simple synopses, and requests such as "Tell me more" or "Then what happened?" All this helps your child organize, interpret, and analyze the sequence of events that goes into an experience. It might sound something like this:

ADULT: Who went to the circus?
CHILD: Me!
ADULT: Yep! Jody went circus. Jody saw . . .

CHILD: Cwown.

ADULT: Yes, funny clowns. And . . .

CHILD: Big monkey.

ADULT: Yes, there was a pretend gorilla . . . gorilla. Jody went . . .

CHILD: Circus.

ADULT: And saw . . .

CHILD: Cwowns and a big monkey.

You can also use toys or other props to reenact an event—sort of like a scene from a mini one-act play. After going to a restaurant, for example, you could do a playback on toy dishes, while you take the part of the waiter and your toddler pretends to be you. When you do these kinds of play reenactments, discuss what happened at the event first, then talk about it while you play-act, then finish by talking about what you did for the play reenactment. Each builds on the next and is a great way to teach.

Hearing Stimulation ◆

"Teddy in a boat." Young children love this game, and there are several variations. Sit next to your child with a teddy on your lap facing you. As you recite a rhyme, bounce teddy on your knee while holding your toddler's hands. The rhyme might go as follows:

Teddy bear in a boat,
Doing what he ought-er (should, can, wants, says, thinks)
A big fish bumped the boat
And Teddy fell in the water.

On the last line, spread your knees and let teddy fall through or perform any other action that goes with your personalized rhyme. Vary the wait between the third and fourth line, so your child will have to pay attention and will anticipate the climax. Then encourage her to hold teddy on her knees and do the same thing, which gives her more responsibility for the song. Gradually give her more to do. Begin by leaving out just the last word and letting your tot supply it as Teddy falls through her knees. While this is a lot of fun, your toddler is also learning about sequencing words and participating in word play. Really laugh when she gives you a word that is different than the one intended. Or change the rhyme and teach her a new verse.

Visual Stimulation ◆

The bear went . . . "The Bear Went Over the Mountain" is a song that can be used a lot to stress vision and observation. It goes like this:

> *The bear went over the mountain,*
> *The bear went over the mountain,*
> *The bear went over the mountain,*
> *To see what he could see.*
> *He saw another mountain,*
> *He saw another mountain,*
> *He saw another mountain,*
> *That's all that he could see.*

Your variations on the song could include family members and familiar objects, for example:

> *Jolie went on a walk (three times)*
> *To see what she could see.*
> *She saw a great big doggie.*
>
> *Mommy drives in the car (three times)*
> *To see what she could see.*
> *She saw the Teletubbies.*
>
> *Daddy flies in an airplane.*
> *He saw pretty birdie.*
>
> *We took a hike in the woods.*
> *We saw a little bunny.*

Occasionally pick things in your immediate environment so you can point them out as you sing—*Mommy saw Jolie's sweater*. Also encourage your tot to point to what the person sees as you sing about it, or even let her point to something beforehand and then include her choice in the song. The book *Brown Bear, Brown Bear, What Do You See?* by Bill Martin is a terrific accompaniment to this activity—either as an introduction or conclusion. It's a classic, rhyming picture book that has a different animal asking, "What do you see?" ("Red bird, red bird, what do you see?") You have to turn the page to find out ("I see a yellow duck looking at me!") Before you turn each page, ask your tot what she thinks the animal will see next—then see if she's right.

Sensory Stimulation ◆

Play fingers, play. Continue with your finger plays. Now that your tot's fine motor skills are much more developed, she should be able to do a lot of the hand movements herself. Finger plays are actually excellent learning tools all through these preschool years, since they have motor and language skills built in, and learning through movement is especially effective for young children. Try any of those in Appendix B—they're all excellent. Once you've sung and done the actions together a few times, you might hear your child practicing when she's off on her own or in her car seat.

Name that sensation. Your toddler has been receiving lots of sensory stimulation so far; now let's ask her to be more active. This time as you help her experience different sounds, tastes, and textures, ask her what she smells, tastes, or feels. Tell her to close her eyes or hold your hand over her eyes (if she doesn't mind) and let her smell or taste things that she knows the words for. (*Vanilla extract* doesn't count.) Try things like yogurt, lemonade, chocolate, peanut butter, orange, peach, cookie, tomato, cheese, pudding, Jell-O, marshmallow fluff, jellies, and the like. Try to avoid strong or offensive smells or tastes. Things like anchovies and escargot are acquired tastes and definitely not kid food.

Feed it to the birds. I know, I know . . . you built a pinecone bird feeder like this way back when you where in preschool. But it will still be a hit with the new birds in town . . . not to mention your fledging bird-watcher. All you need for this project is a pinecone, peanut butter, birdseed, yarn—and, of course, your little helper. Together, spread peanut butter on the pinecone, roll it in the seeds, and tie it outside with the yarn. It's a fail-proof project, and if your child tends to be messy, it's fine. She can't ruin this project. There are lots of opportunities for language while making the feeder and even more while you enjoy watching the birds feed—and it gets your toddler in touch with nature, too. Later on you can watch the birds feed and talk about them. (*Please don't try this if your child is allergic to peanuts.*)

Motor Development ◆

I got you pegged. Manipulating small but safe objects like those in toy pegboards, gear games, and toddler Legos can enhance your child's fine motor abilities and creativity while strengthening her hands for holding and squeezing. (Check Appendix E for specific recommendations.) Building and imaginative playing also offer great opportunities for building language:

> ADULT: What are you making?
> CHILD: Make airplane.
> ADULT: Oh, airplanes can . . .
> CHILD: Fly up high.
> ADULT: Well, that's a good thing for a plane. What's this?
> CHILD: Wing.
> ADULT: Like a bird's wing.
> CHILD: No, a plane's wing!

Batting balloons. Batting colorful balloons back and forth with your toddler is great for hand-eye coordination as well as large-motor development and visual stimulation. Children love it—balloons move slower than a ball, which gives kids a better chance to hit their mark, and balloons are light so nobody ever gets hurt. An all-around winner! Get more than one going at a time, and keep them all in play. (Watch that you're toddler doesn't mouth them, and don't leave her alone with them.)

Footprints in the sand. When you're at the beach, show your toddler how to walk in your footprints. It's terrific for her large muscle development and coordination, and can move into problem-solving territory as well. Plus, she'll find following in an adult's footsteps quite novel and exciting.

Snow works just as well as sand, and wet footprints on concrete or cutout paper footprints taped to the floor are other options. Whichever route you go, remember that your little one has short legs, so keep the footprints close together. After you've done this a few times, you can add some very low obstacles at the end to make it more challenging, and a nice little treat when you're finished is always a welcome ending.

Shared Communication Activities:
Months 19 through 24

MONTHLY ACTIVITIES

Age (Mos.)	Communication	Cognitive Development	Hearing Stimulation
19-20	▲ "My day" book ▲ This one's ON you ▲ Spin and talk ▲ Oh where, oh where . . . ▲ "What would you like?"	▲ Sort and match ▲ Mail call!	▲ Dances with scarves
21-22	▲ Jazzed up "Old MacDonald" ▲ Ins and outs ▲ Let it blow!	▲ Sink or swim in the tub ▲ Match pictures	▲ Look! Books!
23-24	▲ Pass it on ▲ The ever-popular body tracing ▲ Knock, knock. Who's there? ▲ One story building	▲ Not-so-instant replay	▲ "Teddy in a boat"

Shared Communication Reminders
- Keep setting good language examples
- Take advantage of ALL language opportunities
- Have real conversations

Visual Stimulation	Sensory Stimulation	Motor Development
▲ Shine, little flashlight	▲ Pass on something nice	▲ Sliding
	▲ Fed up	▲ Animal moves
	▲ Special cards	▲ Squirrel away
	▲ No-bake cookies	
▲ Simply puzzling	▲ Rip 'em up tear 'em up	▲ Jump, jump, jump
	▲ What a rip off!	▲ To the park
	▲ Finger paint the town	▲ A magnetic personality
	▲ And you thought the other activities were messy!	▲ Spin city
▲ The bear went . . .	▲ Play fingers, play	▲ I got you pegged
	▲ Name the sensation	▲ Batting balloons
	▲ Feed it to the birds	▲ Footprints in the sand

- Sing social songs in which your child can participate
- Be silly
- Provide opportunities for language growth

CHAPTER THIRTEEN

Two Years Old and Beyond

The Wonderful Years Ahead

BY now you should be mightily impressed with your little chatterbox. He may have been slow to start talking, but his pace has been rapidly accelerating and won't slow down until school age. If we were rocking the past few months, we're totally rolling now! At about two years, your preschooler will be adding two or three words a day to his vocabulary, and by the time he enters first grade, he'll be able to regale you with more than 2,500 words. Even more amazing, he'll understand as many as 10,000! By the time he's five years old, his sentences will *average* five to eight words. He'll have learned more than 90 percent of language form (grammar) and mastered almost all difficult speech sounds—even those tricky consonant blends, like *street* or *slippery,* where one consonant loses some of its sound oomph as it mixes with another, won't stop him.

But while your child's sentences will be advanced (though maybe not quite adultlike), they will still be 100 percent pure child in content, and that's wherein the beauty lies. These next years promise lots of fun! You can be as silly and playful as you want to be, and your heartstrings will be tugged every which way. I recently had a little chat with an adorable three-year-old daughter of a good friend who told me all about her feelings for her mom. "I love my mom," she said with a secretlike whisper, "cause she takes care of me, and uh, she makes banana milkshakes, and she . . . she does funny burps." It was so sweet and somehow really moved me to see that loving, caring relationship peeking through. Imagine how you'll feel when you hear things like that about you from your own child—and it's right around the corner.

Over these next few years, your child will learn to support his part of a conversation. He'll be able to initiate topic discussions, maintain a running dialogue, and end conversations appropriately. His communication will be enlivened by stories and pretend. He'll become increasingly verbal, and soon his talking will not only accompany play but actually be the focus of it. He'll begin to take on roles as he plays, pretending to be a baby, mommy, doctor, or my son's former favorite, a fireman. And of course, there's a good chance he'll be imitating you and your favorite expressions more and more—so don't blame him for any four-letter words that might slip out while Grandma's visiting. In addition to swearing off swearing around your little tyke with the big ears, there are some important Shared Communication suggestions to keep in mind over these next few years.

■ *Continue to expand on your child's words and phrases for the next year or so, then gradually taper off*. Rather than correcting your child's less-than-perfect speech, reply in a positive way with a slightly altered, more adultlike version of what he said. For example:

CHILD: We goed zoo.
ADULT: Um-hm, we **went to the** zoo with Grandma. My favorite animal was the lion.
CHILD: I likeded monkeys.
ADULT: You **liked** monkeys? Why?

As your child matures and his language gets more complex, he'll begin learning less from mimicry and more by formulating language rules from the talking he hears around him. That's when this strategy gradually starts losing its effectiveness. So after about three years old, start using it more sparingly.

■ *Reply in a conversational way*. Now that your preschooler is learning to hold his own in a conversation, give him full rein. Concentrate less on providing a model of overall language and more on *facilitating the exchange of information*. Still, don't abandon your shepherding altogether—he'll still need plenty of help from you. He'll have to juggle a lot of linguistic complexities just to keep a conversation going. He has to interpret your speech, decide on an appropriate response, and make sure that response is grammatically correct—all while trying to formulate his own language rules. You can make all this easier for him by using *Conversation extenders* in your responses—which essentially means tossing him new ideas to help him stay involved in the conversation. For example:

CHILD: The horse goes in the barn.
ADULT: She's going to go to sleep. <u>What about the cow?</u>
or
CHILD: And my favorite is French fries.
ADULT: That's my favorite, too. <u>Do you like ketchup on them?</u>

Of course, you don't want to ask questions all the time. That can get tedious for anyone—including your little one. So it's a good idea to incorporate a few other, more creative conversation extenders into your repertoire. You'll find the following five especially effective. The examples for each of the different types of extenders here are in response to a child who says, "My favorite food is French fries."

A fill-in. Let your child *fill in* the last word.

"Ummm . . . and you like French fries with _____."

I wonder statement. As in "I wonder what will happen if . . ." or "I wonder what will happen next."

"Umm. I like them, too. <u>I wonder what</u> you like on them."

I think statement. As in "I think we should . . ." or "I think X will Y."

"<u>I think we should</u> pretend to eat French fries."

Tell me more. *"<u>Tell me more about</u> your favorites."*

Silly statement. *"<u>I like to eat French fries in the bathtub!</u>"*

Give some of these extenders a try; you'll be surprised how creative your child's responses will be. Think of this as conversational turn-taking with a twist.

■ *Ask for clarification.* Be sure to pay full attention to your child when he talks. It will really help you to understand him, and he won't be forced to repeat himself over and over in response to an unending string of "What?" and "Huh?" If you don't understand something he's said, it's perfectly okay to let him know it. He needs to learn that the speaker has a responsibility to transmit clearly—that's part of being a good conversationalist. But help him out a bit! Instead of just saying, "What?" make your question specific to what you didn't understand. For example, "Honey, where did you go?" or "Um-hm, tell me again what she did," or even "I don't understand what he ate." By specifying what information you need, you help your child to respond.

■ *Don't interrupt, hurry, or make fun of your child.* Sometimes well-intentioned parents become too anxious about their child's speech, or too impatient. They attempt to finish his ideas or to hurry him along. They may even make fun of his speech or be overly critical. This latter behavior is more often used with boys to "make" them into little men. Avoid all of these behaviors at all costs. The results can be disastrous. When I first started working as a speech-language pathologist, I was asked to evaluate a five-year-old boy for stuttering. During our session, this small, handsome, inquisitive child, whom we'll call Billy, spoke perfectly; nary a stutter. I maneuvered him into producing complex sentences. I hurried him along some. I tried a variety of speaking tasks. No stuttering. I couldn't imagine why his parents were concerned.

When we went into the waiting room to tell his parents the good news, Billy started to stutter—he just fell apart before my eyes. The bottom line was that Billy was terrified of making a speaking mistake in front of his parents. His older, somewhat formal parents were creating the problem. The three of them were caught in a vicious cycle. The more Billy stumbled over his speech, the more they criticized and finished his sentences and thoughts for him, which resulted in his stumbling even more. Fortunately, once they learned what they were doing wrong, they were able to change their ways—and I learned something, too. Now, whenever I do an evaluation, I always watch the child conversing with his or her parents *first*. I assure you that most children give you the best speech and language they can. Occasionally—usually when there's a new baby in the house—a child will use more juvenile speech and language, but that's generally rectified with a discussion about how important it is to be a big brother or big sister.

■ *Keep those books coming.* As we've discussed, oral language is a precursor to written language. The better your child's speech, the better his reading and writing will be. You can help develop your tot's reading and writing ability by sharing books with him on a daily basis. Get in the habit of reading together before bedtime or napping or during some other quiet time. Make it part of each day's routine. Use the story in the book as a focus for discussing different aspects of its contents, and talk about how it relates to other things in your child's life. (There's a nice long list of terrific books that I'm sure you and your tot will enjoy in Appendix E.)

You will continue to be amazed—and often amused—by your child's language development. But no matter where he is with his words, I'd like to leave you with a really important reminder: Enjoy your child to the fullest.

Children are wonderful little people; this time in their development is precious, and it will never come again. After all my years working with kids, I still melt when I hear them say things like, "Can we play with teddy? He looks lonesome." Children are, in a word, inspiring. Your loving input has already had a tremendously positive impact on your little one, and will continue to be hugely important in the years to come. The Shared Communication principals and techniques that I've set forth here will continue to help his spoken language, reading skills, and cognitive abilities grow and flourish, as they give him a positive self-image and the confidence to successfully wend his way through this complicated yet wondrous world we live in.

I began this book with congratulations to you as a new parent, and I end now with congratulations for having a wonderful, verbal, happy, and engaging two-year-old. I hope you've both had lots of fun, along with some good bonding hugs, snuggles, and giggles as you've played the games and shared the activities. Be assured that your time and efforts have helped your child in ways that will bear fruit throughout his life, and that your ongoing shared *conversations* are the best way to help him continue to learn language and to feel your unparalleled interest, caring, and love. Thank you for allowing me to share this special time with you and to be part of your parental journey. Enjoy and cherish the wonderful years ahead.

F.A.Q.s

Dr. Bob Answers Some of Your Questions

Part of being a parent is that little nagging doubt that often comes in the middle of the night—"Am I doing all that I can for my child?" Trust me, that doesn't go away as your child matures. There will always be questions: it's just the situations that change. Over the years, I've worked with hundreds of parents concerned about their children's ability to communicate; perhaps some of their concerns echo your own. If so, I hope these Q and A's will help alleviate some of your worries, answer some of your questions, or, at the very least, get you on the right track to finding the correct information for your particular situation.

What can I expect in terms of language acquisition if I adopt a child from another culture?
That depends on a few variables: the two languages involved, the age and health of the child, the development of the child in the first language, and the importance placed on each language within the home.

In general, if you adopt an infant younger than the age of one year old, the first language will have little effect on English. Remember, however, that even a seven- to twelve-month-old child has been babbling with many of the sounds of his first language. It may take a short period of adjustment to get accustomed to new sounds. A friend of mine who adopted a one-year-old infant from China noticed how little she babbled when they brought her to the United States compared to the babbling she did in her Chinese orphanage. She was adjusting to her circumstances. Now, at age three, she's fine.

I'm also reminded of a dear friend and fellow speech-language pathologist, Irene, whose first language is Russian. She was asked to evaluate a fifteen-month-old child, adopted from Russia, who, after a few months in the United States, was not speaking—although his new parents reported some incomprehensible babbling. When Irene began to play with the boy, she realized that he was saying a few words, but in Russian, which, not surprisingly, his adopted parents didn't understand. He quickly adapted to English with a little help from Irene. Even children of three or four should be able to learn a second language without special instruction. True, a first language can interfere with the second, but it can also facilitate the second. And remember that a three-year-old hasn't developed his first language fully, so the interference is minimized.

Health is a separate issue and can be a concern in some foreign adoptions, especially if the child comes from an orphanage or similar facility in a developing nation. Institutions may be overcrowded, and health and nutrition concerns secondary. Poorer countries may simply lack the resources to care for these children adequately. Poor health can lead to developmental problems, such as the effects of severe malnutrition on the developing brain, which are difficult or near impossible to reverse.

Most preschool children faced with a new language will take some time to study and analyze the situation. They may go silent for several weeks or even months. Regardless of the child's age, you can apply the Shared Communication ideas that are appropriate for the child's developmental level. Use the month watchlists as a guide. You should also find a good preschool program, and in cases of severe delay, contact a speech-language pathologist through your county health service, local school district, local hospital, or clinic.

Don't try to go it alone. Seek out other adoptive parents for support and encouragement. Here are a few websites that may be helpful:

www.iaapadoption.com/afterhome/afterhome.htm—The International Assistance & Adoption Project (IAAP) provides services for families wishing to adopt children of all ages from either China or Vietnam.

www.adopting.com/countries.html—The International Adoption Information and Support site offers a variety of services for children from various countries, including family support at www.i-a-a.org.

www.adoptlaw.org/tiac htm/7specpro.htm—The International Adoption Center offers links to many other related sites.

Not all professionals agree on what to do with your child's first language, be it Spanish, Korean, Chinese, or what have you. I find it sad that a child should lose this part of his heritage, but I also recognize the difficulty in finding appropriate original culture learning resources. In large urban areas, there may be immigrant communities that take pride in preserving their language and customs. They may even have preschool or after-school programs in churches, mosques, or temples. Investigate. Test your comfort level. Do you feel welcome even though cultural differences exist?

The important aspect of learning two languages is keeping them separate. It's not as if you can tell your two-year-old that he's learning two languages now. So, English at home and in preschool, and Ukrainian or whatever the first language is on Saturdays at the fellowship hall or Ukrainian Orthodox church. Or English in preschool and Urdu at home. There are endless variations, but keep the two language separate.

Will learning two languages at the same time adversely affect my child's development?
No! I'm constantly amazed by the flexibility of young minds. Learning two languages seems to take little more effort than learning one. Far from adversely affecting your child's development, learning two languages greatly enhances a child's educational and employment potential. There is absolutely no research data that suggests that learning two languages simultaneously delays a child's overall language development.

Learning two languages at the same time is most often a concern for parents who are bilingual, speak different languages themselves, or are immigrants who speak English only minimally or not at all. My main cautionary recommendation is similar to that in the previous answer. Keep the two languages separate. For example, Dad speaks Spanish and Mom English. Or Tagalog is spoken at home and English in daycare or preschool. Your child may begin speaking a few months later than I've predicted in this book, but that's to be expected. When your child begins to speak, there will be some initial language mixing of both words and grammatical rules. Be patient and keep using the appropriate language. Around a year after he begins to talk, your child will have sorted it all out. He's on the way to becoming truly bilingual.

Let me tell you the story of Natalia, a very bright preschooler who came to the United States from Colombia when she was five months old with her bilingual Spanish-English, college-educated parents. At home, her parents and their friends spoke in Spanish. When she arrived at English-only daycare around age one, her parents were advised by the teacher to stop speaking Spanish at home. As a family friend—and the "official" U.S. gran'pa—I was asked for my advice. In defiance of the daycare teacher, I recommended continued use of Spanish at home. I saw no benefit in raising her to be monolingual, and frankly, I found it insulting to suggest that she not speak the language of her family and culture.

At first, Natalia spoke very little at school, and continued to use Spanish words at home. When she began to use English at daycare it was often mixed with Spanish, and when she began to combine words, it was often a Spanish one plus an English one. School was of little help, but at home her parents sorted out her speech and spoke to her in Spanish. When Natalia was thirty months old, her grandmother (who speaks limited but serviceable English) and her great-grandmother (who speaks only Spanish) flew in from Bogotá for a visit. Being a close friend of the grandmother, I stopped by frequently. To my utter delight, Natalia conversed easily with her great-grandmother in Spanish, effortlessly switching to English for me. But the real joy came in listening to her negotiate Spanish and English with her grandmother. If Natalia was speaking in English and her grandmother seemed confused, Natalia smoothly switched to Spanish for an explanation, then back to English. Sometimes they spoke in Spanish only, at others English only. To my delight, at age three-and-a-half, Natalia decided on her own to march into the preschool director's office and negotiate to ride the bus to preschool like the four-year-olds because she technically was in the fours' class. Because of her persuasive argument delivered in impeccable English, she is now the only three-year-old on the bus!

Do all children learn language in the same way?
The ways that children learn language is as varied as their personalities. We all differ slightly and so do our methods of deciphering the language code. Some children take a wait-and-see attitude, cautiously speaking only when they're certain of what to say and how to say it. Others are more assertive and forge ahead, seemingly unaware of language conventions. Some children are constructionists, creatively piecing together bits of language, while others construct less but parrot more of what they hear around them. Differences in cognitive processing, perception, sensory ability, personality, family history, environment, and parental education, all combine to affect a child's language learning ability. So don't worry if your child's approach to language is different than that of a sibling or another child.

If my baby starts talking late, will he catch up?
Yes, your child will catch up, unless he has a severe or undetected language impairment—and the odds are against that. About 25 percent of all children are late talkers, and more than half of them catch up and are doing fine by the time they go to school. That leaves only about 12 percent who *may* need some help. Unfortunately, since children don't come with labels and instructions, there's no way of knowing if your child's language development will continue to be delayed. When in doubt, err on the side of caution and seek professional help. Ignoring a communication problem won't make it go away.

How do I know if my child needs professional help?
Approximately 10 to 15 percent of all children will have *some* kind of handicapping condition, many of them speech- and language-related. Although many of these children develop typical speech and language skills without treatment, it's a good idea to have your child evaluated if you think there's a problem. If you wait until school age, it may be too late for

optimal benefit. In addition, your child may be starting school with a real disadvantage—as we discussed, the best indicator of a child's likely success in reading and writing is his oral language skills. Early identification and clinical intervention increases the chance of a child improving his language. Here are some of the signs of possible communication problems to help you judge if professional intervention is warranted:

- At three months, your child doesn't respond to noises or to your voice or doesn't establish eye contact with you.

- At six months, he's not producing speech sounds.

- At twelve months, he's not pointing or reaching and making noises.

- At eighteen months, he doesn't have at least one or two words that you understand.

- At twenty-four months, he has no two-word utterances that you understand or doesn't ask or answer simple questions.

Remember that the range of normal development is very wide. Even the guidelines presented may signal nothing but a late-blooming child.

Factors related to speech and language problems may include, but are not limited to, temporary or permanent hearing loss, prematurity/low birth weight, Fetal Alcohol Syndrome, genetic abnormalities such as Down's syndrome, neurological conditions such as cerebral palsy, neurological accidents, developmental delays, poor learning or health, and lack of opportunity. Temporary hearing loss may result from a middle ear infection caused by colds, upper respiratory infections, or allergies. One middle ear infection will probably not affect language learning, but chronic infections can be a serious factor. None of these conditions automatically dooms a child to speech and language impairment. Most premature infants don't have permanent difficulties. Even Down's syndrome doesn't always mean severe retardation.

If you suspect your child may have problems, put your mind to rest and take him to a professional for an evaluation. As parents, most of us have a bad case of the "Hopes" when it comes to our children. We *hope* that things will be for the better, and often try to wish problems away. That's not good enough when we're talking about critical early development. Even if you feel that your child might be lacking because of something you did—like taking drugs or drinking while pregnant—don't let shame or guilt stop you from seeking professional help. Your child's needs and well-being come first. Whatever you did, it's done. Now you have to move on and take responsibility.

Some parents are also reluctant to seek professional help because of the fear and embarrassment of having a child with a handicapping condition. I knew a pair of very well-educated parents who continued to deny that their preschooler needed to wear glasses because the thought of having a "disabled" child embarrassed them. As far as they were concerned, their child was "perfect" despite his squinting and inability to recognize letters and numbers! I simply can't understand this kind of behavior. If your child has an obvious and potentially handicapping condition, it's all the more reason to seek assistance. Is it really so awful to have a child who wears glasses or signs, when the alternative is a child who communicates very little and may be educationally disadvantaged?

And please, don't hide your child at home. Children with handicapping conditions need to be out and about, having normalizing experiences. It can be argued that such children need even more of these types of encounters because of the less-than-normal ways in which they can interact with the world. Promise me—for the sake of your child, you'll seek professional advice if you have any concerns.

For these concerns or additional questions, consult appropriate child development books, ask development professionals in private practice or at schools and universities, or research online. Use only reputable professional organization websites. A good place to start is the American Speech-Language-Hearing Association (ASHA) at www.asha.org/index. cfm. ASHA offers guidance and links to other sites and can provide a list of certified clinical facilities in your geographic area. Note also that your local government is legally responsible for children's special educational needs and should offer communication ability screenings by a certified speech-language pathologist. Finally, if you're seeking professional input, don't accept prescriptive advice from any professional who has not evaluated your child in person. It is a violation of most professional ethics to prescribe treatment without seeing the child in person. Your child's well-being is incredibly important, and there is no substitute for a thorough, individualized, professional diagnostic evaluation—and, if necessary, specifically tailored, family-centered intervention.

Finger Plays

As a camp counselor (way back when), I can't tell you how many times I hollered "Are you happy?" as an introduction to the old favorite action song, *"If You're Happy and You Know It . . ."* It was obvious that my little campers were having fun, but I never would have guessed how much developmental value they were getting from these kinds of exercises. Finger plays and action songs teach structure, participation, and fine motor skills while strengthening verbal memory—that's a big payoff!

If you attended preschool, daycare, or camp back when you were a child, there's a good chance you'll remember some of the ones I've assembled for you here. I hope that your favorites are among them so you can pass them on to your little tyke. Most one-year-olds (and older) will be able to participate in all the finger plays at some level. The younger your tot, the more you'll want to simplify the hand motions. The activities that involve counting (which I earmarked for you) are more appropriate for ages eighteen months and older. Don't try to do too many at once. Your child is bright but does have limited memory. Learn one together. Play it for a week or two; then, when it seems to lose its spark, move on to a brand-new ditty. Have fun!

Beehive *(counting)*
Here is the beehive, (Make a fist.)
Where are the bees? (Shrug.)
Hiding away where nobody sees.
They are all coming out,
They are all alive.
One! Two! Three! Four! Five!
(Stick up thumb, first finger, second finger, etc. as you say the last line.)

Bunny and the Cabbage
Once there was a bunny (Right fist forms bunny, and two fingers are his
ears.)
And a great big cabbage head (Fist of left hand.)
"I think I'll have some cabbage,"
The little bunny said.
So he nibbled and he nibbled (Nibble cabbage head with fingers of right
hand.)
And he ate all day,
Then pricked up his ears. (Ears straighten up.)
And then he hopped away. (Bounce hand away.)

Chipmunk in a Tree
See the little chipmunk (Hold left hand up, elbow bent to form tree.)
Run up the tree (Right hand runs up left arm like a chipmunk.)
There he finds a hole and hides from me. (Right hand goes through hole
made by left thumb and fingers and disappears.)
Watch and you will see him peek all around. (Put forefinger of right hand
through hole and wiggle.)
And if you'll be quite still, he'll come down. (Right hand runs down.)

The Church
Here is the church, (Fingers of both hands interlaced, pointing down and
folded underneath palms, thumbs together on the outside.)
Here is the steeple. (Index fingers together, sticking up.)
Open the doors (Thumbs separate.)
And see all the people! (Turn hands over and wiggle interlaced fingers.)

The Elephant
The elephant's trunk is a big, long nose, (Hold out arm like trunk.)
And up and down is the way it goes. (Extend arm and raise and lower.)
He wears such a saggy, baggy, gray hide! (Sag and relax body.)
Do you think two elephants would fit inside? (Hold up two fingers.)

Five Little Blue Birds *(Counting)*
Five little blue birds, hopping by my door (Hold up all five fingers.)
One went to build a nest, and then there were four. (Take one away.)
Four little blue birds singing prettily
One got out of tune, and then there were three. (Take one away.)
Three little blue birds, and what should one do,
But go in search for worms, leaving only two. (Take one away.)
Two little blue birds singing for fun
One flew away, and then there was one. (Take one away.)
One little blue bird sitting in the sun
He took a little nap, and then there was none. (Hold palms up to show
*   they're empty.)*

Five Little Chickadees *(Counting)*
Five little chickadees, sitting by a door (Hold up five fingers.)
One flew away, and then there were four (Take one away.)

Chorus: (Have your baby join in.)
Chickadees, chickadees, happy and gay,
Chickadees, chickadees, fly away.

Four little chickadees, sitting in a tree
One flew away, and then there were three. (Take one away.)
Chorus

Three little chickadees, looking at you
One flew away, and then there were two. (Take one away.)
Chorus

Two little chickadees, sitting in the sun
One flew away, and then there was one. (Take one away.)
Chorus

One little chickadee, sitting all alone
That one flew away, and then there was none. (Hold up empty hand.)

Five Little Ducks *(Counting)*
Five little ducks went out one day (Hold up five fingers.)
Over the hills and far away,
Mommy (or Daddy) duck called, "Quack, quack, quack."
But only four little ducks came back. (Take one away.)
Four little ducks went out one day
Over the hills and far away,
Mommy (or Daddy) duck called, "Quack, quack, quack."
But only three little ducks came back. (Take one away.)
Three little ducks went out one day
Over the hills and far away,
Mommy (or Daddy) duck called, "Quack, quack, quack."
But only two little ducks came back. (Take one away.)
Two little ducks went out one day
Over the hills and far away,
Mommy (or Daddy) duck called, "Quack, quack, quack."
But only one little duck came back. (Take one away.)
One little duck went out one day
Over the hills and far away,
Mommy (or Daddy) duck called, "Quack, quack, quack,"
But no little ducks came wandering back. (Empty hand.)
No little ducks went out one day
Over the hills and far away,
Mommy (or Daddy) duck called, "Quack, quack, quack."
And five little ducks came waddling back. (Hold up five fingers.)

Five Little Fishes
Five little fishes swimming in a pool. (Wiggle five fingers.)
The first one said, "The pool's too cool." (Wrap arms around body like
    you're cold.)
The second one said, "The pool's too deep." (Voice deep.)
The third one said, "I want to go to sleep." (Rest head on hands.)
The fourth one said, "Let's dive and dip." (Hand dives and dips.)

The fifth one said, "I see a ship." (Look out under hand.)

Fishing boat comes, (Palms together, zigzag hands as move away from body.)

And its line goes KER-SPLASH, (Mime throwing fishing line.)

Away the five little fishes all dash. (Wiggle five fingers away.)

Five Little Monkeys *(Counting)*

Five little monkeys swinging from a tree, (Hold up five fingers. Swing hand to rhythm of verse.)

Teasing Mr. Alligator, "Can't catch me."

(Whisper) Along comes Mr. Alligator, quiet as can be, (Put palms together, one atop the other, and slither hands like an alligator.)

and . . . (Loudly) SNAPPED A LITTLE MONKEY OUT OF THE TREE. (Clap hands with the word SNAP like an alligator's jaws.)

(Repeat with four, three, two, one little monkeys.)

Five Little Monkeys Jumping on the Bed *(Counting)*

(Kids love the last line. I've even heard kids weave it into their conversations. Try this one while bouncing on the bed. Or you can just bounce your hand.)

Five little monkeys jumping on the bed (Hold up five fingers. Bounce hand to rhythm of verse.)

One fell off and bumped his head (Take one away, then rub your head.)

Mommy called the doctor and the doctor said, (Mime holding phone to ear.)

"NO MORE MONKEYS JUMPING ON THE BED!" (Shake index finger as if chastising.)

(Repeat with four, three, two, one little monkeys.)

Five Little Piggies *(Counting)*

"It's time little piggies for you to go to bed." (Place cheek in palm.)

That's what the great big mother piggy said. (Hunch shoulders and puff self up.)

"So I will count them first, then I can see (Look around.)

If all my piggies came back to me." (Hug as if child in arms.)

One little piggy, two little piggies, three little piggies, OH DEAR! (one, two, three fingers, and hand on mouth for "Oh dear!")

Four little piggies, five little piggies. Yes, they're all here!" (Four, then five fingers. Shake head "yes.")

Five Little Puppies (Counting)
Five little puppies were playing in the sun. (Hold up five fingers.)
This one saw a rabbit, and he began to run. (Take one away.)
This one saw a butterfly, and he began to race. (Take one away.)
This one saw a cat, and he began to chase. (Take one away.)
This one tried to catch his tail, and he went round and round. (Take one away.)
This one was so quiet, he never made a sound. (End with thumb up and cuddle it gently against your cheek.)

Five Little Snowmen (Counting)
(Wintertime variation of "Five Little Monkeys")
Five little snowmen riding on the sled (Hold up five fingers and pretend they are sledding by moving open hand down across body as if going downhill.)
One fell off and bumped his head. (Take one finger away and then rub head with other hand.)
I called Frosty and Frosty said, (Mime holding phone to ear.)
"NO MORE SNOWMEN RIDING ON A SLED!" (Deep voice, shake finger as if chastising.)
(Repeat with four, three, two, one little snowmen.)

Going to Bed
This little boy (girl) is going to bed (Hold up right index finger.)
Down on the pillow he (she) lays his (her) head. (Place right index finger in left palm.)
Wraps himself (herself) in the cover tight. (Close left hand over right index finger.)
This is the way he (she) sleeps all night. (Close eyes.)
Morning comes and he (she) opens his (her) eyes. (Blink eyes as if awakening.)
Back with a toss the cover flies. (Open left fist and quickly raise right index finger.)
Up he (she) jumps and dresses for the day. (Hold up finger.)

*Kisses his (her) mom, then runs to play. (Touch finger to lips, then wiggle it
  and move hand as if running away.)*

Grandma's Glasses

*Here are Grandma's glasses. (Make little circles with each thumb and index
  finger in front of eyes.)*

*Here is Grandma's hat. (Pretend you are tying a bonnet underneath your
  chin.)*

This is the way she folds her hands, (Fold your hands.)

And puts them in her lap. (Daintily drop your hands on your lap.)

*Here are Grandpa's glasses. (Make bigger circles with each thumb and in-
  dex finger.)*

Here is Grandpa's hat. (Mime putting on a hat.)

This is the way he folds his arms! (Cross arms over chest.)

Just like that! (Relax back in chair and give a "Hurrumphing" movement.)

Hands on Shoulders *(Body parts and counting)*

  (Follow the actions as described.)

Hands on shoulders,

Hands on knees.

Hands behind you,

If you please. (Wag a finger.)

Touch your shoulders,

Now your nose,

Now your hair and

Now your toes;

Hands up high

Waving in the air,

Down at your sides,

Then touching your hair;

Hands up high as before,

Now clap them, one, two, three, and (pause) four!

Head and Shoulders

  *(Touch each body part with both hands as named, and remember
  to go slowly with your child.)*

Head and shoulders, knees and toes.
Knees and toes.
Head and shoulders, knees and toes.
Knees and toes.
And eyes and ears, and mouth and nose.
Head and shoulders, knees and toes.
Knees and toes.

Hokey Pokey

(You've probably been embarrassed at least once at a party danc-
ing the Hokey Pokey; it's best in a circle but can be done either fac-
ing or alongside your child.)
You put your right hand in, (Put hand into a pretend circle in front of you,
or toward each other if facing.)
You put your right hand out, (Pull hand out of circle and behind you.)
You put your right hand in, (Put hand into circle, or toward each other.)
And shake it all about. (Shake hand.)
You do the Hokey Pokey (Wiggle body and shake limbs.)
And you turn yourself about, (Turn around while wiggling.)
That's what it's all about.
(Continue by putting in all the other parts of the body, and finish up with
your whole body in and out!)

I can

(Works best with more than one child.)
I can touch my nose, (Touch nose.)
Or even touch your shoe. (Touch shoe.)
I can clap my hands, (Clap.)
Or I can follow you. (Point to your child.)
Now,_____show me something (Say child's name in blank.)
I can try and do. (Imitate your child and begin again.)

If You're Happy *(or other emotions)*

If you're happy and you know it, clap your hands (Clap twice.)
If you're happy and you know it, clap your hands (Clap twice.)
If you're happy and you know it, then your face will surely show it (Smile.)

If you're happy and you know it, clap your hands (Clap twice.)
If you're happy and you know it . . .

> . . . stomp your feet.

> . . . tap your head

> . . . jump up and down.

(Any action that's appropriate.)

I Have Two
I have two eyes to see with, (Touch eyes or blink.)
I have two feet to run, (Touch feet or wiggle them.)
I have two hands to wave with, (Wave hands.)
And nose I have but one. (Touch nose or crinkle it.)
I have two ears to hear with, (Touch ears.)
And a tongue to say "IT'S FUN!" (Shout and hug.)

Johnny Johnny Jingles
Johnny Johnny Jingles
Jumped out of bed (Jump.)
Brushed his teeth and washed his face, (Mime brushing and washing.)
And combed his tousled head, (Pretend to comb hair.)
He put his clothes on carefully (Mime buttoning shirt.)
His shoes he neatly tied, (Pretend to tie shoes.)
Then he went to breakfast, (Pretend to eat.)
And sat by his mother's side. (Give a REAL hug.)

(For variety substitute your child's name and another descriptor for "Jingles," as in "Sally, Sally, sweet smile" or "Nicki, Nicki, bright eyes.")

Little Turtle
There was a little turtle (Make fist like turtle shell.)
That lived in a box (Make a box by tracing a square with your hands.)
He swam through the puddles (Pretend to doggie-paddle.)
And climbed on the rocks. (Walk your finger's across each other.)

He snapped at a mosquito (Make snapping motion with thumb and fingers
   acting as turtle's mouth.)

He snapped at a flea (Make snapping motion again.)
He snapped at a minnow (Make snapping motion again.)
And he snapped at me. (Snap at yourself and act very surprised. Ham it up!)

He caught the mosquito (Tickle your child gently.)
He caught the flea (Tickle child again.)
He caught the minnow (Tickle child again.)
BUT HE DIDN'T CATCH ME!!! (Shake index finger.)

(You can both do the motions on each other, once your child learns them.)

Mrs. Turtle
Mrs. Turtle round and low (Make a circle with your hands.)
We know why you move so slow (Nod yes.)
You carry such a heavy load (Act out carrying something heavy.)
Moving your house (Form upside-down "V" with finger tips together) up and down the road. (Shade eye as if watching her go.)

My Head
This is the place I call my head (Make large circle around your face with your hand.)
This is my mouth where words are said (Point to mouth.)
These are my eyes that help me see (Point to eyes.)
This is my nose that's a part of me (Point to nose.)
This is the hair that grows on my head (Hold some hair.)
When I get embarrassed, my face turns red (Hold hands in front of face.)

(An alternative last line is "When I get tired, I take them all to bed" while placing cheek in hand and closing your eyes.)

Open, Shut Them
Open them, shut them, (Separate then bring together your thumb and fingers like an animal's mouth.)
Open them, shut them, (Again)

Give a little clap. (Clap hands.)
Open them, shut them, (Again.)
Open them, shut them, (Again.)
Put them in your lap. (Drop your hands into your lap.)
Creep them, creep them, creep them, (Crawl up your body with your hands like two "critters.")
Right up to your chin, (Stop at your chin.)
Open wide your little mouth (Open your mouth and pause.)
But do not put them in. (Shake finger.)

Pretty Little Goldfish
Pretty little goldfish (Palms together and weave them left and right as you move them away from your body.)
She can't even talk. (Point to mouth and shake head "no.")
All she does is wiggle (Wiggle body.)
When she tries to walk. (Place palms down and flap hands up and down as if feet are walking.)

Right Hand, Left Hand
This is my right hand, (Show right.)
I'll raise it up high. (Raise right hand over head.)
This is my left hand, (Show left.)
I'll touch the sky. (Raise left hand over head.)
Right hand (Show right palm.)
Left hand (Show left.)
Roll them around (Roll hands over and over.)
Left hand (Show left palm.)
Right hand (Show right.)
Pound, pound, pound (Pound fists together.)

(The left and right distinctions are difficult enough for me. And I dislike fist pounding of any type. Try this variation . . .)

This is my one hand, (Show hand.)
I'll raise it up real high. (Raise hand over head.)
This is my other hand, (Show other hand.)

With it I'll touch the sky (Raise hand over head.)
One hand (Show palm.)
Other hand (Show other.)
Roll them around (Roll hands over and over.)
One hand (Show palm.)
Other hand (Show right.)
Reach down to the ground (Squat down and touch the ground with both hands.)

Round and Round the Garden

Round and round the garden like a teddy bear (Swirl your index finger around palm of child's hand.)
One step, two step (Walk fingers up child's arm.)
He's hiding under there! (Tickle child's underarm.)

Here's a variation with the same motions . . .

Roundabout Wee Mouse

Roundabout, roundabout, little wee mouse
Up the tree, up the tree,
Into your house!

Sleepy Caterpillars

Let's go to sleep, the caterpillar said, (Wiggle right index finger.)
As they tucked themselves into their little beds. (Place right index finger in left palm.)
They will awaken by and by, (Close left hand around right index finger.)
And each one will be a lovely butterfly. (Open hand one and transform it into a butterfly with the thumbs together, palms out and the fingers flapping slowly like wings.)

This Little Froggy

(Hold up five fingers and, as you say each line in succession, fold the finger down, beginning with the pinky.)
This little froggy broke his toe
This little froggy said, "Oh, oh, oh!"

This little froggy laughed and was glad.
This little froggy cried and was sad,
This little froggy did just what he should
He hopped for the doctor as fast as he could. (Wiggle the thumb and have
  it "hop" off to one side.)

Three Little Hot Dogs *(Counting)*
(Place three fingers from your right hand into the palm of your left, patting
  them up and down.)
Three little hot dogs frying in the pan,
The pan got hot and one (Hold up one finger.) went BAM! (Clap on
  "BAM.")

(Place two fingers from your right hand into your left palm . . .)
Two little hot dogs frying in the pan,
The pan got hot and one (Hold up one finger.) went BAM! (Clap.)

(Place one finger from your right hand into your left palm . . .)
One little hot dog frying in the pan,
The pan got hot and one went . . .
"Wait, Wait! Put me on your plate and eat me!"

(If your child is in your lap, this is your cue to pretend to "eat her up" and tickle. Or, if she doesn't like to be tickled, you can pretend to gobble up her finger in an exaggerated fashion. Bonus: This song can sometimes help get an obstinate little eater to chow down. Simply pretend the rejected food is the "hot dog.")

Thumbkin
Where is Thumbkin?
Where is Thumbkin?
Here I am. Here I am. (Hold up and wiggle your thumbs.)
How are you this morning? (Wiggle one thumb.)
Very well and thank you. (Wiggle the other.)
Run and play. Run and play. (Thumbs comes down.)

Where is . . .
. . . Pointer (Hold up and wiggle your index fingers.)

. . . Tall One (Hold up and wiggle your third fingers.)
. . . Ring One (Hold up and wiggle your fourth fingers.)
. . . Pinky (Hold up and wiggle your pinkies.)
. . . the everyone (Hold up both hands and wiggle all fingers.)

Tiny Tim
I had a little turtle, his name was Tiny Tim. (Right fist in left palm.)
I put him in the bathtub, to teach him how to swim (Remove fist and place it off to side.)
He drank up all the water, he ate up all the soap. (Pretend to drink and eat.)
And now when he talks (Move mouth.), there's a bubble in his throat.
Bubble, bubble, . . . bubble, bubble, . . . bubble, bubble . . . (Pause.) POP! (Clap.)

Twelve Little Rabbits *(Counting)*
Twelve little rabbits in a rabbit pen;
Two hopped away and then there were ten. (Hold up ten fingers.)
Ten little rabbits with ears up straight;
Two hopped away and then there were eight. (Bend down two fingers.)
Eight little rabbits doing funny tricks;
Two hopped away and then there were six. (Bend down two more.)
Six little rabbits peeking out the door
Two hopped away and then there were four. (Bend down two more.)
Four little bunnies, I know that this is true,
Two hoped away and then there were two. (Bend down two more.)
Two little rabbits found a new friend;
They hopped away . . . and that is the end. (Bend down the last two.)

Very Nice Place
The fish lives in the brook. (Palms together and wiggle forward.)
The bird lives in the tree. (Flap hands like wings.)
But homes are the nicest place, (Make upside-down "V" with fingers touching.)
For a little girl (boy) like me. (Point to child until she/he can point to self.)

Walking through the Zoo

*Walking through the zoo, (Palms down, alternate up and down movement
    like walking.)*

What did I see? (Shield eyes and look about.)

A big yellow lion,

Roaring at me.

Walking through the zoo,

What did I see? . . .

  A funny little monkey,

  Laughing at me.

  A little baby seal,

  Swimming toward me.

  A big gorilla,

  Waving at me.

  A white, furry bunny,

  Hopping toward me.

Wheels of the Bus

(Perform the actions and sounds suggested by the words.)

The wheels of the bus go round and round,

Round and round, round and round

The wheels of the bus go round and round

All through the town.

The driver of the bus says, "Move on back!"

"Move on back! Move on back!"

The driver of the bus says, "Move on Back!"

All through the town.

The people on the bus go up and down,

Up and down, up and down.

The people on the bus go up and down

All through the town.

Substitute these also:

The horn of the bus goes beep beep beep.
The wipers on the bus go swish, swish, swish.
The doors on the bus go open and shut.
The bell on the bus goes ding-ding-ding.
The lady on the bus says, "Get off my feet."
The baby on the bus goes, "Wa-Wa-Wa."
The people on the bus say, "We had a nice ride."

Use a child's name, as in, <u>Tommy</u> on the bus say, "Let Me Off!"

Zoo
  (Use a mirror.)
At the zoo we saw a bear
He had long, dark fuzzy hair. (Lumber like a bear.)

We saw a lion in a cage.
He was in an awful rage. (Snarl like an angry lion.)

We saw the big, long-necked giraffe,
And the silly monkeys made us laugh. (Pretend to laugh.)

But my favorite animals at the zoo
Are the ones that look like me and you! (Make faces, then end with a big
    hug.)

Easy Words for Babies and Toddlers

Here's a collection of words that your baby will find very easy to say. These short words follow the same format as the *bababa* Consonant-Vowel (CV) babbling, and the *guh, kuh, mmm, buh, puh, wuh,* and *huh* babbling sounds that infants make naturally.

First, very simple CV or CVCV words:

Moo	No	Toy
Bye (or Bye-bye)	Baby	Hi
Shoe	Key	Cookie
Knee	See	Toe
Zoo	Boo (as in Peek-a)	Go
TV	Kitty	Yukky
Potty	Potty	Bunny
CD	Teddy	Pie
Tee (T-shirt)	Who	

These are simple VC syllable words, where the vowel sound is first, followed by the consonant sound:

Up	Eye	Ear
Eat	In	Out
Egg	Off	

Many short English words are of the CVC type—*dog* = *duh* + *aww* + *guhh*. At first, these might come out as CVCV (*cup-ah* for *cup*) or a CV (*cuh* for *cup*) when your tot tries to say them, but he'll catch on quickly, especially with good CVC examples from you. These include:

Book	Ball	Juice
Doll	Cup	Hat
Sock	Mouth	Mine
More	Gone	Car
Boat	Bus	Duck
Dog	Cat	Cow
Light	Night-night	Bed
Big	Hot	Man
Seat	Bite	Run
Bike	Nose	Hair
Bear (Teddy)	Chair	Cap
Sit	Coat	Comb
Door	Good	House
Wash	Fall	Kiss
Push	Pull	Bath
Come	Cake	Fish
Pig	Sheep	Kick
Dig	Teeth	Box
Make	Cook	Fix
Sing	Read	Write
Road	Catch	Foot
Game	Home	Show
Give	Laugh	Leg
Room	Meat	Pear
Ride	Soap	Soup
Walk	Talk	Wet
What	Where	Yes

Easy Two-Word Combinations for Toddlers

TODDLERS combine words in predictable ways based on their limited short-term memory and their organization of ideas. If you use the same combinations when you talk to your six- to twelve-month-old, he'll understand you better.

If you use the combinations with your twelve- to eighteen-month-old, they'll serve as excellent models and help him learn to make his own word combinations more easily. The lists below contain easy-to-say child words in the most common combinations. No doubt, your toddler will have some additional words that will easily fit into the suggested structures.

TALKING ABOUT ACTIONS

Add one from the first group to one from the second to form *noun-plus-verb structures*, such as "*Bear sit*" or "*Doggie eat*." Obviously, not all of these combinations will work. "*Duck read*," for instance, is a bit of a stretch.

Nouns	Verbs
Daddy, Mommy, Kitty (or Cat), Doggie (or Dog), Bunny, Teddy, Duck, Cow, Man, Bear, Fish, Pig, Who	Eat, Go, See, In, On, Out, Wash, Sit, Push, Pull, Kiss, Kick, Make, Fix, Cook, Catch, Laugh, Sing, Fall, Read, Write, Walk, Talk, Run, Bite, Gone

You can also talk about actions using the verb first. Add one from the first group to the second to form verb-plus-noun structures, such as *"Eat pie"* or *"Wash knee."*

Verbs	Nouns
Eat	Cookie, Pie, Egg, Pear, Soup, Meat
Wash	Toe, Eye, Ear, Mouth, Nose, Hair, Teeth, Foot, Leg, Knee
Kiss	Mommy, Daddy, Baby
Push	Car, Ball, Bus
Cut	Pie, Cake, Pear
Read	Book
Throw	Ball

Wanting expressions—those that express desire—are a special type because a child can want a thing or an action. Here are some possibilities.

Want Daddy, Eat, Mommy, Go, Kittie (or Cat), See, Doggie (or Dog), In, Bunny, On, Teddy, Out, Duck, Wash, Cow, Sit, Man, Push, Bear, Pull, Fish, Kiss, Pig, Kick, Make, Fix, Cook, Catch, Sing, Read, Write, Walk, Talk, Run, Cookie, Shoe, More, Pie, Tee, Egg, Book, Ball, Juice, Doll, Cup, Hat, Sock, Car, Boat, Bus, Chair, Cap, Coat, Comb, TV

DESCRIBING THINGS

Add an adjective from column one to a noun from column two for baby-easy *descriptor-plus-noun structures.* You'll get familiar combos like *"Big ball"* or *"More juice"* as well as baby-only possibilities like *"More hat,"* which might be used when playing taking hats off and on. The words *more* and *no* are particularly useful in combination with other words to signify *another*, *do again*, and *not present, disappeared, disagree*, respectively. I've included the most common descriptor words—your tot will probably have others.

Adjectives	Nouns
Big, No, More, My, Hot, Yukky	Cookie, Shoe, Pie, Tea, Egg, Book, Ball, Juice, Doll, Cup, Hat, Sock, Car, Boat, Bus, Chair, Cap, Coat, Comb, House

Adjectives	Verb or Verb-like words
More, No	Eat, Go, See, In, On, Out, Wash, Sit, Push, Pull, Kiss, Kick, Make, Fix, Cook, Catch, Laugh, Sing, Fall, Read, Write, Walk, Talk, Run, Bite

---

OWNING THINGS

Expressing possession—*my ball, my sock*—is a favorite of sixteen-month-olds. Claiming things gives them a pleasant feeling of control in a world where they control so little. Make possessive phrases by adding one from the first group below to one from the second—*"Teddy hat"* for instance, means *"It's teddy's hat."* Toddlers use the possessive pronoun *my* but not all the others (*your, his, her, their*), so *his coat*, for instance, will be signaled by naming the owner, as in *"Daddy coat."*

Possessive word	Noun
Daddy, Mommy, Kitty (or Cat), Doggie (or Dog), Bunny, Teddy, Duck, Cow, Man, Bear, Fish, Pig	Cookie, Shoe, Pie, Tee, Egg, Book, Ball, Juice, Doll, Cup, Hat, Sock, Car, Boat, Bus, Chair
My	Cap, Coat, Comb, House, Toe, Eye, Ear, Mouth, Nose, Hair, Teeth, Foot, Leg, Knee
My	Daddy, Mommy, Baby

LOCATING THINGS

Locations seem to hold a particular importance for young children—it's a frequent subject of "conversation." For young toddlers, the location word usually follows the word for the person, action, or object that is in that location. "*Daddy car*," for example, means "*Daddy's in the car*." ("*Daddy car*" can also mean possession, as in "*It's daddy's car*," but we have to rely on the situation to interpret the meaning.) One of my favorite location-type expressions at this age (so I'm told) was "*Eggie cup*," which clearly meant to me that the egg is in the cup. Anybody else's interpretation was up for grabs. Add one from the first column to one from the second column to express *location*.

Action, person, or thing	Location
Daddy, Mommy, Kitty (or Cat), Doggie (or Dog), Bunny, Teddy, Duck, Cow, Man, Bear, Fish, Pig, Shoe, Pie, Egg, Book, Ball, Juice, Hat, Sock, Tee, Cap, Coat, Comb, Put, Sit	Cup, Car, Book, Boat, In, Out, On, Down
Ride	Car, Bus, Boat, Bike
Go	Potty, Car, Bus, Boat, Bed, Up
Throw	Me (to me)
Come	Here
Wash	Soap (with soap)

Obviously, some of these, such as "*Book book*" or "*Daddy cup*" are nonsense (although "*Daddy cup*" works as an expression of possession), but a child might say "*Book car*" for "*The book is in the car*" or "*Bear book*" for "*The bear (picture of bear) is in the book*."

GREETING FOLKS

And of course, we can't forget greetings. Simply add one from the first column to one from the second.

Hi, Bye, Hey   Mommy, Daddy, Man, Baby

And there you go!

Truly, none of the structures in this section is as odd as it may seem. For example, "*Mommy eat*" or "*Eat cookie*" are in the exact order you would expect in a longer adult sentence, such as "*Mommy is eating a cookie.*" But in the toddler phrase, some of the words are missing. Once you realize that, interpreting your child and modeling language for him becomes very simple. Don't try all the structures at once. Go slow. After you make a few short phrases as you talk with your child, it will become second nature. And before you realize it, thanks to your efforts, your baby will be talking in whole sentences.

Resources: Books, Music, Toys, and More

Terrific Books for Your Baby

SIX TO NINE MONTHS

- *Brown Bear, Brown Bear, What Do You See?,* Bill Martin. (Holt Rinehart & Winston, 1983. www.hrw.com.) The first book in a wonderful series with one bold animal illustration per page.

- *Farm Animals,* and *Pet Animals,* Lucy Cousins. (Candlewick Press, 1999. www.candlewick.com.) Two in a great series with colorful and endearing illustrations, and a minimum of text.

- *I Hear, I See,* and *I Touch,* Helen Oxenbury. (Candlewick Press, 1995. www.candlewick.com.) Three books in a series that explore the senses and offer large, simple, bright pictures of one relevant object at a time—great for shared pointing and chatting.

- *Peek-a-Who,* Nina Laden. (Chronicle Books, 2000. www.chroniclebooks.com.) Simple rhymes that encourage your tot to peak through the cut-out window to find an animal.

NINE TO TWELVE MONTHS

■ *Away We Go,* Rebecca Kai Dotlich. (HarperFestival, 2000. www.harperchildrens.com.) Contains colorful illustrations and cute rhymes about various types of transportation. Great fun for budding globetrotters.

■ *Baby Faces,* Margaret Miller. (Little Simon, 1998.) A delightful child-pleaser with photos of multiethnic baby faces expressing simple emotions.

■ *Happy Baby Words,* by Roger Priddy, Richard Brown, Stephen Shoot, and Priddy Bickne. (VHPS Virginia, 2001.) Superb for helping babies learn words.

■ *Max's Bath*, Rosemary Well. (Dial Books for Young Readers, 1998.) Introduces a simple plot of a routine familiar to your baby. The title says it all.

■ *My Clothes, My Animals, My Toys,* and others, Rebecca Emberley. (Little Brown, 2002. www.twbookmark.com/children/index.html.) A bilingual series (English and Spanish) that features excellent colorful, simple illustrations of common items that your child will easily recognize.

■ *My First Word Board Book*, Angela Wilkes. (Disney Press, 1997. disney.go.com/DisneyBooks/.) Another winning way to learn words.

■ *Touch & Feel: Puppy* and *Touch & Feel: Farm.* (DK Publishing, 1998. www.dk.com.) Offers fun "textured reading" with lots of things to touch.

■ *Where Is Baby's Belly Button?* Karen Katz. (Little Simon, 2000.) Features cutely illustrated babies playing Peek-a-boo with body parts ("Where are baby's eyes? Under her hat!"); a fun way to reinforce learning body parts.

THIRTEEN TO FIFTEEN MONTHS

■ *Everybody Has Feelings,* Charles Avery. (Gryphon House, 1998. www.ghbooks.com.) A wonderful photographic essay on children moods that features a wide range of emotions and simple prose in English and Spanish.

■ *Clap, Tickle, Tickle,* and *All Fall Down,* Helen Oxenbury. (Little Simon, 1999.) Features illustrations of adorable, relatable, multiethnic babies at play and talks about what they're doing in simple phrases. Watch your tot bond with the babies!

■ *That's Not My Teddy, That's Not My Kitten,* and *That's Not My Bunny,* Fiona Watt and Rachel Wells. (Usborne Publishers Ltd. www.usborne.com.) This entire series cleverly uses the process of elimination to describe common animals and objects.

■ *The Very Hungry Caterpillar,* Eric Carle. (Scholastic, 1994. www.scholastic.com/.) A wonderful tale of a lovable caterpillar's last eating frenzy before changing into a beautiful butterfly.

SIXTEEN TO EIGHTEEN MONTHS

■ *Elmo Likes,* Tom Brannon. (Random House, 2000. www.randomhouse.com.) Uses the simple two-word combination in the title to introduce Elmo's favorite things, as in "Elmo likes cookies." The format makes for easy baby participation.

■ *Outside, Inside,* Carolyn Crimi. (Simon & Schuster, 1995. www.simonandschuster.com.) Contrasts things to do indoors and out through beautifully colored eye-catching illustrations.

■ *Where Is Baby's Mommy?* Karen Katz. (Little Simon, 2001.) A lift-a-flap format winner that has a child searching throughout the house for his "missing" mommy—who happily turns up in a bubble-bath taking a deserved soak—is great for introducing an elementary plot.

■ *Where's Spot?* Eric Hill. (Puffin, 2003. www.puffin.co.uk.) A wonderfully illustrated, interactive book with colorful flaps that your child can lift to help search for a missing pup.

NINETEEN TO TWENTY-FOUR MONTHS

■ *Counting Kisses: A Kiss and Read Book,* Karen Katz. (M. K. McElderry, 2001.) This one is as hard to resist as the baby kisses it elicits.

■ *Dinosaur Roar,* Paul and Henrietta Stickland. (Dutton Books, 1997. www.penguinputnam.com.) Offers brilliantly illustrated and non-scary reptiles with lots of good descriptor words.

■ *Is Your Mama a Llama?* Deborah Guarino. (Scholastic, 1991. www.scholastic.com.) A sweet story of a baby's search for his mother is available in both English and Spanish.

■ *Some Things Go Together,* Charlotte Zolotow. (Abelard-Schuman, 1999.) A wonderfully illustrated, rhyming story about how things are linked together that foster feelings of familial love and caring.

■ *When I Get Bigger,* Mercer Mayer. (Golden Books, 1999. www.randomhouse.com/golden.) A real winner with the little folk.

AFTER TWENTY-FOUR MONTHS

■ *Alexander and the Terrible, Horrible, No Good, Very Bad Day,* Judith Viorst. (Aladdin, 1987.) Explores a child's world turned upside-down.

■ *Bright Eyes, Brown Skin,* Cheryl Willis Hudson and Bernedette Ford. (Just Us Books, 1990. www.justusbooks.com.) A wonderful book for brown children on their special inner beauty.

■ *The Doorbell Rang,* Pat Hutchins. (Harper Trophy, 1989. harpertrophy.1.serchbook.net/.) A fun, interesting crowd of characters builds and builds as more and more people arrive.

■ *Froggy Gets Dressed,* Jonathan London. (Viking Children's Books, 1997. www.penguinputnam.com.) An inventive, animal-loving way to learn about clothes. No child can resist laughing at silly old froggy.

■ *Green Wilma,* Tedd Arnold. (Puffin, 2002. www.puffin.co.uk.) This one keeps the little one laughing and anticipating as Wilma deals with the challenges of waking one looking like a frog.

■ *The Grouchy Ladybug,* Eric Carle. (Harper Trophy, 1996. harpertrophy.1.searchbook.net.) A foul-tempered ladybug learns how to be a nicer, happier, better-behaved insect. Another in the fine series of books from this author.

■ *If You Give a Mouse a Cookie,* Laura Joffe Numeroff. (Laura Geringer, 1985. www.harperchildrens.com/hch/aboutus/imprints/geringer.asp.) One in a great series *(If You Give a Pig a Pancake, If You Give a Moose a Muffin)* that keeps your little reader busy predicting what an energetic mouse might need next after an initial cookie offer . . . milk, straw, clean-up stuff. Great pictures, too.

■ *The Little Old Lady Who Was Not Afaid of Anything,* Linda Williams. (HarperTrophy, 1988. harpertrophy.1.searchbook.net/.) A terrific book for the Halloween season. The little old lady goes for a walk in the woods, and then the action begins. Presents lots of opportunities of fun, inventive, dramatic readings.

■ *Never Babysit the Hippopotamuses,* Doug Johnson. (Bt Bound, 1999.) A wonderfully silly and ridiculous story about the perils of babysitting hippos.

■ *Pancakes for Breakfast,* Tomie DePaola. (Voyager Books, 1990.) A classic must-read for pancake aficionados.

■ *The Paper Bag Princess,* Robert Munsch. (Annick Press, 1992. www.annickpress.com.) One of my favorite children's stories. The ultimate lesson in how to outwit a dragon.

■ *Somebody and the Three Blairs,* Marilyn Tolhurst. (Orchard Books, 1994.) A funny, silly twist on an old Goldilocks classic.

■ *Who Sank the Boat?* Pamela Allen. (Puffin, 1996. www.puffin.co.uk.) A group of heavyweights overload their craft, but place the blame on someone smaller when they scuttle the ship. An engaging story with a moral.

BABY FOOD COOKBOOKS

If you love to cook and want to start your baby out on home cooking, these books will give you some great ideas.

■ *Homemade Baby Food Pure and Simple,* Connie and Constantina Linardakis. (Prima Lifestyles, 2001. www.primapublishing.com.)

■ *Organic Baby and Toddler Cookbook,* Lizzie Vann. (DK Publishing, 2001. www.dk.com.)

■ *Super Baby Food,* Ruth Yaron. (F. J. Roberts Publishing, 1998. www.pma-online.org/scripts/showmember.cfm?code=6148.)

■ *Simply Natural Baby Food,* Cathe Olson. (GOCO Publishing, 2002. www.pma-online.org/scripts/showmember.cfm?code=12240.)

■ *Whole Foods for Babies and Toddlers,* Margaret Kenda. (La Leche League, 2001. www.lalecheleague.org/catalog.html.)

BOOKS ABOUT BABY MASSAGE

■ *Baby Massage: The Calming Power of Touch,* Alan Heath, Nicki Bainbridge, and Julie Fisher. (DK Publishing, 2000.)

■ *Infant Massage: A Handbook for Loving Parents,* Vimala Schneider McClure. (Bantam Books, 2000. www.randomhouse.com/home. pperl.)

■ *Loving Hands: The Traditional Art of Baby Massage,* Frederick Leboyer. (Newmarket Prress, 1997. www.newmarketpress.com.)

Music for Your Baby

- *Hot Hot Hot Dance Songs* from Sesame Street: Pure fun and Muppet madness at its best.

- *Playtime Favorites* and *Toddler Favorites* (part of the Music for Little People series. www.mflp.com.): Features all-time kiddy favorites like "Tisket a Tasket," "Hokey Pokey," "Ring Around the Rosy," and the ever-popular "One, Two, Buckle My Shoe." Even the most discerning infant will find these hard to resist—especially once they hear the children's voices in the choruses.

- *The Singable Songs Collection* (Rounder. www.rounder.com.): A three volume set compilation by kiddy song specialist Raffi that contains every child song ever conceived by man—or woman.

Developmental Baby Toys

FOUR TO SIX MONTHS

Kiddie gyms are excellent and provide tykes with a lovely colorful mat to lie on as they play to their hearts' content.

- Gymini activity center gyms

- Carter's Butterfly play gym

- Kookazoo Tunnel Gym

SEVEN TO NINE MONTHS

- Playzone Roll Along Drum Roll (Fisher-Price. www.fisher-pricestore.com/fpecom/plsql/fp1.page): A crawl-and-push toy with colorful balls inside that make noise, music, and different sounds.

- Spin Ball (Leapfrog. www.leapfrog.com/do/findpage?pageID=home_page): Plays various melodies and changes from a stationary ball for spinning to a rolling ball for crawling, sitting, or walking.

TEN TO TWELVE MONTHS

These are all in the $40 to $60 price range, except for Chico's, which is much less.

- *Activity Center with Blocks* (Chico): A bright, colorful activity table with easy to handle blocks for building and stacking.

- *Leap Start Learning Table* (Leapfrog. www.leapfrog.com/do/find page?pageID=home_page): A singing piano with height adjustments for crawling, sitting, or standing is another good one.

- *Megasaucer Activity Center* (Evenflo) and *Little Tike 3-Way Entertainer* (Graco): Kiddy-colorful activity centers full of levers, buttons, and knobs that your tot can manipulate from the adjustable central *command post* seat. Your tot just has to pull, push, turn and twist to activate all kinds of fun lights and sounds. Kiddie heaven!

- *Step and Play Piano* (Fisher-Price. www.fisher-pricestore.com/ fpecom/plsql/fp1.page): A foot-operated piano like the one Tom Hanks played in the movie *Big!*

THIRTEEN TO FIFTEEN MONTHS

- *First Shape Fitter* (Plan Toy. www.plantoys.com/enter.htm): Features colorful chunky square, circular, and triangular blocks than fit perfectly into cut-outs in a wooden tray.

- *Lock-a-block* (BRIO. www.brioplay.com/main.asp): A plastic box with round, square, and triangular holes. Your little shape-sorter has to find the appropriate cubes, balls, and triangles to push through the holes into the box. To retrieve the shapes, she has to open the box with her own child-friendly key.

- *Singing Pop Up Pals* from Sesame Street: A button-pushing, knob-twisting toy that has all your special *Sesame Street* friends ready to pop out and sing a favorite tune.

- *Shape Sorter Cube* (Lights, Camera, and Interaction): A cube with multiple shapes and holes. It's not fancy but offers a real learning-challenge bang for your buck.

SIXTEEN TO EIGHTEEN MONTHS

- *Little Linguist* (Neurosmith. www.neurosmith.com/home): One of the more promising—and more pricey—talking toys for toddlers that I've seen recently. (Comes in English, French, and Japanese versions.) Little Linguist essentially consists of a base unit, a language cartridge, and a variety of familiar objects like cars and animals. Your tot puts one of the objects in the center of the base unit. The unit identifies the object. Then the child presses one of the big buttons and hears something about the object. If he presses the blue button, he gets the name of the object; the red button will give him a short phrase or a sound— a dog bark, for example. (One caution: Early models had some operating problems, so check to see that it does what it's supposed to do before buying one.)

NINETEEN TO TWENTY-FOUR MONTHS

- *Gears Creation Activity Easel* (Fisher-Price. www.fisher-pricestore. com): A fun array of colorful moving and spinning pieces that can creatively fit together in lots of different ways.

- *Legos* (Toddler edition. www.lego.com/eng): Offers endless opportunities to build and design cars, planes, trucks, boats . . . almost anything you can imagine.

- *Geometric Shapes* jumbo knob puzzle (Lights, Camera, Interaction. www.tuttibellakids.com/melissadoug.html): A simple, brightly colored puzzle made with large wooden pieces with knobs that are perfectly suited for tiny hands. There are several other puzzle varieties with animals and vehicles that are pretty terrific, too.

■   *Hide and Slide Climber* and the *Easy Store Activity Gym* (Little Tikes. www.littletikes.com): Excellent sturdy, colorful, plastic slide-climber combinations.

■   *Tall-Stacker Pegs* and *Pegboard Set* (Lauri. learningforallages.com): This one has colorful pegs that attach end-to-end, as well as fit in the crepe rubber pegboard for creative building (ideal for small fingers).

INDEX

ABOUT THE AUTHORS

Robert E. Owens, Jr., Ph.D., is an internationally recognized expert on child language development and language disorders. He is Professor of Communicative Disorders and Sciences and Director of the Graduate Program in Speech-Language Pathology at the State University of New York at Geneseo.

Leah Feldon is a freelance writer, author of five top-selling books, and a longtime journalist. She currently splits her time between Nashville and New York City.